Building stronger communities

Building stronger communities

Connecting research, policy and practice

Edited by
Lesley Doyle
David Adams
John Tibbitt
and Peter Welsh

promoting adult learning

© 2008 National Institute of Adult Continuing Education
(England and Wales)

21 De Montfort Street
Leicester
LE1 7GE

Company registration no. 2603322
Charity registration no. 1002775

NIACE has a broad remit to promote lifelong learning opportunities for adults.
NIACE works to develop increased participation in education and training,
particularly for those who do not have easy access because of class, gender,
age, race, language and culture, learning difficulties or disabilities,
or insufficient financial resources.

You can find NIACE online at www.niace.org.uk

Cataloguing in Publication Data
A CIP record of this title is available from the British Library

Typeset by Avon DataSet Ltd, Bidford-on-Avon, Warwickshire
Printed and bound in the UK by Latimer Trend, Plymouth

ISBN: 978 1 86201 345 2

Contents

Contents

Contents

Foreword

Paul Carter

As Leader of Kent County Council, one of the founding funders of the Pascal International Research Observatory[1], I was delighted to be asked to write the Foreword to this book. Building stronger communities and supporting those that have grown strong is at the heart of our work in Kent. Elected representatives of our communities, like myself and my colleagues, have not only a duty, but also a compulsion to listen, to learn and to do what is best for those who have put their trust in us.

There are many ways by which I test my assumptions and decisions, and these vary, from the powerful insights I get from personally talking to the people of Kent about their experiences, their concerns and their hopes, to the valuable mirror provided by international studies and respected experts. In both of these extremes and across the range of anecdotal and professional research that they span, however, it remains the role and responsibility of policy makers and practitioners to act or not on the evidence.

The links between what we do as policy makers, practitioners and researchers are stronger today than they have ever been. We live in a time of unprecedented levels of communication and knowledge exchange. We are able to tap into these to help understand better the problems that face us and develop more effective solutions. However, the speed at which all of this happens presents policy makers and practitioners with an ever-increasing challenge; that of time. Research findings are published and disseminated in a seemingly constant flow. How are we to make sense of them?

Perhaps even more fundamental is the question of what constitutes research appropriate to the needs of those engaged in delivering frontline public services. How do we judge quality? How do we apply theoretical work to real situations? Here, the answer may lie in the unique community that we call the PASCAL Observatory.

The concept of creating a community of *practising academics and academic practitioners* is beginning to show signs of a new working culture. The chapter by Kilpatrick and her colleagues explores the importance of 'boundary crossers'. This notion may also apply to those who work within PASCAL where the applied view of the practitioner and policy maker is shaping the kind of work being produced in our universities. Equally, I have witnessed a growth of academic research interest and activity from officers within Kent County Council, a trend which is no doubt visible in other PASCAL partner bodies.

One particular area of research identifies a clear need to raise aspirations and self-esteem through inspired learning programmes in schools, in an endeavour to break the repetitive cycles of welfare dependency which often permeate generations of families. This means empowering individuals through the education system by providing them with the appropriate stimulating learning opportunities tailored to their strengths, talents and ambitions and which are relevant to the commercial world.

Another area of work is on community engagement, essential in the political world and in the best interests of democracy. Individuals that make up the communities we serve will be able to access information about our work and its legislative context through the internet and other rapidly evolving media. In Kent we are seizing this opportunity (such as through the introduction of a local broadband TV channel) to ensure the flow of information is working for our communities and the County Council.

It is with all of this in mind that I value my own active participation in PASCAL. This book will not provide all the answers, but it demonstrates the growth and energy in the relationship of once distinct worlds. Policy makers and practitioners have long been encouraged to look to the research, but it is equally important that the research looks to its subject not as something to be studied from afar, but as part of the cycle and the community of knowledge. The chapters in this book go a long way to demonstrating that this idealistic notion is becoming a reality around the world, and further contribute to the debate that is active in PASCAL.

Notes

[1] PASCAL (http://www.obs-pascal.com) is an international research and policy development alliance, which aims to develop, communicate and explain new and emerging ideas about place management, social capital and learning regions. It was initiated by the Royal Melbourne Institute of Technology, the University of Stirling, the Victorian Government, the then Scottish Executive and Kent County Council. PASCAL is funded by its members on the presumption that there is considerable work to be done to enable regional governments and associated policy makers to benefit fully from emerging research and learning about how best to foster balanced and sustainable economic and social development in their regions. (To find out more about the service or to become a subscriber or supporter please contact mary.serafim@rmit.edu.au *or* lyanamacinnes@stir.ac.uk).

Contributors

Professor David Adams
Professor of Management and Innovation, University of Tasmania, Australia

Professor Britt Andersen
Assistant Professor, Programme for Learning in Complex Systems, Akershus University College, Norway

Mr Stuart Auckland
Assistant Director and Lecturer – Community Engagement, Department of Rural Health, University of Tasmania, Australia

Ms Anne Badenhorst
Director, Community and Regional Partnerships, RMIT, Australia

Mr Dave Beck
Lecturer in Community Development, Department of Adult and Continuing Education, University of Glasgow, UK

Dr Carolyn Broadbent
Head, School of Education, Australian Catholic University, Australia

Mr Paul Carter
Leader, Kent County Council, UK

Dr Lesley Doyle
Pascal Research Fellow, Stirling Institute of Education, University of Stirling, UK

Professor Paolo Federighi
Ordinary Professor in Pedagogy, University of Florence, Italy

Mrs Susan Johns
Research Fellow, Department of Rural Health, University of Tasmania, Australia

Mr Peter Kearns
Director, Global Learning Services, Australia

Associate Professor Sue Kilpatrick
Director, Department of Rural Health, University of Tasmania, Australia

Ms Gwenneth Marshall
PhD Student, School of Performance and Cultural Industries, University of Leeds, UK

Professor Barry McGaw
Director, Melbourne Educational Research Institute, University of Melbourne and formerly Director of Education, Organisation for Economic Co-operation and Development (OECD)

Dr Balázs Németh
Reader in Lifelong Learning, Lifelong Learning Research Centre, University of Pécs, Hungary

Ms Jaana Puukka
Analyst, OECD Programme on International Management in Higher Education, Turku Polytechnic, Finland

Dr Denise Reghenzani
Director, Global Learning Services, Australia

Professor Ingunn Sandaker
Professor and Research Director, Programme for Learning in Complex Systems, Akershus University College, Norway

Professor Hans Schuetze
Professor Emeritus, Centre of Policy Studies in Higher Education and Training, University of British Columbia, Canada

Dr Rob Strathdee
Head of School, School of Education Studies, Victoria University of Wellington, New Zealand

Mr Larry Swanson
Director, O'Connor Center for the Rocky Mountain West, University of Montana, USA

Mr John Tibbitt
formerly Senior Principal Research Officer, Scottish Executive

Mr Peter Welsh
Department Head, Analysis and Information, Kent County Council, UK

Ms Jessica Whelan
Lecturer, Department of Rural Health, University of Tasmania, Australia

Chapter 1

Connecting research, policy and practice in building stronger communities

Lesley Doyle and Peter Welsh

Origins and purpose

Building stronger communities is a key objective for government at all levels in many parts of the world. The rapid expansion of cities, the regeneration of existing urban areas and a renewed interest in regional dynamics are prominent features of the social and economic strategies of governments and of increasing interest to businesses and the community sector. These developments bring some major challenges in recognising and responding to the changing needs of the spectrum of urban, rural and remote communities and for the crucial role played by lifelong learning in creating the conditions for well-being and prosperity.

In this fourth publication[1] from PASCAL[2] (the third published by NIACE), researchers, policy makers and practitioners come together to demonstrate, in a wide variety of settings, how improved dialogue between them is benefiting the development of new initiatives to strengthen communities. In demonstrating the beneficial outcomes of knowledge production and transfer, our aim is to encourage those in government, business and in community practice-leading roles to develop further the arrangements to facilitate the collaborative sharing and application of knowledge drawn from reflections on experience and from research. PASCAL operates in a broad cross-disciplinary fashion, with input from spatial geography, education, governance and different notions of social, human and cultural capital. This has produced an eclectic collection of chapters which challenge conventional boundary issues. This book is therefore typical of PASCAL's work – collaborating through and across traditional boundaries to elicit and transfer new knowledge across space and time.

Our attention in this volume is on two related areas and the links between them. The first is with policies and practices for sustainable community development and the understanding and development of the role of lifelong learning. The second is the way new knowledge is produced and incorporated into the first. Both are rooted in current concerns and draw from a conference and policy forum, sponsored respectively by PASCAL and the Department for Victorian Communities which took place in Melbourne, Australia in July 2006. At both events, participants were concerned with new learning, better governance and future directions in building stronger communities. There was a general consensus that stronger communities can accumulate social capital which in turn transfers over into lifelong learning – for example, through greater participation, retention and completion of learning activities with further benefit for the sustainability of the community.

It was apparent that there is a growing understanding of the importance of spatial and in particular local place factors in shaping social and human capital, and of the significance of governance – especially at a local level – in producing and sustaining synergies between them and connecting with national policies. Governments at all levels have a growing interest in place-based strategies, both as drivers of prosperity and well-being and of innovation. But there is recognition, largely as a result of research, that the processes are more complex than hitherto thought with, for example, social capital playing a much greater role than previously credited.

It was also clear at both the Australian events that there is a new, growing mutual respect and shared purpose between policy, practice and research. An earlier PASCAL book, *Making Knowledge Work*[3] reflected the need to find a common language between them. With this new book we are taking the process further through examples of fruitful dialogue. Drawn from ten different countries, each chapter demonstrates that research and academic theory, themselves often derived from practice, are finding ready application to the benefit of new policy and new practice around the concepts of place management, social capital and learning cities and regions. The chapters further offer examples of a productive synergy in the processes of knowledge transfer, brokerage and exchange.

Each of the chapters provides illustrations of the interweaving of the two policy themes of sustainable community development and lifelong learning, but from a particular governance perspective. The impact of international and national policies, their application and reinterpretation at regional and local level, draws attention to the permeating impact of globalisation at a local level

– aptly termed 'glocalization' by Robertson (1995). We have grouped the chapters into sections focused respectively on the international/national and regional/local levels, although inevitably the boundaries become fuzzy, for example where there is regional cooperation across national boundaries. The international/national chapters in Part 1 of the book are characterised by a high level of theory and abstraction, the offer of deduction from theory to some specific cases, and reference to national-level policies. Part 2 offers chapters with a regional/local focus on sub-regional networks and governance. These are mostly case-based; they show case-study methodology, make inductions from cases to the theory and concentrate on 'people and places'.

Knowledge-making and the processes of policy and practice development

We begin here with some observations (reflecting the conversations at the 2006 events in Australia) about the often uncertain relationship between knowledge production and the incorporation of new knowledge and learning into policy and practice development. Whether working at international, national, regional, local or community level, policy makers and practitioners may worry that they are running the danger of missing out on a 'better way' for lack of information, knowledge and analysis.

Good professional practice places great store on reflection, leading to the accumulation of powerful 'practice wisdom' as a guide to practice development, and as a source of influence on policy making. Policy makers also are subject to a number of pressures from lobby groups, politicians and political organisations, professional or other communities of interest including researchers, and from unanticipated events. All will present different kinds of 'evidence' of the need, in their view, for policy initiatives.

During the 1990s governments in many parts of the world committed themselves to improve the evidence base underlying new policies. A number of writers, while accepting governments' intention to use the best available evidence in policy making, nonetheless suggest that the reality is very different. For example, Nutley (2003), based in the Research Unit for Research Utilisation (RURU) in Scotland, observes with reference to the UK that:

> Research evidence does not always, or even often, enter the policy process as part of a rational consideration of policy

options. Instead research tends to become known and discussed within policy networks through a process of advocacy. This suggests that other aspects of the modernising government agenda which seek to open up policy processes, to make them more consultative and inclusive of stakeholder interests, are likely to be a more powerful vehicle for increasing research impact. (Nutley, 2003, abstract)

Nutley's reference to networks and advocacy strongly echos the work of Sabatier (1988), who introduces the concept of 'beliefs systems' as a variable in his analytical approach to the study of policy making. Sabatier focuses on the analysis of change and 'policy learning'. He underlines the importance of the interests of actors, often combined in 'advocacy coalitions' which may not always be concerned simply to find the best solution. Interests may include actors' beliefs concerning the objectives of policies and the means used to meet them. Sabatier sets out a framework for the analysis of policy change which rests upon three criteria:

- understanding policy change requires a time perspective of a decade or more;
- the most useful way to think about policy change is through a focus on the interaction of actors from different institutions interested in the policy area;
- public policies can be conceptualised as sets of value priorities and causal assumptions about how to realise them. (Sabatier, 1988: 131)

Sutton (1999) seems to give more prominence to the political dimension in her analysis of the policy process and she too rejects a 'linear model' of policy making as inadequate. Osborne and Edwards (2003), in relation to policies of lifelong learning, give credence to Weiss's 'interactive model' (1977), suggesting ways research might be used by policy makers as part of a complex process.

So how might research be regarded by those in policy-making roles and by service practitioners? Paul Carter, leader of Kent County Council (England), in the foreword to this volume provides a starting point in stressing the role of research in validating professional practitioner experience, in the investigation of 'customer needs' and the evaluation of service initiatives. Researchers will recognise an immediate tension here, well expressed by Wilson (2006), when he writes: 'research is intended primarily to lead to the production of new knowledge. This is, unfortunately, a tortuous process in which the tasks of defining research questions, gathering data and trying to make sense of it can be very untidy. It can be a real struggle to fit into the framework necessary to meet contractual obligations'.

There is, of course, no certainty that the researchers' research questions will correspond to those issues which policy makers and practitioners identify. Biesta's (2007) paper: 'Why "What Works" Won't Work: Evidence-Based Practice and the Democratic Deficit in Educational Research' illustrates this dilemma. In his critical analysis of the idea of evidence-based practice and the ways in which it has been promoted and implemented in the field of education, he concludes that 'evidence-based practice provides a framework for understanding the role of research in educational practice that not only restricts the scope of decision making to questions about effectivity and effectiveness, but that also restricts the opportunities for participation in educational decision making'. In this way, professional and user involvement can be limited if they are not seen to be approaching policy making from the same perspective as government. Wiliam (2002) takes this much further, offering little hope for educational research having any effect unless the practitioners are involved at every stage: 'the failure of educational research to impact on practice stems from a failure to understand the nature of expertise in teaching, and that traditional models of knowledge transfer can only be effective for those at a relatively limited level of competence'. It is therefore imperative that teachers are: 'involved, collaboratively, with researchers in a joint process of knowledge creation'.

There is a range of other issues identified in the literature which may serve to inhibit the contribution of research to practice and policy. These include knowing where to look for relevant research, differential use and ambiguities in the meaning of terms and language used by practitioners, policy makers and in research, the interpretation of accumulations of research and analysis, and the time frames available for decision making.

These issues are being tackled in a number of ways. Sponsors of research are taking active steps to improve the awareness of and access to research through improved dissemination. But important though this is, there is recognition that 'the passive dissemination of research findings is not sufficient to ensure that they are used to improve service delivery and to inform policy' (National Audit Office, 2003). It is the utilisation of research which is crucial.

There are now a number of research organisations which are devoted to the policy making/practice/research interface, usually with specific foci. For example, the International Development Research Centre (IDRC) is 'a Canadian Crown corporation that works in close collaboration with researchers from the developing world in their search for the means to build healthier, more equitable, and more prosperous societies'. The Research Unit for Research Utilisation (RURU) is a Scotland-based organisation whose stated role is 'to conduct research on research use and provide a research resource for all those interested in using research to improve public policy and services. In addition to its research activities, RURU also provides training in areas relating to the use of research in policy and practice.' Again, the Global Development Network (GDN), based in India, consists of research and policy institutes. Its concerns are with 'generating and sharing knowledge, building research capacity and bridging the gap between ideas and policies for development'.

It is likely, that just as with practitioners, the impact of research on policies and policy makers will be facilitated through partnership and dialogue if the issues identified above are to be overcome. Organisations such as the PASCAL International Observatory act as a repository for research findings, whether commissioned by government departments or other reputable organisations such as research councils, but also through its active engagement with government at all levels, PASCAL seeks to ensure that research is accessible and intelligible. Of course, the corollary of successful research dissemination has to be receptiveness on the part of policy makers and practitioners, and this book provides examples of the effectiveness of such reciprocity. Reciprocity is not confined to the willingness of policy makers and practitioners to 'take research on board'. It extends also to an understanding that reflective practice is an important springboard for ideas for exploration in research and incorporation into wider, more general policy. It also embraces the awareness that local situations likewise are both illustrative of issues for research and contexts in which to understand and explore policy and practice implementation and impact.

As noted earlier, the chapters in this volume traverse a wide range of cases, countries and cooperative endeavours to build community sustainability and promote lifelong learning. The interdependence of these two goals and the common links with the importance of place and social capital are repeated themes. The chapters which follow provide examples of connections between research, policy and practice at all levels from the international to the local, with specific reference to sustainable community development and the role of lifelong learning. The organisation of the chapters into the two categories of international/national and regional/local reflects the differing spatial orientations of the cases being analysed rather than any distinctive theoretical differentiation. Indeed, one of the more interesting issues being canvassed in many of the chapters is the ability to transfer knowledge and practice in both directions, from the local to the regional and international and from the international to the regional and local.

In the foreword, Paul Carter brings home the potential significance of research from the perspective of the policy maker and practitioner, but grounds this within the reality of the dynamic and often reactive world of a large political organisation. He emphasises the importance of research in validating professional, practitioner experience and the further investigation of 'customer needs'. In this way the work of researchers impacts on a policy process, which is driven by external factors. These may include belief systems, events, policy from central government or financial constraints, rather than the ideal of research driving policy from the outset.

Perspectives on sustainable community development and the role of lifelong learning

The authors of the chapters in this book have brought to bear the multi-disciplinary and international perspectives of PASCAL. In the first section of the book, we use a wide lens to offer international and national perspectives, beginning with an exploration of some of the external factors shaping lifelong learning trends by Hans Schuetze (Canada). He argues that beliefs and funding offer particular salience in explaining the nature and directions of lifelong learning. In lifelong learning policy, Schuetze argues that the fundamental ideological choice between state intervention or free-market activity, and any potential mix of the two, forms a starting point for a debate, which in turn impacts upon structures, delivery mechanisms and ultimately determines learners' experiences. He explores this perspective through the means of four models of lifelong learning which he labels emancipatory, cultural, open society and human capital.

Schuetze argues that, through these four models, lifelong learning has been absorbed into policy, culture and language, and that while there may be no universal agreement on what lifelong learning is, the basic principle that the nature of education provision has changed to encompass both formal and informal approaches (life-wide learning), and to this end both policy learning and change may be evidenced.

The impact of lifelong learning on society beyond the public policy makers in government is explored by Rob Strathdee (New Zealand) through a focus on social capital. The relationship between innovation, knowledge transfer, learning communities and social exclusion is examined with reference to the creative sector and to biotechnology. Strathdee argues that one way to advance understanding of these aspects of society is to incorporate Bourdieu's notion of *field* into our research and testing. Bourdieu (1988) saw cultural capital operating in conjunction with economic and social capital in the process of social class reproduction. Economic capital refers to financial assets and finds expression in general terms as property rights, while social capital refers to resources that can be mobilised through network membership. In various configurations and in different ways in different settings, social capital confers advantage. Different resources, or capitals, have different values in different settings (or fields). Although problems exist with field theory, Strathdee builds a case for its utility to understand better the value of social capital operating in different contexts and how it interacts with other forms of capital.

The relationship between New Zealand's research universities and the biotechnology sector serves as a case study in which he examines the different levels of skills required by employers, relative to formal qualifications. His conclusions point towards a situation within this specific sector which takes the formal qualification as the basic requirement, with greater value being placed by employers on intangible, complex notions of reputation, innovation and participation in specialised global networks.

The complex interaction between the formal and informal is developed with reference to several examples of institutions and sectors in Norway and elsewhere. Ingunn Sandaker and Britt Andersen (Norway) explore the utility of complexity theory. They address the dynamic tension between strategies for cooperation and integration across institutional layers, and the complex phenomena emerging from the consequences of agents' behaviours. Both from a policy maker's point of view and from a scientific position, for the success of a 'learning region', the authors argue that it is crucial to analyse the relative proportion of influence of the organisations and the agents responsible for them.

Sandaker and Andersen posit that borders, both geographic and institutional, have become more porous, and informal relations within and between systems have increased exponentially. The consequences may be perceived as a lesser degree of predictability and control. With increased knowledge on how to take advantage of the dynamics of complex systems, combined with evidence-based human performance technology, the objectives of learning regions may be within reach.

While the highly theoretical approach outlined above sets boundaries of understanding, it is important and within the objectives of PASCAL to develop the application of theories to address issues faced by the range of professional disciplines, including educators, planners and policy makers working in the context of community development and lifelong learning. In the following chapters we seek to better understand these applied contexts with examples from Europe and Australasia.

An applied study of the co-location of different schools is presented in the chapter by Barry McGaw (OECD). The lack of systematic evidence about the impact of co-located services on the development of social capital or, indeed, on the social connectedness of these projects is examined. To overcome this lack of evidence, the solution of conducting a number of substantial pilot projects is put forward. Studies of this type would look at systematic and wide-ranging sets of evidence. A set of carefully designed indicators is suggested and indeed is already being applied by private-sector developers in conjunction with government bodies. McGaw argues that such work requires the development of new mechanisms for communities to be involved in determining the shape of their education services. He suggests that all three tiers of Australian government (national, regional and local) need to be involved, together with private developers and service providers.

The lessons learned from the experience of McGaw's study could be of considerable benefit not only for the development of education services in greenfield sites but also for the substantial rationalisation and refurbishment programmes being undertaken with existing facilities, whether in Australia or elsewhere.

While McGaw's focus on the physical co-location of lifelong learning facilities poses questions for those engaged in the urban planning process, the following chapter provides a context for joining up and co-location of policies.

Balázs Németh (Hungary) argues that while there is now a clear framework for lifelong learning through the European Commission's work, initial take-up of the ideas in the EU has been relatively slow and primarily driven by economic concerns – namely to maintain skilled labour and therefore competitive advantage. He argues that lifelong learning strategies need to parallel social objectives (such as social inclusion) and civic objectives (such as more active citizenship) if they are to be successful.

Crucially in the context of this book, Németh also canvasses (through the Hungarian experience) the role of regional strategies in integrating lifelong learning into localised policy objectives around tourism, population settlement and health care. Finally he raises the important issues of how and when there might be a unified EU approach to lifelong learning rather than the current jurisdiction-by-jurisdiction approach.

A further national perspective is provided in Peter Kearns and Denise Reghenzani's analysis of the state of the learning communities' agenda in Australia. They note that in parallel to most international situations, lifelong learning in Australia is poorly understood and that this operates as a barrier to coordinated national policy and development, resulting in an ad hoc growth pattern and in the main, community and regional learning strategies rather than nationally coordinated approaches.

The authors identify two main barriers to integrated local learning com-munities and in doing so strengthen similar findings of others in this volume. Further, they put forward the view that emerging local and international drivers are starting to come together, causing central shifts in policy thinking.

Importantly, Kearns and Reghenzani demonstrate the rich array of local-level initiatives that already exist and which may provide a solid knowledge platform for scaled-up national-level strategies. They conclude that there is a significant role for research in helping to develop local strategies that connect to national reform objectives.

The need for research-led strategy development is echoed by John Tibbitt (Scotland). In contrast to Kearns and Reghenzani, his chapter leans strongly towards the role of the practitioner and reflective learning rather than formal evaluation. He examines the extent to which the Scottish Executive's policy statement on regeneration (Scottish Executive, 2006) has been built on the learning from regeneration programmes in Scotland and elsewhere in the UK over the last 30 years. Tibbitt identifies a number of issues and challenges which the strategy will need to address if it is to achieve its objective of the sustainable regeneration of disadvantaged communities in Scotland.

The strategy document itself offers a number of wider issues and challenges which will have to be addressed. One such example is the role of the Executive itself, and the ways in which local communities engage with the strategy and local voices are heard. In commenting on these last issues, Tibbitt identifies continuing dilemmas over issues of governance, the role of research in informing policy, bridging government and local action, and on the balance to be struck in promoting the economic and social drivers of sustainable regeneration.

These chapters illustrate the relationship between research, policy and practice drawn from the national perspective within the policy arenas of lifelong learning and community regeneration strategy. But the debates cross jurisdiction boundaries as well. By way of example, Paolo Federighi (Italy) draws from a live research project involving several European regional governments (Wales, Andalusia, Vejle, Vastra Gotaland, Vidin, the Basque Country and Tuscany). Writing from a substantially theoretical perspective, he presents a state-of-the-art analysis in the field of transnational institutional learning and provides a detailed model of the management of the innovation of training and lifelong learning policies, based mainly on voluntary and self-governing methodologies. The soft Open Method of Coordination (OMC) model between regional governments is adopted to be utilised in the study. This model makes it possible to adapt methodologies to the institutional norms and procedures existing in each regional government because it depends on collaboration rather that any form of diktat.

In a further cross-national study, Jaana Puukka (Finland and OECD) draws lessons from the OECD study *Supporting the Contribution of Higher Education Institutions to Regional Development*, which involved 14 regions in 12 countries, and was carried out in 2005–06. Puukka's review seeks to understand the rationales, stages of development, drivers and barriers to the engagement of higher education institutions with regional development. This is offered through an examination of strategies, policies and activities at institutional, regional and national levels.

The chapter highlights the different stages of development of capacity to engage with regional development between higher education institutions, and illustrates the tension for many institutions between the pursuit of world-class research and enhanced regional engagement. However, the study points to many cases where these activities complement and reinforce each other. Puukka suggests that institutions need to find a balance between allowing and encouraging individual initiatives, and strengthening institutional management to promote regional engagement in a way which does not infringe academic autonomy. In conclusion, she points nevertheless to a number of challenges for institutions if they are to become more regionally engaged.

Local research projects bring out finer detail and a wider range of cases in which local knowledge is central to the development of learning and community engagement. Anne Badenhorst (Australia) focuses on a project for young people at risk in schools which aims to assist them into pathways in further education, training or employment in Melbourne. She explores the interaction between a programme which grew from local issues and committed organisations, and a national programme with similar objectives 'imposed' from the centre.

Badenhorst demonstrates the power and ability of community collaboration to match and improve the research and development of solutions by government but she also reveals the limitations of the local project. These occur in particular where matching policy responses from government are not forthcoming, resulting in barriers caused by structures and programmes, which are beyond local control. Universities are cited as examples of how organisations support the work of partnerships in promoting the learning of all participants. Badenhorst describes the varied contributions made: universities can provide accommodation and other resources, information and analysis, guide or initiate local research to facilitate the understanding of different stakeholder perspectives on relevant issues and help identify indicators of successful outcomes.

Carolyn Broadbent (Australia) describes a community education project in a suburb of Canberra aimed at strengthening school–community partnerships with a view, among other things, to increasing participation in education of Indigenous people. The successful outcomes from earlier programmes are used to argue that deepening an understanding of, and respect for, Indigenous traditions and culture is essential to improving the achievement levels of Indigenous students and members of the wider Indigenous community.

The chapter examines the way a community-based programme assisted in building mutual trust and respect between participants for the sharing of knowledge and expertise. In reflecting on progress, Broadbent shows how a learner-centred approach and the negotiation of the course content helped build active engagement in the learning process to build a strong community of learners.

Knowledge about how government policy levers can shape desired features of communities, such as places to turn to others for support, is increasing. David Adams (Australia) examines the policy-practice dynamic through an analysis of how governments are now able to link policy objectives with community-level strategies. Context to this study is provided through an examination of how the State of Victoria Government, Australia, has been exploring ways of using information communication technology (ICT) to create 'virtual' communities for young people. Just like place-based communities, these new communities can provide a range of benefits to young people.

Adams argues that the logical extension of the communities' agenda is to privilege those local institutions that can be close to the people, democratic-ally responsible, general-purpose and responsive to local risks and oppor-tunities. In principle, this pushes towards a greater role for local governments. He concludes that entities such as PASCAL have an important international role in observing and analysing these new developments around community, around governance and around new technologies – to build better theory and to understand better the policy implications.

Partnerships for developing rural health services in Tasmania are examined in the work of Sue Kilpatrick, Stuart Auckland, Susan Johns and Jessica Whelan (Australia). The authors draw on experiences in two rural community coalitions working to negotiate and plan health service provision. Using a set of indicators of maturity for partnership working drawn from the group development and partnership research literature, the authors illustrate the key role of the behaviour of 'boundary crossers' in mature partnership working. Boundary crossers are people who can move freely between community and professional domains and have the trust of both because they understand their values, cultures and languages. The authors argue that an understanding of the characteristics and behaviours of boundary crossers can provide valuable insights for external agents in formulating their approach to partnerships to build community capacity for health.

Kilpatrick *et al.* point to the gains to be obtained from the development of sustainable partnerships based on reciprocity and trust among participants, but make it clear that the difficulties in achieving such partnerships should not be underestimated.

The central role played by individual actors, their skills and understanding of the environment in which they function is further explored by Dave Beck (Scotland). His contribution reflects on a programme to develop community capacity, working with a group of unemployed people who were active in community work on a voluntary basis in Inverclyde near Glasgow. Based on a Freirean approach, students, together with a project worker and a university worker, collectively examined their experience and understanding of social capital. The group went on to identify both the strengths and downsides of the notion and found that even when people had apparently high levels of social capital through friendships, family and workplaces, it did not necessarily give them access to influence on policy making or the allocation of resources.

Beck reflects that community learning and development might provide a critical analysis and the organisational skills to better harness those stocks of social capital to effect change. He also points to the need for policy and practice to be grounded in a clear appreciation of the perspective of those likely to be most affected by a policy initiative. He draws attention to a view among his course participants that much activity with a legitimate aim of developing social capital in communities can be seen as tokenistic, more focused on human capital than social capital, and runs the risk of being counterproductive through further marginalisation of disempowered groups, if stronger efforts are not made to 'let the community in'.

Local leadership may provide clues as to how community engagement can be made a reality. Larry Swanson's (USA) contribution combines commercial and public-service perspectives, offering a means of advancing local leadership skills and broader community learning. Paying due regard to national-, state- and sub-state-level economic developments in the United States, the goal of Swanson's suggested approach is to link up key decision makers and decision making as they affect community vitality and future development. In Billings, Montana a process is being carried forward by a private–public leadership partnership called *Celebrate Billings* which is serving as the planner, organiser, and convener of multiple forums and community workshops. It includes representatives of the communities' two large hospitals, the largest bank, a local university, a college of technology, a daily newspaper and the City of Billings through its mayor's office.

Swanson has been involved in this process from the beginning as a significant resource, assisting in area learning regarding economic change and factors in future economic success by the community. He explains how the O'Connor Center for the Rocky Mountain West at the University of Montana developed a Regional Economies Assessment Database (READ), a computerised database and analysis system designed for local leaders to facilitate visualisation and comprehension of the economy and economic activity.

The chapters outlined above place significant value on the dynamic of social relations within the exercise of power and influence as part of the processes of building stronger communities. However, this dimension appears absent in many of the policy approaches cited in the national and even regional cases presented in this work. It is from this perspective that Gwenneth Marshall's (England) work may be seen contribute most to the present volume.

Examples from England provide the context for Marshall's critical analysis of identity implications within current strategy-led governance practice by planners, development agencies, arts managers and others in the UK, as they respond to regional, national, international and global agendas. Her challenging analysis demonstrates that the strategies adopted are imbued with what may be unacknowledged understandings of identity, which can in turn influence and constrain future identities. The chapter considers interventions that could be made in this process and suggests a theoretical framework for the development of systemic, practical and dynamic processes that could be adopted, in contrast to the layering of add-on consultative procedures that have become a standard, though in some cases ineffective, feature of master planning processes. The interventions may point towards the need for different approaches to development processes, event management, codes of practice and professional and occupational training.

The research/policy/practice relationship

It is through the understanding of projects and research thinking across many countries that PASCAL facilitates processes of knowledge transfer and policy learning. In these chapters, policy makers and practitioners endeavour to engage with the research world where recognition of complexity through analytical thought can frequently be the greatest contribution academics can make – though it may not always be particularly appreciated at the time! But researchers have to learn to explain themselves, to ensure their analysis is made accessible (as well as easy to find) so that it contributes to the collective thinking which makes up the policy process. At the same time they need to recognise that what they think of as good research for policy makers is not necessarily what makes good policy in terms of either method, content or practicality. By the same token, an increased awareness is required from researchers, policy makers and practitioners as to which role research is endeavouring to fulfil at any given time: Is to critique a policy? Is it to aid the making of new policy? Is it to evaluate existing policy or practice? This is particularly important to ensure that the expansive thinking which Biesta

(2007) refers to is not squeezed out by the highly selective and perhaps rather suspect approach, at least in the eyes of some, advocated by 'evidence-based' and 'rational' policy making.

This is where the PASCAL International Observatory comes into its own – not only as a repository and access point for research findings but also in its provision of a relatively neutral space for debate. The development of the PASCAL associateship, embracing different players by profession and occupation, has resulted in a network of multidisciplinary experts coming from a wide range of theoretical as well as political and organisational perspectives across the world. Its constructive, mediating approach facilitates conferences, books, hot topics and a website, all bringing research, policy and delivery together. For all their different starting points, collectively, the chapters in this volume offer consistent and important threads and conclusions which are highlighted in the final chapter.

Notes

[1] C. Duke, M. Osborne and B. Wilson (eds), *Rebalancing the Social and Economic: Learning, Partnership and Place* (Leicester: NIACE, 2005);. (2) C. Duke, L. Doyle and B. Wilson (eds), *Making Knowledge Work* (Leicester: NIACE, 2006); (3) M. Osborne, K. Sankey and B. Wilson (eds), *Social Capital, Lifelong Learning and the Management of Place: An International Perspective* (London: Routledge, 2007).

[2] PASCAL (http://www.obs-pascal.com) is an international research and policy development alliance, which aims to develop, communicate and explain new and emerging ideas about place management, social capital and learning regions. It was initiated by the Royal Melbourne Institute of Technology, the University of Stirling, the Victorian Government, the Scottish Executive, Communities Scotland and Kent County Council. PASCAL is funded by its members on the presumption that there is considerable work to be done to enable regional governments and associated policy makers to benefit fully from emerging research and learning about how best to foster balanced and sustainable economic and social development in their regions. (To find out more about the service or to become a subscriber or supporter please contact mary.serafim@rmit.edu.au *or* lyanamacinnes@stir.ac.uk).

[3] C. Duke, L. Doyle and B. Wilson (eds) (Leicester: NIACE, 2006).

References

Biesta, G. (2007) 'Why "what works" won't work: evidence-based practice and the democratic deficit in educational research', *Educational Theory*, 57(1): 1–22.

Bourdieu, P. (1988) *Homo Academicus*. Trans. Peter Collier. Stanford, CA: Stanford University Press.

Duke, C., and Charles, D. (2006) 'Old wheels and new: cyclical progress in the use of language, metaphors, networks and projects to enhance learning and city governance', in C. Duke, L. Doyle and B. Wilson (eds), *Making Knowledge Work: Sustaining Learning Communities and Regions*. Leicester: NIACE.

Global Development Network (2007) (http://www.gdnet.org/pdf/global_research_projects/br&p/BRP_synthesis.pdf), accessed May 2007.

International Development Research Centre (http://www.idrc.ca/en/ev-1-201-1-DO_TOPIC.html, accessed June 2007).

National Audit Office (2003) *Getting the Evidence: Using Research in Policy Making*. London: Stationery Office.

Nutley, S. (2003) 'Bridging the policy/research divide: reflections and lessons from the UK', keynote paper presented at *Facing the Future: Engaging Stakeholders and Citizens in Developing Public Policy*, National Institute of Governance Conference, Canberra, Australia, 23–24 April.

Osborne, M., and Edwards, R. (2003) 'Inquiring into lifelong learning', *Journal of Adult and Continuing Education*, 8(2): 165–78.

Research Unit for Research Utilisation (http://www.ruru.ac.uk), accessed June 2007.

Robertson, R. (1995) 'Glocalization: time-space and homogeneity-heterogeneity', in M. Featherstone, S. Lash and R. Robertson (eds), *Global Modernities*. London: Sage, pp. 25–44.

Sabatier, P. (1988) 'An advocacy coalition model of policy making and change and the role of policy oriented learning therein', *Policy Sciences*, 1: 129–68.

Scottish Executive (2006) *People and Place: Regeneration Policy Statement* (http://www.scotland.gov.uk/Publications/2006/06/01145839/0).

Sutton, R. (1999) *The Policy Process: An Overview*. Working Paper 118, London: Overseas Development Institute (http://www.odi.org.uk/publications/abswp118.html), accessed May 2007.

Weiss, C. (1977) 'Research for policy's sake: the enlightenment function of social research', *Policy Analysis*, 3(4): 531–45.

Wiliam, D. (2002) 'Linking research and practice: knowledge transfer or knowledge creation?', plenary presentation at the annual conference of the North American Chapter of the International Group for the Psychology of Mathematics Education, Athens, Georgia, USA, October.

Wilson, B. (2006) 'Policy-makers and researchers working together: dilemmas in making the connection', in C. Duke, L. Doyle and B. Wilson (eds), *Making Knowledge Work: Sustaining Learning Communities and Regions*. Leicester: NIACE.

Part 1

An International/national perspective

Chapter 2

Lifelong learning and the learning society: from concept to policy to practice?

Hans G. Schuetze

Lifelong learning (LLL) has become commonplace in current policy discourse. A wide range of actors – academics, employers, policy makers, educators – talk about the necessity for and the many benefits of LLL. Continuous learning after school and preparation for working life has become essential for everyone who wants to find, or hold on to, a skilled job in the 'knowledge-based economy', progress on the career ladder or participate actively in cultural and civic life. Benefits for the economy more generally are a highly trained and flexible workforce, greater productivity and therefore competitiveness in the market; and for society, LLL translates into a higher tax income, lower expenditure on unemployment, health and other social benefits, more active citizens, and ultimately greater social cohesion and more social justice. Prescriptions are made by various organisations and interest groups about what is needed to make LLL a reality and to reach the elusive goal of a learning society in which everybody learns from the cradle to the grave: more kindergarten places, better schools, more post-secondary education, more learner choice and hence greater diversification among the various educational institutions and programs, more opportunities for adult education and for self-learning, more training in the workplace. It follows from this wide array of propositions and the lack of precision that LLL is an elusive term. With this variety of objectives, LLL has been described as 'both a cliché and an empty theoretical label: Motherhood and apple pie, all things to all people' (Frost and Taylor, 2001: 51), as 'a panacea for solving all kinds of social ills and economic problems' (Tuijnman and Boström, 2002: 105). Paradoxically, this overly broad understanding makes it easy for various stakeholders to define LLL from a much narrower perspective, such as adult or continuing studies, or in terms of human resource development, using the concept as a convenient policy label.

This chapter reviews the concepts and meanings of LLL and examines its main features, drawing on the literature and policy reports and papers on LLL in theory and practice. I shall then discuss some of the organisational changes as well as the resources that would be required to put the theoretical frame into action.

Models and meanings

The concept of LLL is based on three principles which break with the traditional notion of 'front-end' formal education: LLL is life-long, 'life-wide', and centred on 'learning' and the learner rather than on 'education' and educational institutions.

LLL implies that people continue learning throughout their lives, not just in informal ways as everybody does anyway ('everyday learning'), but also through organised learning in formal and non-formal settings.[1] Most analysts take this to mean further or continuous learning after the phase of initial (compulsory) education and therefore concentrate on post-compulsory or post-secondary learning activities. However, the extent and quality of education during the earlier, 'formative' years are considered of crucial importance for the ability and motivation to engage in further learning later in life (e.g. Istance, 2004; Hargreaves, 2002). Therefore, a strategy of LLL must include these formative years. While this may not be obvious to the so-called 'developed' countries with ten years of compulsory schooling and universal school attendance, elementary and secondary schooling and literacy education for adults beyond school age may be the top priority within an agenda of LLL in less developed countries (see for example Alvarez Mendiola, 2006; World Bank, 2002).

The 'life-wide' component recognises the fact that organised learning occurs not just in schools, colleges, universities and training institutions, but in a variety of forms and in many different settings, many of them outside the formal educational system. In a system of 'life-wide' learning the assessment and recognition of knowledge learned outside the formal education system becomes a fundamental necessity. Simple as this may appear, this proposition poses a major challenge to the established hierarchy and traditional validation of different kinds of knowledge, that is both the places where, and the mode in which, knowledge and know-how (i.e. the applied form of knowledge) have been acquired. If all forms and types of know-how are treated the same way no matter where and how they have been acquired, mechanisms are needed for assessing and recognising skills and competencies (OECD, 1996). These mechanisms must assess individual knowledge and abilities, instead of formal qualifications, or the reputation and quality of accredited or otherwise recognised formal educational institutions and their programs. That formal qualifications and actual abilities are not identical has been demonstrated impressively by the International Adult Literacy Survey (IALS), which was designed to assess literacy levels of the adult population in various countries (OECD, 2000). The surveys showed that discrepancies of certified and actual know-how exist on both ends of the spectrum: while a relatively sizable per-centage of holders of high school or even advanced education qualifications have only minimal levels of literacy, others with few formal qualifications have demonstrated literacy competence at advanced levels. Under a LLL aspect, both groups are ill served by the present system of front end educa-tion: the former group relying on qualifications acquired during their youth which are no longer adequate, the latter with knowledge acquired in non-formal settings and modes without the formal certification that is required for both admission to continuous studies in the formal system and access to good jobs in the labour market.

The change of perspective from 'education' and 'schooling' to 'learning' entails an even more radical departure from the present system. This shift emphasises the individual process of learning and de-emphasises its social dimension that is associated with education and schooling. It has a number of consequences. The first of these is the recognition that there is little room for prescribed and rigidly structured and sequenced curricula or programs that apply to every individual belonging to the same age group. With the exception of the early years of formal learning, what is learned, and when, where and how it is learned, is determined, in principle, by learners themselves – thus 'choice' has become a key term associated with this emphasis on learning and learner-centred programs. Secondly, in a learner-based system the individuals have not only more choice but also a greater personal agency for taking action and making meaningful choices among the various options open to them. To make an informed choice can be very difficult as information is often incomplete, misleading or outright wrong, and may be – even if it is correct – too complex for an individual to assess the costs versus the benefits.

Individual motivation and ability to engage in learning beyond compulsory schooling is also crucial to exercise choice. Motivation and capacity for learning are factors that are dependent on others, especially the individual's socioeconomic background, endowment with cultural and social capital, and the quality of people's childhood and primary education experience. From a lifelong angle, the capacity and motivation of further learning are also closely related to the structure and processes of day-to-day situations, especially the workplace (Rubenson and Schuetze, 2000).

Principal models

In summary, we can distinguish several basic models, all located under the same banner of LLL yet demonstrating differences.[2] These models advocate different scenarios of education and learning, of work, and ultimately of society:

- an emancipatory or social justice model which pushes the notion of equality of opportunity and life chances through education in a democratic society ('LLL for ALL');
- a cultural model where learning is a lifelong process aiming at an individual's fulfilment of life and self-realisation ('LLL for self-fulfilment');
- an 'open society' model in which LLL is seen as an adequate learning system for developed, multicultural and democratic countries; and
- a human capital model where LLL connotes continuous work-related training and skill development to meet the needs of the economy and employers for a qualified, flexible and adaptable workforce ('LLL for employment').

Of the four models, the first is an idealistic, normative and somewhat utopian concept, promoting LLL for *all*. The second and third are more limited in scope, and the fourth is most specific about which types of learning activities, work and employment oriented, are included.

The cultural model does not advocate a social policy like the first nor does it contain utilitarian elements: it is designed to promote learning for learning's sake, towards cultural ends, and for leisure time (Okamoto, 1994). The 'open society' model is descriptive and typical of the situation in modern and open societies. It is normative in the sense that there should be no institutional barriers to learning opportunities for anyone who wants to learn. It embraces all developments that tend to eliminate such barriers, especially the modern information and communication technologies and education and learning at a distance, especially online learning. In contrast to the first model, which would achieve its objectives by targeting specific populations that face specific barriers of a dispositional and situational nature and are therefore under-represented in formal and non-formal education and training activities, the second model emphasises the role and responsibility of the individual.

The human capital model, now appearing to be most prominently advocated, sees LLL as a continuous training system appropriate for a knowledge-based economy in which a well-educated and adaptable workforce is seen as a principal prerequisite for industrial innovation and international competitiveness (Preston and Dyer, 2003). In contrast to the traditional view that saw initial and continuing vocational or professional training largely as a responsibility of industry, the human capital notion of LLL regards individual workers as primarily responsible for acquiring and updating their skills and qualifications in order to enhance their employability and career chances.

As with all models or ideal types, none of these exists in its pure form, rather one finds hybrid forms with different emphases on one or several of these principal directions. The official policy discourse and rationale also tend to change over time, and countries that in the 1970s aspired to becoming inclusive 'learning societies' such as New Zealand, embraced a human capital-oriented strategy in the 1990s (see for example Casey, 2006). Thus, to assess country strategies towards LLL, it may be more appropriate to look at different, broader types of societal models that distinguish countries' or groups of countries' political culture and their understanding of the respective roles of the (welfare) state and of markets.

Any analysis must identify the contextual factors, forces and influences that have led to their adoption and implementation. Differences between countries may be due to different regional and country patterns of education and training, changing policy objectives and priorities, the role of the state, as well as the influence of culture.

Thus, other authors distinguish different regional models of LLL and the knowledge economy/society that depend on certain regional socioeconomic contexts. Green (2006) makes a case for a threefold typology of knowledge societies. Besides the neo-liberal model, prevalent in the USA, Australia, the UK and the Republic of Ireland (for the latter see Healy and Slowey, 2006), and the social market model of Germany and France, he argues that the third, Nordic model combines economic competitiveness and social cohesion by emphasising educational equality and hence more equal distribution of life chances.

Green's classification is very useful for the discussion of how and under what circumstances LLL is being implemented, and what the effects of the different models are regarding the distribution of educational opportunities and of income. His neo-liberal model, in many ways similar to the human capital model as mentioned above, puts the emphasis on employers and individual workers as the main actors, even if the state has an important role in providing the resources for basic education and training as well as the legislative framework for a market-oriented system. In contrast, the Nordic model is closer to the 'social justice' model which is not only different from, but, in many ways, the antithesis of the current policy pursued in the Anglo-Saxon countries. The state assumes an active role here as it establishes and, together with the 'social partners', enforces binding standards of equity rather than just setting the rules of the market and sitting on the sidelines to watch the free play of market forces (Rubenson, 2006).

As has been argued elsewhere (Schuetze, 2006), this neo-liberal or human capital model is also close to that advocated by some international organisations such as the World Bank, which, for a long time, has insisted on reducing public financing for education beyond basic education and enhancing greater private investments in post-secondary education and training. While other international organisations differ in their general direction and detailed prescription, they all reflect the policies of their members, and in particular the more influential ones among them. Thus, UNESCO (1996) advocates a more comprehensive and partly utopian model that is in some respects close to the 'social justice' concept with an emphasis on reducing inequalities between the rich and the poorer countries, while the European Commission was, at least initially, advocating a model that bore many similarities with the human capital model (ECC, 1995). Somewhat surprisingly for many analysts who see the OECD as the spearhead of global capitalism, its 1996 policy report was entitled 'Lifelong Learning for All' and stressed the need for improving the foundations of LLL, including the quality of early childhood and school education, in order to reduce educational disadvantage (OECD, 1996).

When discussing models and meanings of LLL, it should be noted that these are not static but have developed over time. Today's dominance of an economic and human capital rationale is in contrast to the strong egalitarian thrust and rationale for reforming the front-end, school-based education system of the earlier reform concepts as supported in the early 1970s by UNESCO (1972) and the OECD (1973). Whereas these recognised the need for workers to adjust their skills to changing workplace requirements, the objective of the proposed reform was primarily aimed at expanding access to general learning opportunities for people from less privileged socioeconomic backgrounds with little or no previous formal education. Thus the early model of LLL was primarily a social justice and emancipatory proposition, with a strong emphasis on advancement of an equitable society through equal opportunity regarding education and other life chances. Thus, the dominant emancipatory-utopian or social justice concept of the first generation has shifted to a more market-oriented model thirty years later, that emphasises continuous learning for increasing productivity and adjusting workers' skills to the requirements of changing production processes and global market conditions.

Organisational requirements: how much state and how much 'market'?

The lifelong aspect of learning raises questions about the structure and interrelationships between different sectors of the educational system. Since a crucial prerequisite for lifelong education is a system that allows and promotes smooth progression, which has multiple access and exit points, pathways and transitions, with no programs leading to dead ends, this would require some fundamental reforms. The challenge becomes even greater when one includes the life-wide dimension. Flexible access and transitions do not only require recognised links and solid bridges between different parts of the education system itself but also mechanisms for the passage from school to work as well as, conversely, between work, and education and training.

Closely related is the problem of transferring knowledge from one place of learning to another, or of using knowledge in a place and context different from where it was acquired. As was pointed out already, assessing and recognising knowledge that has not been acquired within and certified by the formal education system is a major conceptual as well as a practical problem. There are a variety of mechanisms that try to deal with this problem ranging from national systems of qualifications to institutional rules for the assessment and recognition of prior learning (PLAR),[3] yet, in spite of many models and different approaches and concepts, there is so far little progress overall in terms of consistency and practicality.

The coordination of various programs and institutions is another major challenge. If learning is to become 'life-wide,' the organisation, regulation, financing and promotion of learning activities do not fall exclusively into the domain of ministers of education, but fall into the responsibility of other government departments such as culture, economic and social affairs, health, and employment. Such a government-wide learning system requires a certain degree of consistency regarding policies, procedures and standards of the various agencies concerned, and also efficient mechanisms of coordination.

Moreover, articulation and coordination is not required solely between different public agencies. With a great amount of non-formal adult education occurring in the workplace, and in many other settings in which people learn not just incidentally, public and private roles, rules and responsibilities need to be defined, clarified and articulated to a greater extent than in the past. Whether a fully integrated system of LLL is possible or considered necessary or desirable, is debatable. The answer depends probably as much on the feasibility and practicality as on the respective observer's trust in market mechanisms and voluntary arrangements as opposed to a coordinating role of the state or other public body.

It is clear that such a complex scheme would also need a transparent system of comprehensive and reliable information, guidance and counselling that would enable the lifelong learner to find out about available options and make informed choices. The brevity of this statement should not belie the great difficulties that the setting up of such a system would pose.

Of course, the various models discussed above require different organisa-tional arrangements. It is obvious that it is the 'social justice' model that would need a very different, much more complex array of structures and mechanisms than the other three which are more or less substantial extensions of existing education and learning systems, even if in need of better articulation and linkages between the disparate parts than at present.

The need for better and more transparent structures, articulation and co-ordination, and comprehensive and impartial information does not answer the question of who should be providing these. Under the regime of the welfare state public authorities would have played the dominant role, and the literature of the 1970s suggested or, at least, implied a strong role for the state. Yet the shift at the end of the twentieth century has put the emphasis on 'market forces' and public-private partnerships changing the role that governments play in the production and marketing of 'services' such as education (see for example Dale, 2005). Thus the answer will depend on the political context and attitudes towards equality and social cohesion, as argued by Green (2006), above, and will therefore be different under the Anglo-Saxon than the Nordic model.

Costs and financing: who pays, and how much does it cost?

LLL covers various forms of formal and non-formal learning which are now largely separate and operate in isolation from each other, including the way they are financed. Table 1 shows various activities that are part of a LLL system and who pays for them.

Presently, financing systems for the different learning activities vary a great deal, depending not only on type of programme or institution, but also on factors such as personal background (especially age, socio-economic background, national or ethnic origin), geographical location, and employment status. The question of whether a financing system for LLL should be comprehensive in the sense that it includes all learning activities and learners, or allow for a variety of financing schemes so long as they are consistent and equitable, again depends on the scenario or model that is to be implemented.

Financing models

From the beginning of the discussion of concepts of lifelong education or learning, economists have proposed different financing models, ranging from specific to comprehensive models. Vouchers, income contingent loans, drawing rights and, more recently, individual learning accounts suggested as adequate forms for more learner-centred and broader-based systems (for details of these see Schuetze, 2007). Some of them were put to a test in the form of pilot schemes in a number of countries. The most successful of these was probably the income contingent loan scheme for Higher Education in Australia (Higher Education Contribution System – HECS). The Australian model has been emulated, or is under discussion in several other countries which wish to shift public funding for post-secondary education, or parts thereof, from educational institutions to students. The most unsuccessful pilot scheme was the individual learning accounts (ILAs) in Britain, which was closed down after only a year because of inefficiency, irregularities and fraud (Schuetze, 2007). Financial incentives, such as public grants or subsidies from employers, which are put into individual learning accounts, are thought to motivate individuals to participate in education and training activities in which they would otherwise not participate. However, the failure of ILAs has shown that good intentions alone are not enough, and that new models must not only be coordinated with other existing funding schemes, but also carefully designed to prevent misuse.

As with these two schemes, most of the proposed models do not cover the whole gamut of learning activities that would fall under a comprehensive LLL concept, nor do all cover all costs incurred by the learners, both the direct ones such as tuition and other closely associated cost, and the indirect cost, primarily the cost of living while learning (and therefore not being in full time employment). Thus the different models vary widely with respect to their comprehensiveness and coverage. While some support specific activities, or target specific groups (for example labour-market training for the unemployed, or language education for immigrants), others provide a single financing system for all LLL activities.

It is clear from the discussion of the models of LLL that there is no 'ideal' financing system that would benefit all potential lifelong learners. However it is possible to apply a number of different criteria in assessing various financing models with respect to the multiple objectives comprehensive LLL systems are expected to realise (see for example Timmermann, 1996). It is fairly obvious that the objective of providing incentives for further learning for those falling out of the high school system and adults with severe literacy difficulties will require different mechanisms than inciting highly educated professionals to engage in continuing professional education. Most important here, therefore, is the question of 'financing what?' – this brings us right back to the discussion about the different models and their objectives and agendas.

The costs of LLL

A similar question – the costs of what? – applies to the assessment of what resources would be needed for putting a LLL system into practice. Answers depend not only on what model is pursued, but also on a number of defining factors such as the existing social and economic realities, the learning infrastructure, and the level of formal educational attainment among the population. It seems obvious that the bill in lower income countries and regions (see for example Walters, 2005; Alvarez Mendiola, 2006) would be considerably higher than in other, economically and educationally more advanced ones if the same levels of attainment were envisaged.[4] However, the calculations of costs is difficult as they depend not only on the volume of the expansion of learning opportunities but also on such factors like the level of additional education, unit costs, age and motivation of learners, types of learning, and indirect and opportunity costs. In the end it seems an inevitable conclusion that more education and organised learning will cost more money, even if there are cost savings that can be realised through innovation, re-organisation and coordination (see for example OECD, 1996, 1999, 2000, 2001).

From (which) concept to (what) practice?

LLL is a concept for rethinking and remodelling established systems of education and non-formal learning. Although it is confusing in its broad claim and scope, it has proven rather resilient and influential for two reasons: first, it has adapted to a new political, socioeconomic and cultural environment, in which it can play the role as a 'master concept' for educational and social reform; and secondly because industry, and by extension ministers of economic affairs and finance, are seeing it as a necessary instrument for advancing their countries or regions towards a more knowledge-based economy. Although that objective is different and narrower than that of the broader social justice model, it should be acknowledged as *one*, but not the exclusive, interpretation of LLL. As pointed out above, the flag of LLL flies over different interests, political cultures and notions of society. The models that have been discussed earlier are partly incompatible with each other but also partly overlapping.

Notes

[1] 'Formal' settings comprise the education system, i.e. schools, colleges and univer-sities, whereas 'non-formal' settings are other places outside the formal education sector where organised learning takes place (e.g. the workplace, museums, com-munity centres, trade unions, sports clubs). By contrast, 'informal' learning is learning that takes place anywhere, yet in an unplanned, unorganised, and mostly incidental manner. Although it is also a major form of learning, this informal 'everyday learning' is not included here as it is impossible to draw a clear boundary between what can be considered 'learning' and the range of other behavioural and experiential activities in which people engage (Tuijnman and Boström, 2002).

[2] Jarvis (2004) finds the concept of LLL confusing as the different meanings –

institutionalised and individual learning – make it 'impossible to have a policy for LLL' (p. 65).

[3] There is some variation of names, e.g. Accreditation of Prior Experiential Learning – APEL in the UK.

[4] While wealthier countries, regions and municipalities can probably be convinced that benefits from further investments in education and learning will generate benefits that might offset the costs, at least in part, low-income countries will not be able to invest as it would be necessary to catch up with the more developed countries. Thus, investments in LLL in the developed countries can accentuate the problem of widening gaps and increasing levels of inequality between countries that, unless it can be stopped through aid and other measures of international solidarity, might lead to increased mobility and a 'brain drain' of especially younger people from third world countries into the countries of the 'first world'.

References

Alvarez Mendiola, G. (2006) 'Lifelong learning policies in Mexico: context, challenges and comparisons', *Compare*, 36(3): 379–99.

Casey, C. (2006) 'A knowledge economy and a learning society: a comparative analysis on New Zealand and Australian experiences', *Compare*, 36(3): 343–57.

Dale, R. (2005) 'Globalization, knowledge economy and comparative education', *Comparative Education*, 41, 117–149.

European Commission (1995) *Teaching and Learning: Towards the Learning Society* (White Paper on education and training), Luxembourg: Office for Official Publications of the European Commission.

Frost, N. and Taylor, R. (2001) 'Pattern of change in the university: the impact of "Lifelong Learning" and the "World of Work" ', *Studies in the Education of Adults*, 33(1): 49–59.

Green, A. (2006) 'Models of lifelong learning and the "knowledge society"', *Compare*, 36(3): 307–25.

Hargreaves, D.H. (2002) 'Effective schooling for lifelong learning', in D. Istance, H.G. Schuetze and T. Schuller (eds), *International Perspectives of Lifelong Learning: From Recurrent Education to the Knowledge Society*, pp. 49–62. Buckingham: Open University Press.

Healy, T. and Slowey, M. (2006) 'Social exclusion and adult engagement in lifelong learning: some comparative implications for European states based on Ireland's Celtic Tiger experience', *Compare*, 36(3), 359–78.

Istance, D. (2004) 'How well do schools contribute to lifelong learning?' In OECD (ed.), *Educational Policy Analysis*, pp. 75–95. Paris: OECD.

Jarvis, P. (2004) *Adult Education and LLL: Theory and Practice*, 3rd edn. London and New York: RoutledgeFalmer.

Okamoto, K. (1994) *Lifelong Learning Movement in Japan: Strategies, Practices and Challenges*. Tokyo: Sun Printing.

Organization for Economic Cooperation and Development (1973) *Recurrent Education: A Strategy for Lifelong Learning*. Paris: OECD.

Organization for Economic Cooperation and Development (OECD) (1996) *Lifelong Learning for All: Meeting of the Education Committee at Ministerial Level*. Paris: OECD.

Organization for Economic Cooperation and Development (OECD) (1999) 'Resources for lifelong learning: What might be needed and how might it be funded?' In OECD (ed), *Education Policy Analysis*, pp. 7–26. Paris: OECD.

Organization for Economic Cooperation and Development (OECD) and Statistics Canada (2000) *Literacy in the Information Age: Final Report of the International Adult Literacy Survey*. Paris: OECD.

Organization for Economic Cooperation and Development (2001) *Economics and Finance of Lifelong Learning*. Paris: OECD.

Preston, R. and Dyer, C. (2003) 'Human capital, social capital and lifelong learning: an editorial introduction', *Compare*, 33(4): 429–36.

Rubenson, K. (2006) 'The Nordic model of lifelong learning', *Compare*, 36(3): 327–41.

Rubenson, K. and Schuetze, H.G. (2000) 'Lifelong learning for the knowledge society: demand, supply, and policy dilemmas', in K. Rubenson and H.G. Schuetze (eds), *Transition to the Knowledge Society: Policies and Strategies for Individual Participation and Learning*, pp. 355–76. Vancouver: UBC (Institute for European Studies).

Schuetze, H.G. (2006) 'International concepts and agendas of lifelong learning', *Compare*, 36(3): 289–306.

Schuetze, H.G. (2007) 'Individual learning accounts and other models of financing lifelong learning', *International Journal of Lifelong Learning*, 26(1), 5–23.

Timmermann, D. (1996) 'Lifelong education: financing mechanisms', in A. Tuijnman (ed), *International Encyclopedia of Adult Education and Training*, pp. 300–3. Oxford: Pergamon.

Tuijnman, A. and Boström, A.K. (2002) 'Changing notions of lifelong education and lifelong learning', *International Review of Education*, 48 (1/2): 93–110.

UNESCO Commission on Education for the Twenty-first Century (1996) *Learning: The Treasure from Within*, Paris: UNESCO (Delors Report).

UNESCO Commission on The World of Education Today and Tomorrow (1972) *Learning to be*, Paris: UNESCO (Faure Report).

World Bank (2003) *Lifelong Learning in the Global Knowledge Economy: Challenge for Developing Countries*. Washington, DC (http://siteresources. worldbank.org/EDUCATION/Resources/278200-1099079877269/547664-1099079984605/lifelonglearning_GKE.pdf), accessed 1 March 2004.

Walters, S. (2005) 'South Africa's Learning Cape aspirations: the idea of a learning region and the use of indicators in a middle-income country', in C. Duke, M. Osborne and B. Wilson (eds), *Rebalancing the Social and Economic: Learning, Partnership and Space*: Leicester: NIACE, pp. 126–42.

Chapter 3

Social networks and social exclusion: the case of biotechnology in New Zealand

Rob Strathdee

This chapter explores the relationship between innovation and social capital, in the form of social networks. Although more nuanced accounts accept that the relationship between these aspects of society is complex, in general much popular (and some academic) literature on social capital either promotes the view that social capital is inherently valuable, or that the conception of social network capital is so vague it renders it almost meaningless. The work of Florida (2002; 2005a; 2005b) provides a good illustration of such problems. One of his major arguments is that regional advantage is enhanced through creating creative ecologies. Such ecologies emerge in the presence of what he refers to as the 'three Ts' – 'tolerance', 'talent' and 'technology' – and in the presence of social capital in the form of weak ties. These ties allow a 'basic level of information sharing and collaboration while permitting newcomers with different ideas to be accepted quickly into the social network' (Florida, 2002: 20). Florida's work is illustrative for two reasons. First, he has little to say in detail about the kinds of ties needed to create creative ecologies. This means his analysis does not progress beyond the very basic claim that ties matter. Second, even if such ecologies boost the capacity to innovate and advance the interests of creative workers, they appear to not advance the interests of some groups very far. For example, creative ecologies appear to increase demand for low-waged workers to service the needs of creative workers. This point is acknowledged by Florida (2002), but in somewhat of a utopian position, he believes the creative class will grow out of their residual 'self-centeredness' and increasingly come to represent the interests of all classes (Florida, 2002: 71). As Brown and Lauder (2002) point out, social capital theorists have yet to properly consider the positional nature of social capital. In this respect, while social capital theorists and those working in cognate disciplines might applaud the creation of better networking (including partnering), we know little about how valuable these partnerships are, how they might be developed in different contexts, how their use might vary across time and space, and how they might undermine the realisation of other goals.

This chapter draws upon current empirical work on social capital and knowledge transfer between biotechnology firms and providers of tertiary education in the Auckland region of New Zealand to explore some of the tensions in the social capital debate. In the case explored here, the attempt to promote innovation through partnering can be theorised as undermining one of the founding aims of public education – the promotion of open competition between students for advancement. Although it will not resolve fundamental problems at the heart of the debate, this contribution also argues that one way to advance our understanding is to incorporate Bourdieu's notion of 'field' into our social capital research (Bourdieu and Wacquant, 1992). Although there are some problems within field theory, it nevertheless provides a way for sociologists to better theorise the value of social capital operating in different contexts.

Before proceeding further, it should be stressed that the chapter draws upon both Bourdieu (1997) and Coleman's (1988) approach to social capital. In contrast to the more communitarian perspective and the open networks this implies, such as that adopted by Putnam, Leonardi and Nanetti (1993), both Bourdieu and Coleman see social capital as providing access to resources through social relationships. In this respect, social networks can be considered a form of social capital when they facilitate productive activity. Social networks, for example, are productive when they provide trustworthy advice to individuals about the quality and the availability of particular forms of employment.[1] There are, of course, important differences between Bourdieu and Coleman on the subject of social capital. For example, Bourdieu sees social capital as an individual asset, which is used by elites to advance their interests. In contrast, Coleman is more interested in using the concept to help explain why students from similarly disadvantaged backgrounds have dissimilar rates of school retention. Also in contrast to Bourdieu, Coleman tends to deemphasise the positional nature of social capital.

The first section of this contribution draws upon earlier work to explore the relationship between innovation, knowledge transfer and partnering (Strathdee, 2005). The second advances field theory as means of better understanding the value of social capital in different contexts. The third section briefly describes the research project on which this contribution is based and outlines some of the issues that the preliminary research has raised. The contribution concludes by considering the implications of partnering on the competition for advancement through education and by raising questions about social capital research.

Innovation, knowledge transfer and partnering

Interdisciplinary research is increasing throughout the world. So much knowledge is coming on that it's impossible for one individual to have all the knowledge at their fingertips. You can do excellent developmental research by yourself, but to make major breakthroughs you have to collaborate (Dekker, 2007).

As the contributions in this collection and the quote from the late Nobel Laureate and New Zealand scientist, Alan MacDiarmid, attest, greater partnering and the resulting increase in collaboration can increase the likelihood that goals (shared or otherwise) will be realised. In the area of tertiary education, for example, it is argued that innovation and competitive advantage is more likely to emerge from interactions between knowledge generators, firms, investors, and other actors working together in clusters, or learning communities (Etzkowitz and Leydesdorff, 2000). This idea that knowledge transfer is best facilitated through social interaction is based, in part, on the belief that some kinds of knowledge are tacit in nature.[2]

In contrast to explicit codified knowledge (Simmie, 2003), tacit knowledge is embodied in experts and its use is not governed by rules. Tacit knowledge is often critical to innovation in knowledge societies because it involves the generation of new knowledge and discovery, for instance, through acting on intuition. Moreover, because much embedded knowledge is tacit in nature, relationships between knowledge generators and employers are developing, such as those that exist between universities and businesses. Although university-business partnerships have existed in various forms for a long time (Bok, 2003), their value has recently been accepted by politicians and their policy makers in New Zealand and the UK. These parties have developed numerous interventions to bring knowledge creators into closer association with business to create geographies of talent (Florida, 2002). Examples of these interventions include the knowledge transfer networks in the UK (Department for Trade and Industry, 2007) and regional facilitation in New Zealand (Tertiary Education Commission, 2007).

Although it is possible to accept the argument that partnering can increase the capacity to innovate, the precise relationship between partnering and innovation varies considerably. Moreover, although politicians and social capital theorists tend to see positive social outcomes from partnering, further consideration reveals that the case is not so straightforward and it is far from clear that partnering and social inclusion are necessarily compatible objectives. For example, the idea that partnering can increase the capacity to innovate and improve the efficiency of the tertiary sector underpins the new regional facilitation model of tertiary planning in New Zealand. The idea is that by working together, better quality information will flow between providers of tertiary education and those who refer to or base decisions on qualifications, such as employers. The result of this collaboration will be a funding system that will reflect better the needs of all users of education and training. For its part, the government will fund those courses it deems necessary to meet these needs. In contrast to the practice adopted since the development of neo-liberal training strategy in the early 1990s, the government will not fund different providers to offer the same courses in competition with each other. Instead, it will fund a network of provision and will carefully monitor the cost, the quality, and the value of the training offered.

However, it is worth remembering that one purpose of education is to promote social mobility through separating individuals from their social origins. A network of provision might sound reasonable, but the social implications remain unclear. For example, to what extent the new regionalism will ease the inequality residing in spatial differences, and the resulting differences in access to tertiary education, has yet to be addressed. In addition, just because theorists can find associations between social capital and improved efficiency, this does not mean we should try and build social capital in all contexts. For example, educational qualifications are needed to advance in the field of biotechnology. It matters little how richly endowed in social capital an individual is, if they lack the required qualifications, their likelihood of advancement is debatable. Consequently, it seems reasonable for individuals and governments to invest in the production of relevant qualifications for this field. In contrast, educational qualifications are likely to place a lesser role in advancement into the creative sector, such as film and theatre, where the signals of competency resist codification. As Peter Jackson, director of several major films including the *Lord of the Rings* trilogy is reputed to have put it, 'if you want to get into film, don't go to film school'. Although the relationship between different forms of capital and advancement in the creative sector remains an empirical question, Jackson's comment is at least suggestive; indicating that investment in formal education and training in the creative sector is questionable.

In general, what matters in terms of advancement are the signals of competency (and the various capitals this implies) that are in use in particular fields. These are evolving and differ across time and space. This issue is explored in greater depth in the following section.

Field theory

As argued above, our understanding of social capital is to look at it within fields. Bourdieu (1997) developed a model of class in which he saw cultural capital operating in conjunction with economic and social capital in processes of social class reproduction. Economic capital refers to financial assets and finds expression in general terms as property rights, while social capital refers to resources that can be mobilised through network membership. In various configurations and in different ways in different settings, social capital confers advantage.[3]

An important contribution made by Bourdieu to our understanding of social capital was to give emphasis to the ways in which the different resources, or capitals, have different values in different settings (or fields). Bourdieu argued that social formations, and the institutions these give rise to, are structured around a complex ensemble of social fields. Fields are structured as a 'network, or configuration, of objective relations' among positions (Bourdieu and Wacquant, 1992: 97). The idea that different capitals have different values in different fields is helpful because it allows a better understanding that social capital has different effects in contrasting settings and contexts. Furthermore, while it is possible to describe the contest at a macro level, it is important to recognise that the way the contest is played out is best understood locally. A key reason for this is that although changes in the overall framework can occur at a macro level, for example, in the shift from social democracy to Third Way approaches to political management (Giddens, 1998), the precise mix of the resources needed for advancement (or the rules of advancement) can only be understood locally.

Fields are structured in a hierarchical fashion, with different forms of capital being of greater or lesser value in different fields.[4] However, whatever the field, some combination of economic, cultural and social capital, as well as other forms of capital, is required for advancement. So, for example, given the importance of personal referrals to their work, real estate agents arguably rely more heavily upon social capital, than on embodied cultural capital (for example, in the form of educational credentials) to be successful. In contrast (and in theory at least), academics rely more heavily upon human capital and social capital, than on economic capital to advance in their field.

Unfortunately, there has been relatively little empirical research exploring the relationship between different capitals operating in different settings. One problem is that it has proved difficult to isolate the cause of observed effects. For example, in their study of American citizenship and political power, Nie, Junn and Stehlik-Barry (1996) argue that there exist a limited number of positions of power in any network and that educational attainment is the best predictor of 'network centrality'. However, their results may further confound educational achievement with the social origins of the network participants.

Although the conceptualisation of the competition for advancement as conducted in different ways within different fields is an important development, Bourdieu (1997) did not give much indication about how the boundaries between fields should be drawn. This remains a challenge for sociologists. One solution advanced in the literature as a way of coping with problems identifying boundaries between fields is to let participants who are engaged in competition drive the boundaries of fields. This means the boundaries of a field are fluid and the subject of research and testing, and suggests we should define fields on the grounds of the interactions found, rather than on the basis of abstract principles established prior to research and testing (DiMaggio and Powell, 1983).

Another solution is to draw upon existing knowledge to define fields ahead of empirical research and testing, as does Naidoo (2003) in her work on higher education. On the one hand, this approach seems sensible (indeed, Bourdieu conceived higher education as a field), as institutions of higher education complete similar functions. For example, they all award degree qualifications and undertake research. However, on the other hand, the 'field' of higher education is diverse. For example, the economic returns from completing tertiary education differ from institution to institution and from programme to programme (Smetherham, 2006). Similarly, the entry requirements into universities also differ markedly, with some institutions being highly selective, and others less so.[5]

Finally, it is important to note that the rules of advancement are subject to change over time. In the case of regional facilitation that was noted above, arguably the move to a network provision is going to increase the selectivity of tertiary education providers. The Government has already signalled that it wishes to fund fewer student places, but at increased levels. One advantage of the previous market-orientated system of provision was that it encouraged providers to maximise recruitment into their programmes. Although the merits of this approach can be debated, by expanding provision dramatically, it did provide a way for those who might have otherwise been excluded on the basis of their relatively poor performance at school from gaining access to tertiary education, even if they tend not to convert this participation into achievement.[6] One outcome of the new funding model is that social capital will be of increased value in determining what courses receive funding. A key reason for this is that regional facilitation requires providers to seek agreement from other providers to offer courses. Another is that embodied cultural capital, in the form of educational credentials, will be of increased significance in gaining access to tertiary-level study, as providers will be encouraged to be more selective about whom they admit to their programmes.

Despite its weaknesses, such as those noted above, Bourdieu's conception of fields provides a way to understand how different kinds of capital can be combined in different ways to produce patterns of advantage and disadvantage. The following section considers its value in relation to the 'field' of biotechnology in New Zealand.

Partnering in biotechnology

> *One of the main reasons I chose to attend the University of Auckland was its emphasis on quality research. It employs some of the most highly regarded scientific researchers in the world and has established, or is collaborating with, many outstanding research bodies both at home and abroad. I also saw it as a portal to the international arena.* Cherrie Kong (Auckland University, 2007)

As the testimony from Cherrie Kong attests, delivered to readers of a large daily newspaper in Wellington in the form of a glossy advertisement brochure, the University of Auckland is promoting itself as New Zealand's pre-eminent university. According to the brochure, those who choose (or who are chosen) to study at the University of Auckland benefit not only from accessing the best knowledge on offer in New Zealand, they also benefit from access to high quality social resources, which increases their chances of winning high quality employment. These social resources include developing a network of contacts and gaining access to the leading employers, clustered in the Auckland area.

There is some evidence supporting the University of Auckland's position that it is the top university in New Zealand. According to the Performance Based Research Fund's 2004 review, the University of Auckland is the country's leading university on virtually every quality measure, including earning the most in external sources of revenue and having the greatest share of A-rated researchers. Moreover, according to the Times Educational Supplement, the University of Auckland is ranked in the top 50 research universities in the world – the only university in New Zealand to achieve this (Auckland University, 2007).

In relation to the themes prominent in this chapter, Cherrie Kong's testimony is also interesting because it situates the University as offering advantages to students derived from collaborations between individual researchers and between the University and other research bodies. As stated in the brochure, Cherrie sees the University of Auckland as providing her with a 'portal' into the global labour market. Thus, attendance at the University of Auckland provides graduates with more than educational qualifications: it provides an entry point to employment networks not available to those who graduate from other universities. Partnering in the form of university-business links has been widely encouraged by government policy. Although it is encouraged in every sector, the biotechnology sector has been identified as an area of strategic importance in the government's policy of developing an innovative New Zealand (Office of the Prime Minister, 2002).

For this reason, the biotechnology cluster that has developed around Auckland was selected as a case study exploring the formation of social capital and knowledge transfer. Space limitations preclude a full explanation of the nature of business-university links; interested readers should consult the large (and growing) literature on the subject.[7] However, the basic idea is that partnering will benefit both parties: the universities gain from sources of income and investment from commercial firms, while the firms gain from access to both innovative knowledge and suitably trained new workers.

The central research question that the project is attempting to answer is: how do bio-technology firms make and use networks to solve their human resource issues and to remain innovative? Though the research is at a preliminary stage, the evidence gathered points to the importance of networks as a means of gaining access to resources of varying kinds at most stages of production. In the initial, or 'start up' stages, circumstances of time and place, combined with innovative knowledge created in universities, produce commercial activity. For example, in one firm, an encounter between a scientist, who had spent much of his life searching for a solution to an enduring medical problem, and a wealthy investor who participated in the scientist's networks, led to the development of a new drug. In part, it was the scientist's ability to speak the language of both science and commerce, or to 'span boundaries' between academic and economic 'fields' that led to the commercial activity.[8]

One further reason identified by participants for the importance of networks is that the skills needed to innovate are highly specialised and that relatively few individuals in the world hold them. Thus, in contrast to Durkhemian-inspired functionalism, in which it is predicted that the use of open recruitment methods will increase as production becomes more technocratic and scientific, the evidence gathered as part of this project suggests the importance of closed recruitment methods. Indeed, as the demand for highly skilled and specialised staff increases, the use of networks becomes more important because the size of the potential pool of workers is very small. In this context, knowing who is innovative and who might be looking for a new opportunity requires insider status.

Beyond the start up phase, networks continue to be of importance. For example, although the process of recruiting new scientific and technical staff is formally open in that the positions are advertised, the chief scientific officers in several companies reported that they usually had people 'lined up' for the positions. Information about the capacity of the potential recruits was often obtained through the social networks in which the chief scientific officers operated. If they did not know applicants personally, they had contacts from whom they could gain information about candidates.

However, in contrast to the arguments outlined above concerning the flow of tacit knowledge, it does not appear to matter where the training was gained. So long as the employers had reliable evidence about the potential of new recruits concerning their training and their social skills, they were considered suitable employees. A critical point, however, is that the training needed to innovate was not available at every university. Recruits needed to have developed the technical skills needed and training in these are not offered at all universities.

Another reason networks were important in the recruitment process was that not all of the qualities needed to be successful in innovative firms were measured by educational qualifications, including those at doctoral level. Thus, although potential recruits may complete high-level postgraduate training in relevant areas, merely holding a qualification did not signal to employers that they necessarily had the skills required to be innovative. Employers reported that innovation depended upon workers holding both technical skills and other dispositions and attitudes, including, for example, an ability to make connections between science and business and the ability to be a 'team player'. Other forms of evidence were required to assess if potential recruits had these qualities and this was sourced through social networks.

Beyond the start up and development phases, new human resource needs were identified. For example, in contrast to the needs present at earlier stages of development, during the production phase biotechnology firms reported an increased need for technicians and decreased need for scientists. At this stage, the process changes and there is less emphasis upon networks and more emphasis upon advertising and recruitment. However, in the Auckland region, technicians were seen as difficult to recruit and the quality of potential recruits was perceived as mixed. To resolve this, employers were also recruiting skilled workers from overseas. Here, companies reported forming a view about the quality of the qualifications produced by the tertiary education systems in foreign countries which aides their decision-making. However, at all levels of production firms overseas workers were seen to bring advantages in terms of their global connections. For example, a recent appointment in sales and marketing was made precisely because of their global network of potential clients, and their ability to span networks.

Finally, at every phase of development, partnering was important. Right from the initial funding of an innovative idea at the start up phase, right through to full-scale production, partners were seen as vital. Partnering was an important way to gain access to new ideas and new sources of funding. It may be that, as the industry widens and capacity in the tertiary education sector increases, the rules of advancement will alter.

Concluding comments

The literature and the evidence gathered in the biotechnology project draws strong links between innovation and partnering. The preliminary data show that partnering is needed both to gain access to new forms of technology developed in universities, particularly at the start up and the development phases, and to gain access to forms of financial capital at all phases. In terms of gaining access to capital, an ability to span boundaries was significant. The ability to present scientific ideas in a credible and accessible manner to investors was particularly important.[9]

At various phases of production, from start up through to full production, networks also played a role in the recruitment of staff. At the start up phase, the interviewees reported that finding scientists, who had the ability to innovate, required being well embedded in the field. The highly specialised nature of the work meant that there was not a wide pool of suitable candidates and recruiters often relied upon word of mouth to identify suitable recruits. Even where positions were formally advertised, recruiters reported they usually had candidates lined up for positions. Although holding high-level qualifications, usually doctoral level, was a basic requirement at the start up phase, interviewees reported that the potential to be innovative was poorly measured by qualifications. Thus, potential recruits needed to hold high-level qualifications relevant to the area in which they would eventually work, hold other qualities linked to innovation and have valuable social networks.

At the same time, as these comments suggest, it is important not to characterise the biotechnology industry as homogenous. Instead, the sector is highly differentiated with firms varying in numerous ways, including size, target market, and stages of development. Moreover, as the sector and individual firms within it, evolve, the mix of resources needed to advance alter correspondingly. The human resources needed at the start up phase are different to those needed at the production phase. It is also useful to think of boundary spanning as leading to the formation of new fields. To be effective chief scientific officers in the emerging field of biotechnology, it is necessary to work effectively in two fields; science and business.

Research universities that are strong in bio-technology in New Zealand, such as the University of Auckland, provide both the initial innovative idea and the individuals who initially champion these ideas. However, beyond this stage, the evidence gathered so far suggests that there is little that is unique provided by this university in terms of skilled labour that can not be sourced elsewhere. Indeed, recruitment tends to take on a global, rather than local character, with interviewees reporting the quality of overseas graduates in some areas as being of superior quality. Thus, although the University of Auckland may be developing and trading on its 'reputational' capital (Brown and Hesketh, 2004), the evidence gathered so far in this research project does not support the claim that this institution provides graduates with an explicit portal into the biotechnology sector in the region in which it is situated.

One possible explanation for the trends found in the data, is that during the start up phase, the skills needed to develop innovation rely upon highly specialised knowledge that is only held by very small number of scientists who participate in global labour markets. Beyond the start up phase, workers need to have high levels of skills, but these can be codified and taught in institutions that do not necessarily have research capacity. In the production phase, the sources of innovation shift away from labour and skills towards other sources, such as the cost of labour and investment in scale. However, even at this latter stage in the development of biotechnology firms, interviewees reported some preference for overseas labour, reporting that both the technical expertise and the dependability of these workers were superior. As local training capacity increases, firms may look locally for some of their skilled workers. However, in the interim, for many firms, their recruitment strategy is global in character.

It was argued above that one way to understand better the competition for advancement through the biotechnology sector is to draw upon field theory. One benefit of field theory is that it provides a way to understand how various forms of capital might interact in different contexts. Although field theory provides some insights, it may prove to be the case that, ultimately, providing answers to these questions is likely to be an exercise in frustration for those who want to properly understand social capital because it inheres in human relationships and can not be understood in abstraction. To paraphrase E.P. Thompson's (Thompson, 1968) comments about pitfalls of defining social class mathematically, the finest sociological mess will not give us a perfect understanding of social capital. The relationship between these capitals must always be understood as embodied in real people and in real contexts, and must be understood locally.

Notes

[1] Coleman uses rational choice theory as a way to better understand the deployment of these capitals. While this approach brings with it its own set of problems and dilemmas (Boudon, 1998), nevertheless, it provides one way to better understand the relationship between social capital and innovation.

[2] For a more detailed analysis see Strathdee (2005).

[3] For Coleman (1988) social capital is embedded in concrete social relations that

permit individuals and groups to access resources. Moreover, creation of social capital is context specific and can be built up through repeated exchange in which process-based trust is established (Zucker, 1986). Thus, social capital can be a product of investment strategies (such as the cultivation of social networks through partnering) employed by groups, individuals, and the state.

[4] In addition, conceptualisations of 'elite' are field-specific.

[5] It is possible that both methods of identifying fields produce similar patterns of networks. The extent to which this occurs is possibly an outcome of the nature of the 'field' in the first place.

[6] See Blanden *et al.* (2005) for a discussion of the situation in the UK.

[7] For an extensive discussion of the literature, see Bok (2003).

[8] In this context, it is interesting to note that MacDiarmid attributed some of his success in the interdisciplinary nature of his research to the collaborations he developed with other researchers (New Zealand Press Association, 2007; Dekker, 2007).

[9] The University of Auckland now offers a postgraduate degree in Bioscience Enterprise (see http://www.science.auckland.ac.nz/uoa/science/about/subjects/bioscience_enterprise.cfm).

References

Auckland University (2007) 'A top university is closer than you think', Auckland University.

Blanden, J., Gregg, P. and Machin, S. (2005) 'Social mobility in Britain: low and falling', *CentrePiece*, Spring: 18–20.

Bok, D. (2003) *Universities in the Marketplace: The Commercialization of Higher Education*. Princeton, NJ: Princeton University Press.

Boudon, R. (1998) 'Limitations of rational choice theory', *American Journal of Sociology*, 104(3): 817–28.

Bourdieu, P. (1997) 'The forms of capital', in A.H. Halsey, H. Lauder, P. Brown and A. Wells (eds), *Education: Culture, Economy, Society*. Oxford: Oxford University Press.

Bourdieu, P. and Wacquant, L. (1992) *An Invitation to Reflexive Sociology*. Chicago: University of Chicago Press.

Brown, P. and Hesketh, A. (2004) *The Mismanagement of Talent: Employ-ability and Jobs in the Knowledge Economy*. Oxford: Oxford University Press.

Brown, P. and Lauder, H. (2002) 'Human capital, social capital, and collective intelligence', in T. Schuller, S. Baron and J. Field (eds), *Social Capital: Critical Perspectives*. Oxford: Oxford University Press.

Coleman, J. (1988) 'Social capital in the creation of human capital', *American Journal of Sociology*, 94 (Suppl.): S95–S120.

Dekker, D. (2007) 'MacDiarmid valued sharing', *Dominion Post*, obituaries, 15 February.

Department for Trade and Industry (2007) *Knowledge Transfer Networks 2007*, cited 27 February, http://www.dti.gov.uk/innovation/technology strategy/technologyprogramme/KTN/page12567.html

DiMaggio, P. and Powell, W. (1983) 'The iron cage revisited: institutional isomorphism and collective rationality in organizational fields', *American Sociological Review*, 48(2): 147–60.

Etzkowitz, H. and Leydesdorff, L. (2000) 'The dynamics of innovation: from national systems and 'mode 2' to a triple helix of university–industry–government relations', *Research Policy*, 29(2): 109–23.

Florida, R. (2002) 'The economic geography of talent', *Annals of the Association of American Geographers*, 92(4): 743–55.

Florida, R. (2005a) *The Flight of the Creative Class: The New Global Competition for Talent*. New York: Harper Collins.

Florida, R. (2005b) *Cities and the Creative Class*. New York: Routledge.

Giddens, A. (1998) *The Third Way*. Cambridge: Polity Press.

Naidoo, R. (2003) 'Repositioning higher education as a global commodity: opportunities and challenges for future sociology of education work', *British Journal of Sociology of Education*, 24(2): 249–59.

New Zealand Press Association (2007) *NZ Nobel Prize winner dies*, cited 20 March, http://www.stuff.co.nz/3955234a10.html

Nie, N., Junn, J. and Stehlik-Barry, K. (1996) *Education and Democratic Citizenship in America*. Chicago: University of Chicago Press.

Office of the Prime Minister (2002) 'Growing an innovative New Zealand'. Wellington: Office of the Prime Minister.

Putnam, R., with Leonardi, R. and Nanetti, R. (1993) *Making Democracy Work: Civic Traditions in Modern Italy*. Princeton, NJ: Princeton University Press.

Simmie, J. (2003) 'Innovation and urban regions as national and international nodes for the transfer and sharing of knowledge', *Regional Studies*, 37(6/7): 607–20.

Smetherham, C. (2006) 'First among equals? Evidence on the contemporary relationship between educational credentials and the occupational structure', *Journal of Education and Work*, 19(1): 29–45.

Strathdee, R. (2005) 'Globalisation, innovation and the declining significance of qualifications led social and economic change', *Journal of Education Policy*, 20(4): 437–56.

Tertiary Education Commission (2007) *Regional Facilitation* 2007, cited 27 February 2007, http://www.tec.govt.nz/templates/standard.aspx?id=483

Thompson, E.P. (1968) *The Making of the English Working Class*. Harmondsworth: Pelican.

Zucker, L. (1986) 'Production of trust: Institutional sources of economic structure, 1840–1920', *Research in Organisational Behaviour*, 8: 53–111.

Chapter 4

Complexity and learning regions: learning regions as complex adaptive systems

Ingunn Sandaker and Britt Andersen

Introduction

The year 2006 marked ten years of a growing political interest in lifelong learning. In 1996, the European Commission declared the European Year for Lifelong Learning. In the so-called White Book published in late 1995 called *Teaching and Learning Towards the Learning Society* (European Commission, 1996), the Commission emphasised the importance of learning as a means to building a competitive edge in a global knowledge society. The same year UNESCO published *Learning: The Treasure Within* (Delores, 1996). The UN pointed to knowledge development as a prerequisite for stabilisation and democratic development of the world as a means to modify the differences between the rich and the developing regions of the global society. In 1996, the OECD published their report, *Lifelong Learning for All* (OECD, 1996). The importance of knowledge development was stressed and prescribed as *the* means to a sustainable economic growth for their member countries. Within industry, learning has been prescribed as critical for business survival: 'The knowledge society of the twenty-first century will discover that learning is the source of wealth, welfare and competitive advantage. We are experiencing a paradigm shift. The evidence suggests that the development of learning organisations is not merely desirable, but essential to the survival of companies in the twenty-first century' (Ball and Stewart, 1995).

The common message from these three actors in the global arena is that learning, both individually and as a part of the global system, is critical in preparing for challenges in the twenty-first century. Typically, the perspectives of these three policy-making agents differ, depending on the mission of the organisation.

Looking back on the past ten years, the characteristics of the 'knowledge society debate' are dominated by perspectives and objectives as different as political stability, sustainable economic growth, the battle against social exclusion and the facilitation of workforce employability.

Buzzwords like 'knowledge society', 'learning organisations' and 'learning regions' have flourished during the last two decades. In this chapter we will discuss the learning unit as a complex adaptive system, extended with examples from network theory. We want to separate the *unit of analysis* (system, network, organisation and region) from the *learning unit* (humans). We are aware that systems undergo dynamic changes and may profit from using the metaphor of 'learning organisation'; we believe that strategies to develop 'learning cities', 'learning regions' and 'learning organisations' have to take into account that systems change, and this is inevitably linked to the change of individual behaviour. Our second concern is the tension between what can be deliberately planned or designed and the evolutionary nature of complex social systems, making it difficult to predict how efforts of influencing the system eventually will turn out. 'A learning town, city or region recognises and understands the key role of learning in the development of basic prosperity, social stability, and personal fulfilment, and mobilises all its human, physical and financial resources creatively and sensitively to develop the full human potential of all its citizens' (European Commission, 1996).

Learning regions

One way of defining a region is as a geographical entity. Such an entity is a region by design, and its success will be judged according to some defined objectives over time. This implies a *structural or an institutional* way of approaching regions. Another way to define the region is as a functional unit, depending on a mandate or on delivering certain services, interacting with other agents within some defined area, *a social systems approach*. The first way of defining a region will to a large extent depend on political considerations. A functional definition of a region will be based on to what extent agents interact in a way that gives added value to the area, compared to any other structural unit.

A region, whether it is defined structurally or functionally, may act as a unit, expected to be adding value to the lives of its inhabitants (along some dimension), and contributing to a larger system, like a nation or clusters of nations, like Norway or the EU.

In this light, the notion of a 'learning region' is understood as a normative concept, with an underlying assumption that the learning is goal-directed. 'Regions are becoming focal points for knowledge creation and learning in the new age of global, knowledge-intensive capitalism, as they in effect become learning regions. The learning regions function as collectors and repositories of knowledge and ideas, and provide the underlying environment or infrastructure which facilitates the flow of knowledge, ideas and learning' (Florida, 1995, p. 527, quoted in Hofmaier, 2001, p. 1).

Does a region learn?

Strictly speaking, individuals learn. Whether systems can learn is a difficult question. We will not discuss this question in any depth here. The most common definition of learning is 'a relative enduring change of *behaviour* due to experience' (Kimble, 1961). The term *behaviour* is used in many different meanings and settings. Hull, Langman and Glenn (2001) make a distinction between 'behaviour of a phenomenon' and 'behaviour of behaviours'. They describe the distinction as follows:

> scientists discuss the behavior of volcanoes, proteins, hurricanes, the immune system, etc. When change in the phenomena of interest is the object of scientific study, the scientists are said to be studying the behavior of the phenomena. If the phenomena of interest under investigation are the activities of organisms and those phenomena are themselves exemplified by change, then behavior change or the behavior of behavior is the object of scientific study. (Hull, Langman and Glenn, 2001, p. 521)

When investigating systems changes we are studying the 'behavior of the phenomenon', and when our interest is in the changed behavior of the organism, we are studying the 'behaviour of behaviour'.

Some argue that organisations can learn. We disagree. We think that when using the term learning in connection with organisations, regions, cities, and so on, one is confusing 'behaviour of a phenomenon' and 'behaviour of behaviour'. In our view, the learning unit in social systems is the individual. Although a system may change, a system as such does not learn. A system consists of many interacting, behaving individuals. In order to change a 'systems behaviour', enough people (critical mass) in the system have to change their behaviour. An additional result of changed behaviour of the individual members of the system is that the system itself changes behaviour. What constitutes critical mass varies from system to system. In this respect the terms 'learning region', 'learning city' and 'learning organisation' are the result of the learning, or changed behaviour, of the individuals constituting the region, city, organisation, and so on. In this perspective 'the learning region' is a metaphor, since the learning unit, strictly speaking, is the individual member of the region.

Furthermore, the conditions under which individuals learn will vary, depending on the characteristics of the systems to which they belong. The contingencies specific for different systems will, in their turn, determine whether the behaviour, and hence the systems, are robust or vulnerable to external changes.

The learning and teaching controversy

Neither the format nor the space allow us to elaborate on the controversy of the positivist and anti-positivist position in the domain of teaching and learning. We will, however, briefly point out that much of the philosophical and sociological contributions to the field of behavioural change and learning mainly have been of descriptive character. The contribution from post-modernists and theories of social constructivists – for example, Baudrillard (1995), Derrida (1994) and Rorty (1989) – seems more based on philosophy than science. The field of learning in systems and regions calls for a scientifically sound and empirically based approach as to what really makes people change their behaviour, and in turn change the system of which they are a part. Concepts like tacit knowledge (e.g. Polyani, 1967) or cultural capital (e.g. Bourdieu and Passeron, 1990) no doubt are interesting descriptive approaches, but they do not offer much guidance as to how to intervene and make measurable changes in people's lives.

One common lesson to be learned from both a complexity and a behavioural approach is that if the relations of agents within the system are insufficiently varied and flexible to match the complexity of the tasks the system should handle, the institution becomes dysfunctional. The more complex the surroundings, the shorter the life cycle of the institution, unless it evolves at a speed that matches the systems with which it interacts (Bar-Yam, 1997).

Basic and advanced learning principles constitute one central body of knowledge (Donahoe and Palmer, 1994; Catania, 1998), with extensions to organisational behaviour (Sandaker, 2003; Foxall, 2003). Research in heuristics and decision making will provide input both on agent and systems properties (Gigerenzer and Selten, 2001; Gigerenzer and Todd, 1999). Research on criticality (Bak and Sneppen, 1993; Jánosi and Kertesz, 1993) and networks (Rosvall and Sneppen, 2003; Bernardes and Stauffer, 2002; Albert and Barabasi, 2002; Mendes, Dorovgotsev and Ioffe, 2003) will contribute to the development of new concepts to describe central phenomena. Learning, understood as the selection of behaviour on the individual and systems level, is to be the main focus (Glenn, 2003; Edelmann, 1988), as selection is a process that is common to a number of fields and is observed at many levels of scientific reduction (Hull, 2001).

Statements in science about the lawful relations between behaviour and environmental events, how behaviour is learned, maintained and changed are based on empirical research and may be expressed in technical terms.

The breaking down of barriers

Even though the EU, UN and OECD still differ in 2007 about their approaches to how and why lifelong learning is of crucial importance, they agree on one central issue: If we are to succeed in developing lifelong learners within regions, organisations or businesses, a critical prerequisite will be the ability of the institutions and differing administrative layers to co-operate (i. e. European Commission, 2007; Schwartz, Wurtzel, and Olson, 2007; UNESCO, 2007) Schools, universities, working life and even elected bodies will need to make common efforts to secure employability, social cohesion and stability. Not only do they have to co-operate and establish new kinds of partnerships, they will have to interact across borders and institutional layers in a fashion that changes the flow of influence in ways that we are unable to predict.

The breakdown of traditional barriers between sectors and administrative layers is not just a matter of designing systems for co-operation. It is also a result of the evolution and selection of behaviours within systems by the consequences of globalisation of capital, information and knowledge. Thus, this may not be as much the result of a deliberate organisational strategy as we would like to think it is, but rather results of an evolutionary process based on the selection of behaviours by its consequences.

There are two main areas in which it is interesting to observe the urge for breaking down traditional barriers: (1) the breaking down of barriers between institutions and administrative layers and (2) between scientific disciplines.

From institutions to systems

The trend of traditional divisions between institutions and sectors having progressively less effect on social and behaviour systems has been termed *New Institutionalism* (e.g. Scott, 2001). One basic assumption of New Institutionalism is that relations between agent behaviour and its consequences change dramatically if institutional and organisational barriers between agents are weakened.

A system in which agent behaviour has immediate, important, direct and partly unpredictable consequences requires sophisticated analytical concepts and tools. In institutions, temporal delay has an impact on behaviour. The effects of mechanisms of behavioural selection change dramatically if this buffer between the consequences of direct interaction among agents becomes less important. The instantaneous interactions between agents will cause changes both within systems and between systems, and will function as important behavioural consequences; i.e. in the selection variables (Axelrod and Cohen, 1999).

In this perspective, the unit of analysis is more likely to be networks and complex adaptive systems than studies of geographical and organisational entities, traditionally offered by the social sciences (Bar-Yam, 1997).

Looking back on the ten years preceding 2007, it is not only the evolution of new systems based on the breakdown of institutional barriers that is apparent. The need to investigate complex phenomena with a multidisciplinary approach seems more important than ever, even though complexity studies which originated decades ago show great promise. Postmodernism urges us to abandon the traditional scientific ambitions of measurability, economics, heuristics and repeatability, advocated by, among others, biologist E.O. Wilson (1999). The dominant anti-positivist position leads us to philosophy and a rejection of traditional scientific standards. The multidisciplinary approach offered by complexity science seems a fruitful alternative to the rejection of empiricism, when facing the difficulties of analysing complexity in systems.

Complex adaptive systems: a multidisciplinary approach

The more complex the surroundings, the shorter the life cycle of the institution, unless it evolves at a speed that matches the systems with which it interacts (Bar-Yam, 1997).

There exists no distinct and agreed definition of complex systems (Axelrod and Cohen, 2000; Bar-Yam, 1997), and the term complexity can have different meanings (for a discussion of the different meanings and the relation to complicatedness see, for example, Price (2004)). Complexity theory can be regarded as a science (Bar-Yam, 1997), 'a way of thinking, and a way of seeing the world' (Mitleton-Kelly, 2003, p. 26), or a fad (Price, 2004). Complex Systems Theory (CST) is not a single theory, it has its origins in natural science (Bar-Yam, 1997; Mitleton-Kelly, 2003). It is multidisciplinary, and has its roots in biology, physics and chemistry, among other disciplines (Bar-Yam, 1997; Mitleton-Kelly, 2003; Morel and Ramanujam, 1999). Complexity research involves a diversity of domains, such as physics, evolutionary biology, social-scientific modeling of heterogeneous populations, cellular automata, artificial life and mathematical theories (Axelrod and Cohen, 2000). One of the important contributions of complexity theory has been the nonlinear dynamics in understanding behaviour in living adaptive systems (Morel and Ramanujam, 1999). The new science of networks is an important part of this.

A complex system consists of many components, and the behavior of the system is an emergent property. This means that the system's behavior cannot be described solely through the description of its components (Bar-Yam, 1997). The interaction between the entities in the system is critical, and complexity emerges (Cilliers, 1998). Complexity, therefore, deals with systems composed of many interacting agents. And as Bar-Yam (1997) points out, the more agents, the more complex the system is. According to Bar-Yam the most central properties of complex systems are (a) elements (and their number), (b) interactions (and their strength), (c) formation/operation (and their time scales), (d) diversity/variability, (e) environment (and its demands), and (f) activity(ies) (and its/their objective/s). In brief, since complex adaptive systems include many agents, adapting to each other and the emerging future for the system, behaviour is hard to predict (Axelrod and Cohen, 2000).

The more complex the surroundings, however, the shorter the life cycle of the institution, unless it evolves at a speed that matches the systems with which it interacts (Bar-Yam, 1997). The predictability of the system is also reduced by the fact that changes in one part of the system, may have, and often has, implications for other parts of the system, or other systems. These consequences are often unintended; the cause and effect are uncertain (Chapman, 2004). The behavior of a system (Y) is then a function (*f*) of the interdependent and interacting variables, as shown in Figure 4.1.

Figure 4.1: The behaviour of a system (Y) as a function of many interdependent variables (X_1, X_2, X_3, etc.).

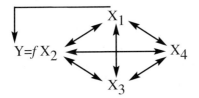

Note: The arrows between X_1, X_2, etc. indicate the interdependency between the various variables.
Source: Gharajedaghi, 2006

It is hypothesised that dynamics of complex systems are founded on universal principles (Bar-Yam, 1997), and that the principles in systems dynamics are valid for systems ranging from physics to economies and societies (Bar-Yam, 1997; Bertalanffy, 1969).

Complex Adaptive Systems

CAS (Complex Adaptive Systems) are characterised by many participants, and often many different kinds of participants, who interact and co-evolve. CAS are complex systems that can adapt, and subsequently the systems can cope better in their interaction with the environment (Axelrod and Cohen, 2000), but not always. They can also change the environment to suit themselves. Two perspectives are possible in CAS: (1) from within the system; and (2) from outside the system (Axelrod and Cohen, 2000).

An agent in CAS is anything that is interacting with the environment, and it has the ability to respond to changes in the environment, and also to other agents (Axelrod and Cohen, 1999). An agent can be a person, an animal, cells, organisations, and so on. Here we use the term related to humans and human organisations. Real situations often include more than just a single population of agents.

The agents have different properties such as location (where the agent operates, i.e. the context), capabilities (how the agent can affect the world, and memory or experience). Because of the many relevant variables in such systems, they are difficult to understand and to predict. Strategy is also important in CAS. Axelrod and Cohen (2000) define strategy as 'the way an agent responds to its surroundings and pursues its goals' (p. 4). 'For a system to exhibit adaptation that enhances survival (or other measure of success), it must increase the likelihood of effective strategies and reduce the likelihood of ineffective strategies' (Axelrod and Cohen, 2000, p. 19).

CAS concerns adaptation and the evolution of systems. Organisations do not operate in isolation from the environment, and when different organisations are adapting to each other the result is a co-evolutionary process. The key processes in CAS are variation, interaction and selection (Axelrod and Cohen, 2000). These processes operate in any population or organisation. For selection to operate there has to be variation (for example, different strategies). Further, the different variations have to interact with their environment. The resulting selection can generate productive processes within and between organisations.

This brings our attention to the ever more important tension between organisations by design and organisations by evolution (Axelrod and Cohen, 1999). In the real world many organisations represent both perspectives, they are organisations by design, but evolutionary processes also affect their development (Campbell, 1965). Organisations by design and organisations by evolution may be considered as two ends at a continuum, but in reality different organisations will place themselves at different places along the continuum.

Networks and complex systems

To understand the dynamics and the behaviours of systems, it is important to understand the fundamental interactions in the systems or between systems. A network is a set of 'points' which are connected to each other by exchange or transport of information, communication, people, material, and so on. The transport is the function of the network (*Network Science*, 2005). The members are nodes (e.g. people, organisations) and the connections are links (Barabási, 2003; Newman, 2003). The connectivity and exchange of resources between the nodes are some of the important features of networks. The structure of a network gives direct information about the dynamics in the network (Albert and Barabási, 2002; Hofmaier, 2001; *Network Science*, 2005).

A network can consist of structural subunits or communities (clusters) (Palla, Derényi, and Farkas, 2005). The communities are characterised by a set of nodes that have a higher degree of connections between them. The communities may overlap but do not have to, an individual may be member of two or more communities, and connections may exist between two or more people (nodes) in the different communities (ibid.; see Figure 4.2). In a learning region, different networks in the region are connected and different communities (sub-networks) may or may not overlap.

Figure 4.2: A representation of a network consisting of 4 sub-networks (or communities/organisations). Some of the sub-networks overlap and have nodes (black dots) in common (for example the upper and lower sub-networks to the right). The sub-networks have links (black lines) to nodes in some of the other sub-networks (for example the upper and lower sub-networks to the left) (after Palla, Derényi and Farkas, 2005, Figure 1c, p. 814)

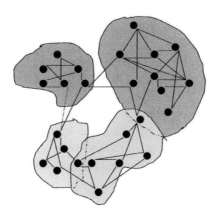

Different categories of networks have been identified. In addition to social networks, which are in focus here, there also exists information networks, knowledge networks, technological networks and biological networks (Newman, 2003). Social networks are characterised by a 'set of people or groups of people with some pattern of contacts or interactions between them' (ibid.). Networks can also be categorised according to their structure. For further readings, see for example Barabási (2003) and Newman (2003).

Networks are non-static entities. Important features in networks are the interaction between the nodes and the mutual interdependency between the nodes to form a network. To constitute a network, there has to be added value for the nodes in the network (*Network Science*, 2005). If value is not added, the network will fall apart.

A complexity perspective on learning regions

'An interrelationship exists between all elements and constituent of society. The essential factors in public problems, issues, policies, and programs must always be considered and evaluated as interdependent components of a total system' (a Canadian premier, cited after Manning (1967), in Bertalanffy (1969, p. 4).

The term 'learning regions' has in many respects become a slogan. In this context, 'region' may be viewed as a geographical entity, or as a social system. A learning region can consist of a wide range of systems/organisations, schools/higher education institutions, further education organisations, big companies, small and medium-sized enterprises, financial services, police, cultural institutions, child-care institutions, health and hospital services, social welfare services, administrative and elective local/regional authorities, voluntary centres and organisations, and so on. The 'learning region' may also be regarded and analysed by the intended or emergent interactions between the agents mentioned above. To form a society all these entities must co-operate in one way or another, and they are dependent on each other in order to achieve the outcomes described in the European Commission's definition of a learning region (see above). No single entity can achieve one of the outcomes described in isolation. This calls for interactions: the interdependency between the entities is apparent and the number of interactions increases as a result of overlapping policy areas (Chapman, 2004) in the definition of a learning region (see above).

A complexity perspective on learning regions

Complexity and networks emerge. A learning region is not a static system; the behaviour of the members in the region, both at individual and system level, changes depending on the focus at a given time, and on the added value networks can offer for the entities. A learning region constitutes a CAS, a system divided into sub-systems consisting of numerous sub-networks. The interconnection and interdependence of these sub-systems and sub-networks determine the degree of learning and adaptation. According to Axelrod and Cohen (2000), to accomplish selection and thereby evolution to meet the requirements in a changing environment, there also has to be variation in addition to interaction.

Defining characteristics of learning regions are (a) networks; (b) some kind of agreement, formal or informal; (c) interaction; (d) added value for the organisations and society; and (e) democratisation and equalisation (Hofmaier, 2001). The different features above indicate that the concept is a *relational concept*. That is; the basis for the learning regions is the relationship between people/organisations, their interconnectedness and interdependency. A learning region is therefore built on relations between people and organisations.

It is not only the single agent that is of interest in CAS, but also the population of agents. A group of agents in organisations that cooperate learn from their experiences. A population of agents is crucial because when an agent is interacting with other agents, this interaction is a condition for learning or adapting by copying and/or modelling each other, shaping behaviours and following rules. A population of agents also represents a variation of strategies or behaviours (Axelrod and Cohen, 1999). The learning region is a system where the mutual result of the behaviours of the individuals in the system leads to an aggregate result that exceeds what the behaviours of the individuals could account for individually, more than the sum of its parts. The behaviour of the system learning region and its results becomes an emergent property, the result of many interacting entities. And hence, regions of learning systems may achieve the outcomes The European Commission has outlined to meet the challenges in an ever changing environment.

The science of networks teaches us a third lesson: that such systems, from power grids to businesses, and even entire economies, are both more vulnerable and more robust than populations of isolated entities. Networks share resources and distribute loads, but they also spread disease and transmit failure – they are both good and bad. But unless we can understand exactly how connected systems are connected, we cannot predict how they will behave (Watts, 2003, p. B7).

Conclusions/summary comments

This chapter has sought to address the dynamic tension between the intended strategies for cooperation and integration across sectors and institutional layers, and the complex phenomena emerging from the 'blind' selection by consequences of agents' behaviours.

Both from a policy maker's point of view and from a scientific position it is crucial to analyse the relative proportion of influence responsible for the success of a 'learning region'. Taking into account both the results from a deliberate planning process and the emergent outcomes of interaction in a complex adaptive system will be of paramount importance to success.

The tension between design and evolution, regulations and deregulations is not a new one. In the ten years since the European Year of Lifelong Learning was announced, societal complexity and scientific interest in complexity have escalated.

Borders, both geographic and institutional, have become more porous and informal relations within and between systems have increased exponentially. The consequences may be perceived as a lesser degree of predictability and control. With increased knowledge on how to take advantage of the dynamics of complex systems, combined with evidence-based human performance technology, the objectives of learning regions may be within reach.

References

Albert, R. and Barabási, A.-L. (2002) 'Statistical mechanics of complex networks', *Reviews of Modern Physics*, 74: 47–97.

Axelrod, R. and Cohen, M.D. (1999) *Harnessing Complexity: Organizational Implications of Scientific Findings*. New York: The Free Press.

Axelrod, R. and Cohen, M.D. (2000) *Harnessing Complexity: Organizational Implications of a Scientific Frontier*. New York: Basic Books.

Bak, P. and Sneppen, K. (1993) 'Punctuated equilibrium and criticality in a simple model of evolution', *Physical Review Letters*, 71: 4083–6.

Ball, C. and Stewart, D. (1995) *An Action Agenda for Lifelong Learning for the 21st Century*. Report from the First Global Conference on Lifelong Learning, ed. N. Longworth. Brussels: World Initiative on Lifelong Learning.

Bar-Yam, Y. (1997) *Dynamics of complex systems* (http://necsi.org/publications/dcs/index.html), accessed 1 December 2004.

Barabási, A.-L. (2003) *Linked: How Everything Is Connected to Everything Else and What It Means for Business, Science, and Everyday Life*. New York: Plume.

Baudrillard, J. (1995) *Simulacra and Simulation: The Body, In Theory. Histories of Cultural Materialism*. Ann Arbor: University of Michigan Press.

Bernardes, A.T., Stauffer, D. and Kertész, J. (2002) 'Election results and the Sznajd model on Barabasi networks', *European Physical Journal B*, 25: 123–7.

Bertalanffy, L. von (1969) *General System Theory. Foundations, Development, Applications*, revised edn. New York: George Braziller.

Bourdieu, P. and Passeron, J.-C. (1990) *Reproduction in Education, Society and Culture*. London: Sage.

Campbell, D.T. (1965) 'Variation and selective retention in socio-cultural evolution', in H.R. Barringer, G.I. Blanksten and R.W. Mack (eds), *Social Change in Developing Areas: A Reinterpretation of Evolutionary Theory*, pp. 19–49. Cambridge: Schenkman.

Catania, A.C.C. (1998) *Learning*, 4th edn. Englewood Cliffs, NJ: Prentice-Hall.

Chapman, J. (2004) *System Failure: Why Governments Must Learn to Think Differently*, 2nd edn. London: DEMOS.

Cilliers, P. (1998) *Complexity and Postmodernism: Understanding Complex Systems*. New York: Routledge.

Delores, J. (1996) *Learning: The Treasure Within*. Report to UNESCO of the International Commission on Education for the Twenty-First Century. Paris: UNESCO.

Derrida, J. (1994) 'The deconstruction of actuality', *Radical Philosophy*, 68: 28–41.

Donahoe, J. and Palmer, D. (1994) *Learning and Complex Behavior*. Boston: Allyn & Bacon.

Edelmann, G. (1988) *Neural Darwinism: The Theory of Neuronal Group Selection*. New York: Basic Books.

European Commission (1996) *Teaching and Learning: Towards the Learning Society*. European Commission White Paper. **ELLI** (European Lifelong Learning Initiative) (http://www.noesis.se/elli/).

European Commission (2007) *Work Programme 2007–2008 Cooperation – Theme 8 – Socioeconomic Sciences and Humanities* (ec.europa.eu/atwork/programmes/index_en.htm).

Foxall, G.R. (2003) *Context and Cognition: Interpreting Complex Behavior*. Reno, NV: Context Press.

Gharajedaghi, J. (2006) *Systems Thinking: Managing Chaos and Complexity: A Platform for Designing Business Architecture*, 2nd edn. Amsterdam: Elsevier.

Gigerenzer, G. and Selten, R. (eds) (2001) *Bounded Rationality: The Adaptive Toolbox*. Cambridge: MIT Press.

Gigerenzer, G. and Todd, P.M. (1999) *Simple Heuristics That Make Us Smart*. New York: Oxford University Press.

Glenn, S.S. (2003) 'Operant contingencies and the origin of culture', in K.A. Lattal and P.N. Chase (eds), *Behavior Theory and Philosophy*, pp. 223–42. Dordrecht: Kluwer Academic.

Hofmaier, B. (2001) *Learning Regions: Concepts, Visions and Examples*, report from Forskiningsplattformen TEII: Technology, Entrepreneurship, Innovation and Industry. Halmstad: Högskolan Halmstad.

Hull, D.L. (2001) *Science and Selection: Essays on Biological Evolution and the Philosophy of Science*. Cambridge: Cambridge University Press.

Hull, D.L., Langman, R.E. and Glenn, S.S. (2001). 'A general account of selection: biology, immunology and behavior', *Behavioral and Brain Sciences*, 24(2): 511–27.

Jánosi, I.M., and Kertész, J. (1993) 'Self-organized criticality with and without conservation', *Physica A*, 200: 179–88.

Kimble, G.A. (1961) *Hilgard and Marquis' Conditioning and Learning*, 2nd edn. Englewood Cliffs, NJ: Prentice-Hall.

Mendes, J.F.F., Dorovgotsev S.N. and Ioffe, A.F. (eds) (2003). *Evolution of Networks: From ... Nets to the Internet and WWW*. Oxford: Oxford University Press.

Mitleton-Kelly, E. (2003) 'Ten principles of complexity and enabling infrastructures', in E. Mitleton-Kelly (ed), *Complex Systems and Evolutionary Perspectives on Organisations: The Application of Complexity Theory to Organisations*, pp. 23–51. Amsterdam: Elsevier Science.

Morel, B. and Ramanujam, R. (1999) 'Through the looking-glass of complexity: The dynamics of organizations as adaptive and evolving systems', *Organization Science*, 10(3): 278–93.

Network Science (2005) Washington, DC: National Research Council, National Academies Press.

Newman, M.E.J. (2003) 'The structure and function of complex networks', *SIAM Review*, 45: 167–256.

OECD (1996) *Lifelong Learning for All*. Paris: OECD.

Palla, G., Derényi, I., Farkas, I. and Tamás, V. (2005) 'Uncovering the overlapping community structures of complex networks in nature and society', *Nature*, 435 (9 June): 814–18.

Polyani, M. (1967) *The Tacit Dimension*. New York: Doubleday.

Price, I. (2004) 'Complexity, complicatedness and complexity: a new science behind organizational intervention?', *Emergence*, 6: 40–8 (http://emergence.org/ECO_site/ECO_Archive/issue-6-1-2/Price.pdf), accessed 14 December 2004.

Rorty, R. (1989) *Contingency, Irony, and Solidarity*. Cambridge: Cambridge University Press.

Rosvall, M. and Sneppen, K. (2003) 'Modeling dynamics of information networks', *Phys. Rev. Lett.*, 91(178701).

Sandaker, I. (2003) 'Et seleksjonsperspektiv på atferdsendring og læring i systemer', in E. Svein and S. Frode (eds), *Anvendt atferdsanalyse*, pp. 417–34. Gjøvik: Gyldendal Norsk Forlag AS.

Schwartz, R.B.W., Wurtzel, J. and Olson, L. (2007) 'Attracting and retaining teachers', *OECD Observer*, 261 (May) (http://www.oecdobserver.org/news/fullstory.php/aid/2235/Attracting_and_retaining_teachers.html).

Scott, R.W. (2001) *Institutions and Organizations*, 2nd edn. Thousand Oaks: Sage.

UNESCO (2007) *Education for All Monitoring Report 2007*. UN.

Watts, D.J. (2003) 'Unravelling the mysteries of the connected age', *Chronicle of Higher Education*, 49(23): B7.

Wilson, E.O. (1999) *Consilience*. New York: Vintage.

Chapter 5

Building human and social capital in communities through education

Barry McGaw

The contribution of education to economic health is well understood. The annual publication of international, comparative education statistics and indicators by the Organisation for Economic Co-operation and Development (OECD) documents the benefits of additional education and higher levels of skill of individuals for nations, in higher levels of national wealth measured as gross domestic product (OECD, 2006: 155–7) and for individuals, in higher employment rates, lower unemployment rates and higher average earnings (OECD, 2006: 112–15, 135–6).

The contribution of education to the development of social capital and the contribution of social capital to outcomes such as improved child welfare, individual health and well-being, better government and reduced crime are also well documented (OECD, 2001b).

In Australia, where public education at school level is provided by relatively centralised state government agencies and private schools are largely operated independently at the institutional level, there is limited capacity to coordinate education services at the community level in the hope of improving their economic and social impact. The available evidence on the quality of schooling in Australia shows that there are marked inequities that reflect differences among communities.

Quality of learning in schools

Good, internationally comparable evidence on the quality of learning in schools is provided by the OECD's Programme for International Student

Assessment (PISA), for which details are available on www.pisa.oecd.org.

PISA collects assessments of the performances of 15-year-olds in schools of any type in reading literacy, mathematics and science on a three-yearly cycle that commenced in 2000. In that year, reading literacy was the main domain of assessment and mathematics and science were minor domains. In PISA 2003, mathematics was the main domain and reading and science minor domains, together with problem solving, which was an additional domain. In PISA 2006, the three original domains were being assessed, with science as the main domain. Individual students are tested for two hours and spend an additional half an hour answering a questionnaire on their family back-grounds and on their learning habits, environment and engagement. More assessment materials are used than with any individual student, so around three and a half hours of assessment are obtained in the major domain and around one hour in each of the minor domains.

PISA does not assess whether students have learned the specific content of their curricula but rather their capacity to use the knowledge and skills they have acquired. Both open-ended and multiple-choice questions are used. In the PISA 2003 mathematics assessments, for example, there were 85 items, 17 of them simple multiple choice, 11 complex multiple choice and 57 items that required students to construct their response. Sample items, illustrating the content and form of assessment, are provided on the PISA website.

Considerable efforts are made in the design of the materials to avoid tasks that could be culturally biased, and all materials are examined for cultural bias in analyses of data obtained in trials conducted in participating countries in the year before each PISA assessment.

To illustrate, the mean performances of OECD countries in reading in PISA 2000 are shown in Figure 5.1. The line in the middle of the box for each country gives the mean performance of 15-year-olds in the country. The size of a box reflects the precision with which a country's mean is estimated, the least precise in PISA 2000 being that for the USA. Where the boxes overlap on the vertical dimension, there is no significant difference between the means for the countries.

The results reveal marked differences among countries in the quality of students' learning, although the comparisons are best interpreted from the perspective of a particular country. Australia ranked in fourth place, but its mean is not significantly different from those of Canada and New Zealand

Figure 5.1: Mean performances of OECD countries in reading literacy in PISA 2000

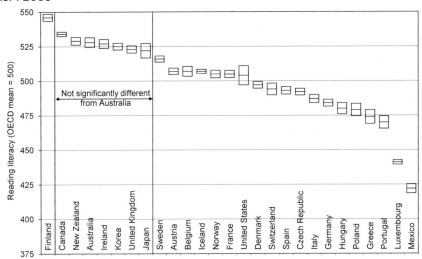

Source: OECD (2001a, Figure 2.4, p. 53).

ranking above it, or Ireland, Korea, the UK and Japan ranking below it. It is appropriate, therefore, to say that Australia ranked between second and eighth or that Australia tied in second place with six other countries.

In PISA 2003 in which mathematics was the main domain of assessment, Australia ranked eighth among the OECD countries in mathematics but, taking account of non-significant differences, could be said to have ranked in fourth place behind Finland, Korea and the Netherlands with others (Japan, Canada, Belgium, Switzerland, New Zealand and the Czech Republic) and significantly ahead of 19 others (OECD, 2004, p. 92).

Inequities in the quality of learning in schools

An important indicator of the equity of educational achievements in a country is the strength of the relationship between students' achievements and their social background.

The 15-year-old participants in PISA complete a questionnaire that collects information on personal characteristics, such as gender, economic and social background, and activities at home and school. The information on economic and social background – parents' education and occupation, cultural artefacts in the home – permits the construction of an index of social background that ranges from socially disadvantaged to socially advantaged. This scale is comparable across countries.

For the OECD as a whole, the correlation between social background and reading literacy is relatively high (around 0.45) and the slope of the regression line that summarises the relationship is quite steep, indicating that increased social advantage, in general, pays off with considerable increase in educational performance. This result has been long established in research in many individual countries and it can lead to a counsel of despair with education seen as impotent and unable to make a difference in the face of such a strong influence of social background. Comparison of the lines for different countries, however, tells a more encouraging story.

The relationships between social background and reading literacy in PISA 2000 for seven OECD countries are shown in Figure 5.2. The steeper the slope, the less equitable the results. The lines for Finland, Korea and Canada are significantly less steep than the one (not shown) for the OECD as a whole. Increased social advantage in these countries is associated with less increase in educational achievement than in the OECD as a whole. That is, these countries ameliorate the influence of social background and produce a more equitable outcome than others in the OECD.

Figure 5.2: Regression of reading literacy on social background in PISA 2000

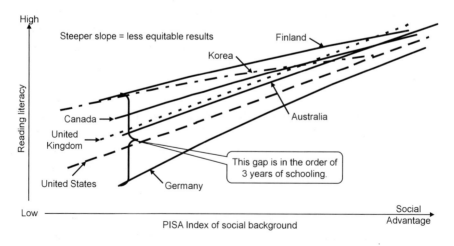

Source: OECD (2001a, p. 308).

The lines for the UK, Australia, the USA and Germany are all significantly steeper than the one for the OECD as a whole. In all of these countries, social background is more substantially related to educational achievement than in the OECD as a whole. Their results are inequitable in the sense that differences among students in their literacy levels reflect to a marked extent differences in their social background.

The differences between these six lines at the left-hand end of the diagram are substantial. Socially disadvantaged students do very much worse in some of these countries (most notably Germany but also the USA, Australia and the UK) than in the other three. The gap in educational achievement between socially disadvantaged students in Germany and similarly socially disadvantaged students in Finland and Korea represents around three years of schooling.

More detailed analysis of the German data shows the pattern to be strongly related to the organisation of schooling. From the age of 11, students are separated into vocational and academic schools of various types on the basis of the educational future judged to be most appropriate for them. Students from socially disadvantaged backgrounds generally end up in low-status vocational schools and achieve poor educational results. Students from socially advantaged backgrounds are directed to high-status academic schools where they achieve high-quality results. The schooling system largely reproduces the existing social arrangements, conferring privilege where it already exists and denying it where it does not.

If lines for more countries were to be added to Figure 5.2, the pattern would become difficult to discern. A clear picture is provided in Figure 5.3 in which mean performances of countries in reading literacy are represented on the vertical axis and the slope of the regression line for social equity on reading literacy is represented on the horizontal axis as the difference between the slope for the OECD as a whole and a country's own slope. This places to the left countries where the slope is steeper than in the OECD as a whole (that is, countries in which social background is most substantially related to educational achievement) and, to the right, countries where the slope is less steep than that for the OECD as a whole (that is, countries in which social background is least related to educational achievement).

Countries high on the chart are high-quality and those to the far right are high-equity. The graph is divided into four quadrants on the basis of the OECD average on the two measures. The presence of countries in the 'high-quality,

Figure 5.3: Relationship between quality and equity in reading performance in PISA 2000

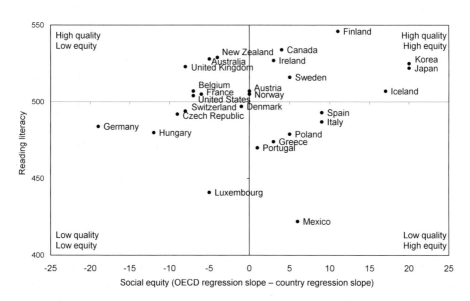

Source: OECD (2001a, p. 253).

high-equity' quadrant (top right) demonstrates that there is no necessary trade-off between quality and equity. They show that it is possible to achieve both together. Korea, Japan, Finland and Canada are among them. As indicated in Figures 5.1 and 5.2, Australia and the UK are 'high-quality, low-equity'. The USA is average quality but it is low-equity. Germany, as a low-quality, low-equity country, is in the bottom-left quadrant along with a number of other countries that also begin to separate students into schools of different types as early as ages 11–12.

A further way in which to examine the equity of educational outcomes is through an analysis of the sources of variation in student performances. In Figure 5.4, the variation in student performance in mathematics in PISA 2003 for each country is divided into a component owing to differences among students within schools, shown above the zero line, and a component owing to differences between schools shown below that line.

In Iceland, Finland and Norway there is very little variation in scores between schools. For parents in these countries, choice of school is not very important because there is so little difference among schools. Among the countries in which there is a large component of variation between schools, there are some in which this occurs by design. In Hungary, Belgium and Germany, for example, students are sorted into schools of different types according to their school performance as early as the age of 12. The intention is to group similar students within schools differentiated by the extent of academic or vocational emphasis in their curriculum. This is intended to minimise variation within schools in order then to provide the curricula considered most appropriate for the differentiated student groups. It has the consequence of maximising the variation between schools. In some other countries, the grouping of students is less deliberate but, nevertheless, results in substantial between-school variation. In Japan, for example, 53 per cent of the overall variation is between schools. In Korea, 42 per cent is between schools. In Australia, 20 per cent is between schools.

For Poland, in PISA 2000, 63 per cent of the variation in reading was between schools whereas in PISA 2003 in mathematics only 13 per cent was between schools. This remarkable difference was due to a reform in which early streaming of students into schools of different types was abandoned in favour of comprehensive schools for students up to the age at which PISA measures their performance. It is worth noting also that not only was the between-school variation reduced, but Poland was the only country to improve its average performance significantly on all measures used in both PISA 2000 and PISA 2003. It did so largely by raising the achievement levels of its poorer performing students.

A further way in which to examine equity is to determine the extent to which the variation between schools can be explained in terms of differences in the social backgrounds of the students. This is done in Figure 5.4 with the between-school variation subdivided into three components:

   (a) variation that can be accounted for in terms of the social back-grounds of the individual students in the schools;
   (b) variation that can be accounted for in terms of the average social background of the students in the schools; and
   (c) variation that cannot be accounted for in terms of the social backgrounds of the students.

Component (a) indicates the impact of students' own social backgrounds on their educational outcomes. Component (b) indicates the impact of the company the students keep in school. In Australia, 70 per cent of the variation between

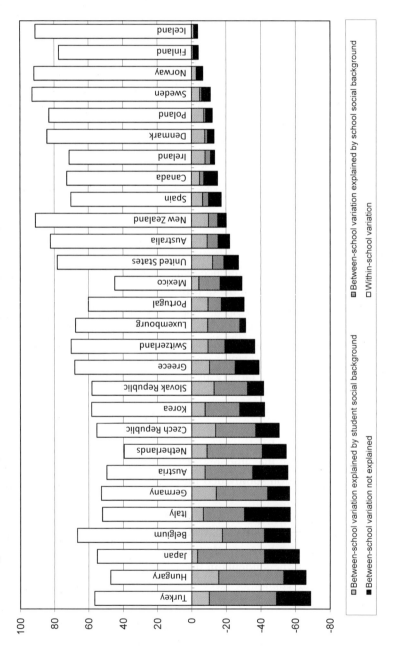

Figure 5.4: Decomposition of variation in mathematics performance in PISA 2003

■ Between-school variation explained by student social background   ■ Between-school variation explained by school social background

■ Between-school variation not explained   □ Within-school variation

Source: OECD (2004, p. 383).

schools can be accounted for in terms of differences between schools in the social background of their students, 40 per cent individual social background and 30 per cent the average social background of students in the schools.

Where differences in social background account for a large percentage of the between-school variation, this suggests that the educational arrangements in the country are inequitable. Where much of the account derives from the social background of other students in the school, it suggests that there is a benefit for advantaged students in keeping company with similarly advantaged students but a compounded disadvantage for disadvantaged students keeping company with others like themselves.

That finding suggests that there is a very difficult policy conundrum for those who might want to move to heterogeneous groupings to ameliorate the influence of social background on disadvantaged students because it implies that reduction in disadvantage for them could only be won by a reduction in advantage for the advantaged. Additional analyses of the PISA 2000 data for Austria, however, offer a more encouraging conclusion. These analyses suggest 'that students with lower skills benefit more from being exposed to clever peers, whereas those with higher skills do not seem to be affected much. Social heterogeneity, moreover, has no big adverse effect on academic outcomes. These results imply considerable social gains of reducing stratification in educational settings' (Schneeweis and Winter-Ebmer, 2005, p. 2).

Concern about the contribution of schools to social cohesion

When an education system produces results that are relatively strongly related to students' social backgrounds it is essentially reproducing existing social arrangements. In some countries refugees and other immigrant groups are heavily represented among the socially disadvantaged so an education system that does not systematically ameliorate the effects of disadvantage can leave them outside the mainstream through several generations.

In these circumstances societies can face progressive decline in social cohesion. Concern about that was evident when the OECD convened the chief executives of the national education ministries for the first time in February 2003. In advance of that meeting, the chief executives had been invited to nominate the major policy issues with which they expected to deal over the following three to five years. They identified continuing work on issues of quality and efficiency, which had already been elevated in OECD's work program on education with the implementation of PISA, but they nominated also work on the contribution that education might make to the development of social cohesion.

The OECD Directorate for Education, through its Centre for Educational Research and Innovation, had already reviewed the evidence on the impact of social capital on human well-being, in health and education as well as on economic development (OECD, 2001b). One of the consultants for this work was Robert Putnam, whose work on social capital had become well known and influential (Putnam, 2000). In a presentation to a Forum for OECD Education Ministers and senior officials in 2004, Putnam set out the standard definition of social capital as 'networks and norms of reciprocity and trust' and added the distinction he makes between three different forms of social capital:

(a) *bonding social capital:* ties with a given social or ethnic group;
(b) *bridging social capital:* ties between groups;
(c) *linking social capital:* vertical links to powerful people, institutions, and agencies;

and considered the roles of schools in the development of each of them (Putnam, 2004). Putnam also points out that, while the different forms of social capital are conceptually distinct, they are not independent. He reported that 'Dutch researchers, for example, have found that the Turkish immigrants who are most actively involved in broader Dutch society are precisely those who are also most actively involved in the life of the Turkish community itself. Bonding, in short, can be a prelude to bridging, rather than precluding bridging' (Putnam, 2004).

It is often claimed that, in contemporary developed countries, many of the experiences that used to be shared by young people growing up are no longer available. It is then often asserted that school is the one common experience building shared understandings. In fact, schools in many countries divide on the basis of gender, faith, social background, wealth, geography, and so on. It is schooling, not school, that is the common experience.

In this circumstance, it is easiest for schools to build bonding social capital, particularly where they deal with a restricted student body drawn from communities in which social capital is already strong but the other two are in many ways more important: 'Bridging and linking social capital are weaker in the sense that they are likely to be less intimate than bonding ties, they are stronger in the sense that they provide access to valued forms of economic and cultural capital' (Gewirtz *et al.*, 2005).

School differentiation and collaboration

School differentiation has increased in some developed countries through the growth of a strong private sector in which those able to afford the fees enrol their children in preference to the public-sector alternative. The distributions of 15-year-olds in the PISA 2003 sample are shown in Figure 5.5.

In the OECD data, three categories of schools are distinguished:

(a) *public schools:* funded and managed by government agencies;
(b) *government dependent private schools:* privately managed but with some government finances;
(c) *private schools:* privately managed and fully privately funded.

The percentage of students in public schools ranges from 100 per cent in Ireland to 24 per cent in the Netherlands. The other 76 per cent of students in the Netherlands are enrolled in government-dependent private schools. In Australia, 65 per cent of students are enrolled in public schools and the remaining 35 per cent are enrolled in government-dependent private schools. In both countries there are no fully private schools. There is an important difference, however, in the relative funding levels of public and government-dependent private schools in the two countries. In the Netherlands, all schools are fully publicly funded. In Australia, the government-dependent private schools receive government support but also charge fees. In the Netherlands, government-dependent private schools differentiate themselves from public schools and from each other on the basis of values, faith commitment or pedagogy, but not resources. In Australia, government-dependent private schools differentiate themselves from public schools and from each other on a similar basis but also on resource levels. While their government funding per student is at a lower level than in public schools, they can reduce their costs by restricting the types of students they enrol and can increase their resources through the fees they charge.

Under the Australian funding arrangements, there is a growing differentiation of schools and an increase in the proportion of students enrolling in government-dependent private schools. The private schools typically recruit

Figure 5.5: Percentages of lower secondary students in schools of different types

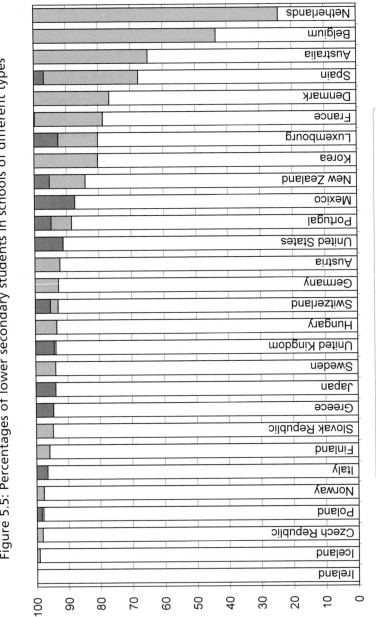

Source: OECD (2006, p. 280).

□ Public ▨ Government-dependent private ■ Independent private

a selective student cohort reflecting parental wealth (to the extent to which fees are set at a level beyond the reach of poorer families), religious faith and, in some cases, gender. They are well set up to enhance the social capital that many of their students and their families will already have but they are not well placed to contribute to the development of bridging social capital for their students.

The exception is a small, but growing, number of cases where public and private schools in Australia retain their distinctiveness but also actively collaborate because they are co-located. To date, they are mostly in greenfield sites where the benefits of collaboration are clearer because all schools are in an initial start-up phase when the collaboration commences. This approach was pioneered by a property developer, Delfin, and the South Australian government in the 1980s.

An early example is the community of Golden Grove on the outskirts of Adelaide, where a new community with around 10,000 inhabitants and 3,000 dwellings was developed over the period from 1985 to 2002. In this community, there is one secondary-school site on which there is one public school and two private schools; one Catholic and one Protestant. The schools are accessed at different points on the perimeter of the site and their students' identity is made clear by the use of distinct school uniforms for the three schools. In the centre of the site, between the three schools, there are shared facilities including a library and senior science laboratories. Shared use of these facilities is coordinated by a staff member in one of the schools, with responsibility taken in rotation by the schools. More recently the schools have developed shared programmes. To increase their capacity to offer languages other than English they timetable their language classes at the same time. Students then move to whichever school is offering the language they wish to study. Funds change hands but the net flows are not large.

In addition to the shared facilities and academic programmes, the schools also collaborate on co-curricular activities. There is, for example, one choir and one annual musical production for the three schools together. The schools also share playing fields with the community with the result that local government also shares the costs of maintenance.

One other consequence of co-location and shared use of facilities with the community is that less land needs to be purchased for schools and more and better education services can be obtained for the same level of expenditure.

In more recent developments, Delfin (now part of Lend Lease) seeks to sponsor the development of an education service that meets the learning needs of all in a community, not just those of school age. In Caroline Springs on the outskirts of Melbourne, a former office and sales facility has been redeveloped to meet some of the needs of more than 200 home-based businesses operating in the community. It provides space for meetings with clients or other business owners, virtual office services and training courses offered by the University of Ballarat. In Mawson Lakes in South Australia, a government primary school, a Lutheran secondary school and a campus of the University of South Australia are essentially jointly located around the Mawson Centre. The university is a majority owner of the centre but the primary school and the City of Salisbury are joint minority owners. The centre houses the primary school principal, the university pro vice-chancellor and the city manager for the community and the school uses its elaborately equipped lecture theatre for its assemblies and other activities. The school and community libraries and their staff are integrated in a single facility in the centre that is available seven days a week. Some of the proceeds from each land sale are placed in a trust fund to which the city also contributes and, from that fund, a 'learning broker' has been appointed with the task of matching learning needs of individuals and enterprises with learning opportunities.

There is now growing experience with this kind of co-location and obvious examples of the collaboration between schools of a type not typically seen in Australia. There is little systematic evidence, however, about its impact on the development of social capital or, indeed, social connectedness. Delfin–Lend Lease is currently exploring, with various government authorities, the possibility of conducting a number of substantial pilot projects in which systematic evidence of impact will be sought using a set of carefully designed indicators. This work will require the development of new mechanisms for communities to be involved in determining the shape of their education services. All three tiers of government will need to be involved together with the full range of private providers.

The lessons learned could be of considerable benefit not only for the development of education services in greenfield sites but also for the substantial rationalisation and refurbishment programmes being undertaken with existing facilities, and not only in Australia. While these programmes are currently restricted to public schools, there is no reason that they could not also cover existing private schools where they are in need of redevelopment.

References

Gewirtz, S., Dickson, M., Power, S., Halpin, D. and Whitty, G. (2005) 'The deployment of social capital theory in educational policy and provision: the case of education action zones in England', *British Educational Research Journal*, 31: 651–73.

OECD (2001a) *Knowledge and Skills for Life: First Results from PISA 2000*. Paris: OECD.

OECD (2001b) *The Well-being of Nations: The Role of Human and Social Capital*. Paris: OECD.

OECD (2004) *Learning for Tomorrow's World: First Results from PISA 2003*. Paris: OECD.

OECD (2006) *Education at a Glance 2006*. Paris: OECD.

Putnam, R. (2000) *Bowling Alone: The Collapse and Revival of American Community*. New York: Simon & Schuster.

Putnam, R. (2004) 'Education, diversity, social cohesion and "social capital"', paper presented to an OECD Education Ministers Forum on Education and Social Cohesion, Dublin (http://www.oecd.org/edumin2004).

Schneeweis, N. and Winter-Ebmer, R. (2005) *Peer Effects in Austrian Schools*, Working Paper No. 0502. Department of Economics, Johannes Kepler University of Linz, Austria.

The document highlighted the following points:

- higher education institutions have a key role to play in the recon-
struction and quality of continuing and adult education, including
the improvement of adult educators' competence and learner-
centred assessment;
- higher education institutions should be involved in the construction of lifelong learning strategies;
- the tendency at both European and national level is for higher
education institutions to be excluded from the implementation of
lifelong learning, so their innovative capacity is not sufficiently
exploited;
- in the strategies of most universities in central Europe lifelong
learning is not embedded as a concept or an important objective;
- the issue of lifelong learning has resulted in the increased cooperation of higher education with market-oriented actors, but
some academic groups remain critical where there is a lack of
clarity on what their role should be;
- even in countries like the UK, France and Finland, where issues
like continuing education and lifelong learning have become
important elements in higher education activity, they are still not
accorded the same status as other academic activities, with
insufficient research capacity (European Universities Association, 2003, p. 99).

In support of these approaches to the role of higher education in the
knowledge market, Jarvis (2001) wrote:

> diversified higher education has no alternative, but searching for
> and finding effective solutions for the challenges affecting educa-
> tion and training. In countries where state roles are exaggerated
> and exceed a convenient status together with the existence of a
> reduced or non-functioning autonomy of higher education
> institutions, a quite artificial and not really self-sustained higher
> education will not, consequently, be able to harmonise its func-
> tions and services to the expectations of the knowledge market.
> The question is, for how long the state can continue its traditional
> role, while universities representing a flexible training policy and
> innovation can maintain and involve significant groups of
> students in their educational and training programmes and
> challenging all rigidly operating higher education institutions.

Universities, which recognise and represent the concept and strategic approach of lifelong learning, establish a contentful partnership with their local environment through the support and development of effective forms of learning (Jarvis, 2001, p. 36).

Effective strategic thinking on lifelong learning connects up social objectives, such as active citizenship, individual fulfilment and social inclusion, as well as employment priorities. At the same time, it points to the importance of coherent national strategies in which a significant role is given to higher education institutions. Current surveys concerning university lifelong learning indicate that the term lifelong learning is misleading for many universities. This reflects inherent multiplicities of understandings and uses of the term within the university sector (Osborne, 2003, pp. 16–17). Osborne argues that lifelong learning has 'lost any narrow definition around age, purpose and location' and 'in the present age is not simply an adult phenomenon, but is about learning across the lifespan'. Nonetheless, conflating continuing education activities that pertain to continuing professional development with part-time initial education for disadvantaged groups (European Universities Association, 2007, p. 62) undoubtedly caused conceptual confusion.

Lifelong learning is still not a core issue in the institutional reforms of many universities. Moreover, features that exemplify a lifelong learning institution, such as adult education in the liberal tradition, have had to be reconfigured as core activities connected to the labour market, thereby moving away from the margins and into the centre of processes. It is clear that, as observed in the Trends V report, it is mainly because of economic imperatives that universities embrace lifelong learning as a means to generating a more educated and skilled workforce for the labour market (European Universities Association, 2007, p. 62).

Today, widening access to learning opportunities is the key agenda. To achieve this, universities must work closely with local and regional stakeholders for a better and more settled social and economic status in the future. Therefore, the strategic development of lifelong learning is combined today with key social and economic objectives in regional development and co-operation (European Universities Association, 2007, p. 65).

A variety of stakeholders have become interested in updating the skills and knowledge of staff and the broader workforce to either compete on the market with better products or to develop better services for the public (Longworth, 2006, pp. 196–200; Learning in Local and Regional Authorities, 2007).

Today, most higher education institutions of the EU member states have already adopted the language of lifelong learning and have given high priority to it. But while many of the universities offer a variety of educational services and refer to their roles in regional development, either through distance education or through networking with local and regional stakeholders (European Universities Association, 2007, p. 65), very little attention has as yet been paid to the need to critically analyse national lifelong learning strategies at a European level.

The Trends IV report (European Universities Association, 2007) on the implementation of the Bologna Structure in 2005 underlined the importance of recognising non-formal/non-academic qualifications. It stated that 'the wider theme of lifelong learning...has been very much neglected so far in the Bologna discussions'. This is despite a number of factors which should be making this more likely, for example, APEL (Accreditation of Prior Experimental Learning) and APL (Accreditation of Prior Learning) are becoming more visible (because of the Lisbon agenda), there is an ageing European population and there is a European Quality Framework (EQF) for higher education and vocational training. Prior learning is another issue that has been underestimated by higher education institutions, apart from the development of the ECTS (European Credit Transfer System). This is despite the fact that local and regional circumstances identify that issue as one of the most important factors to stimulate learning in adult and later life (European Universities Association, 2005, p. 25; van der Hijden, 2007, pp. 5–7).

In 2005, the European Universities Association announced the Glasgow Declaration (EUA, 2005b). The Declaration, by striving for strong universities within a strong Europe, promoted their role in networking in order to enhance innovation and transfer at regional level (EUA, 2005a, p. 4). But a problem with such declarations is that they rarely identify strategies which can then influence politicians and ministries at a national level to ensure that the roles of lifelong learning are understood coherently and holistically. The narrow understanding of lifelong learning is still, therefore, a problem for policy makers, stakeholders and for many traditional academics within higher education, especially in the former socialist countries.

One reason for this is the historical shift from a monolithic political and economic structure into the hegemonistic and ever-changing global world of a market economy. In the former, critical thinking and active citizenship are closed and marginalised as intellectual approaches.

These thoughts are worth elaborating on in the context of the Hungarian higher education sector.

Lifelong learning in Hungary

In Hungary, lifelong learning usually refers to widening participation and the acceleration of part-time and distance/e-education and learning, strongly attached to the needs of the labour market and economic activity. This approach and understanding have been clearly reflected in the main components of the Hungarian government's lifelong learning strategy and in the slowly emerging forum of national university lifelong learning since the turn of the millennium.

Seven years ago, there were at the most five universities interested in endorsing the Memorandum on Lifelong Learning dealing with Employability and Active Citizenship. Today, lifelong learning has become one of the rallying points promoting European initiatives in education, training and learning. This is evidenced, for example by the establishment in 2003 of the MELLearN, the Hungarian Universities Lifelong Learning Network, in 2003 (MELLearN, 2007; see Figure 6.1). Fifteen Hungarian state universities came together to form the network by making use of their 'continuing education networks'. MELLearN is part of a wider European network, the European Thematic Network of University Lifelong Learning (EULLearN, 2007). The aim is to strengthen the role of universities in the development of lifelong learning both within and outside higher education.

MELLearN is a key academic forum for initiating discussion on issues related to lifelong learning in Europe, and especially in Hungary. Through working groups it scrutinises a range of topics on the theory and practice of lifelong learning. This network for Hungarian universities has become very successful and has so far held three annual national and international conferences on lifelong learning related to current themes, most recently on the issue of lifelong learning networking and the cooperation of higher education institutions as regional knowledge centres.

However, as Jarvis (2007) notes in his book on globalisation, lifelong learning and the learning society, it would probably be true to say that the initiators of learning cities and regions are educators. Support for the movement, however, needs to come from a wider field (Jarvis, 2007, p. 117).

Figure 6.1: The Hungarian Universities Lifelong Learning Network (MELLearN)

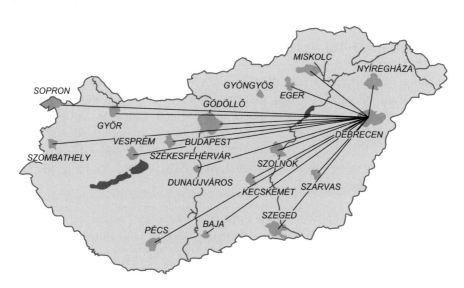

Source: www.mellearn.hu

A similar issue arises in the promotion of a holistic lifelong learning strategy and its implications in a national context. Maybe educators, most of whom come from an adult education background, expect that policy makers will understand and advocate this in national strategy making. But more immediate concerns, such as employment issues, which are of greater importance to them, make this unlikely.

Nonetheless, it is increasingly being recognised by policy makers, business leaders and some universities and researchers that additional, wider and more modern channels are needed to promote an advanced flow of knowledge to support practice and commercialisation. Further, the relevance of university education and research to regional development needs to be a central issue of university reform (Reichert, 2006, p. 16). Local and regional alliances could be used for implementing strategies through partnerships between universities, regional public agencies/authorities and businesses.

The knowledge economy and knowledge production have become important policy issues. Many countries, regions and cities have active citizens wanting to influence their communities' future. Reichert underlines the importance of incorporating the public into framing alliances at local and regional level. Taking the public's concerns and ideas seriously can become part of the knowledge-creation process (Reichert, 2006, p. 17).

Hungarian universities could move to the centre of more innovative economic and cultural modelling since, at least in principle, they are the holders of innovation capacity and could play an interfacing role in the promotion of research and development in a more 'applicability-centred' approach. Some Hungarian universities have resisted those changes, and it is generally clear that universities as institutions have been playing a rather reactive role when responding to new demands. This is clearly reflected in the low use of ICT and of distance education or e-learning and blended learning models in general. However, a significant application of distance-learning models does appear through the use of media and web-based lecturing in some Hungarian universities (e.g. UNIV TV at the University of Pécs).

The formation of the Hungarian Universities Lifelong Learning Network (MELLearN, 2007) has meant that the focus has turned to new areas of institutional development discussions and decision making, and has led to the enhancement of new and adaptable professional competences of academic and administrative staff. New demands on universities are emerging through partnership and cooperation models in the region. These are resulting in projects and experiments using new cooperation instruments and method-ologies (Reichert, 2006, p. 21).

Reichert identifies four roles for universities in lifelong learning, and these can be found within Hungarian universities with varying degrees of emphasis. They are:

- *The sober view*: in this model, the university is a purely know-ledge-based institution, and does not differ significantly from other knowledge-based businesses, although it has more experts.
- *Role*: exchanging knowledge and knowledge workers with other institutions in the region.
- *The social view* of the university sees the institution as an important critical actor providing balance to prevailing governing forces and attitudes. It focuses on the public role of the university to widen access to knowledge.
- *Role*: dialogue with regional actors so as to uncover needs and react to them.
- *The creative view* of the university reflects an institution focusing

on the creative potential of individuals and of teams in continuous dialogue with relevant partners.

○ *Role*: the university acts in a mutually supportive manner with regional actors to benefit from creative environments.

○ *The purist view* of the university is a traditional one by reflecting a university which keeps a critical distance from its social, political and economic environment in order to preserve its innovative potential.

○ *Role*: unidirectional knowledge transfer (Reichert, 2006, p. 23).

Each of these approaches is variously reflected in Hungarian university management culture, in education and training and in research and development. However, in relation to lifelong learning in Hungary the first approach dominates, followed by the second and fourth approaches. Only since 2000 has the third approach begun to emerge, bringing with it innovative and co-operative management, together with developments in policy. These are explored below.

Towards a Hungarian lifelong learning strategy

Reductionist or closed coordination is a label to describe a kind of strategy-making which does not involve enough policy experts and researchers to represent relevant higher education-based research ideas and interests. To date this has resulted in strategies completely and exclusively subordinated to employment policy and human resources development.

Planning for a Hungarian lifelong learning strategy has not yet formally incorporated higher education institutions to legitimate either the process or the content of the strategy.

Options for Hungary

However, there are some useful and appropriate changes that could be initiated in the Hungarian lifelong learning strategy. The strategy should clearly refer to the influences of major EU documents such as the seminal EC White Papers – Growth, Employability and Competitiveness (EC, 1993) and Teaching and Learning: Towards the Learning Society (EC, 1995) – which underlined the impact of education and training and a modern understanding of continuous learning as keys to European development.

The influential working paper Memorandum on Lifelong Learning (2000) heralded a European strategy on lifelong learning. Following the European Year of Lifelong Learning (1996) and the Memorandum Debate, employ-

Figure 6.2: The Hungarian lifelong learning strategy, 2005

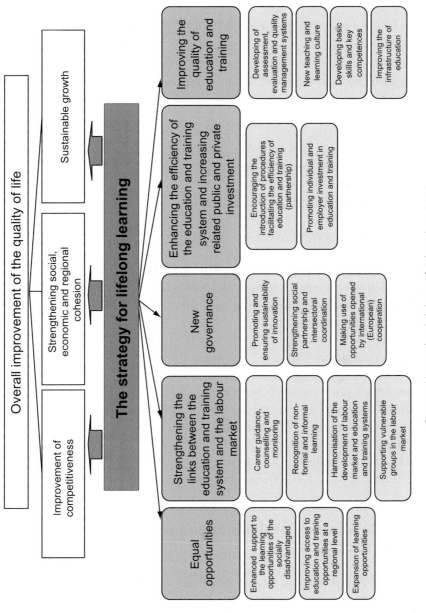

Source: Hungarian Ministry of Education, 2005.

ability and active citizenship had been identified as linked objectives of lifelong learning through six key messages. A year later these became action priorities.

Figure 6.2 shows the structure of the Hungarian lifelong learning strategy from 2005, including the priorities for action. They are a mixture of European strategic priorities of lifelong learning and the economic drivers of competitiveness and growth. There are missing links: active citizenship and social cohesion programmes through regional partnerships and new governance.

Further, it is suggested here that the strategy should openly respond to the three objectives of the Open Method of Coordination (OMC)[1]. These are:

- the development of quality assurance for education and training systems;
- the development of access to education and training; and
- the development of cooperation and partnership inside and especially outside the education and training system, vertically and horizontally, focusing on close relations with the economic, civic and political sectors and, finally, towards the individual. (Szilágyi, 2005)

It would seem from Figure 6.2 that some of these objectives have not yet been taken into account. Specifically, cooperation is needed between the various branches of government to support the implementation of lifelong learning policy. Without this, a Hungarian strategy on lifelong learning may only result in a partial paradigm shift, reflected in education and training and employment policy, but not in other related policy areas including youth, culture, the environment and health. It is argued here that cooperation could be a policy development focus for 2008 and beyond.

The Pole Strategy of Competitiveness and the role of higher education

From 2007 until 2013, in the second phase of the National Development Plan and using resources provided by the EU, the Hungarian government plans to invest approximately 100 billion Hungarian forints (around €400 million) in each regional centre across the country, so it can counterbalance the Budapest-centred national economy with other poles of growth and

Figure 6.3: Regional development poles and axes in Hungary

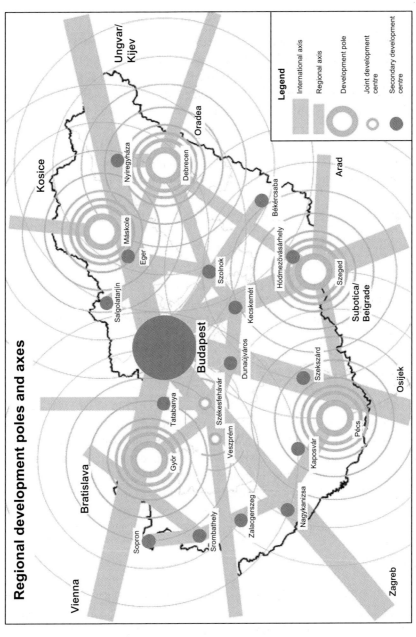

Regional development poles and axes

Legend

Ungvar/Kijev

Kosice

Nyíregyháza

Debrecen

Oradea

Mískole

Eger

Szolnok

Salgótarján

Békéscsaba

Hódmezővásárhely

Arad

Szeged

Budapest

Kecskemét

Subotica/Belgrade

Tatabánya

Székesfehérvár

Dunaújváros

Szekszárd

Osijek

Győr

Veszprém

Kaposvár

Pécs

Bratislava

Sopron

Szombathely

Zalaegerszeg

Nagykanizsa

Vienna

Zagreb

International axis

Regional axis

Development pole

Joint development centre

Secondary development centre

Source: VÁTI PBC Budapest (VÁTI Hungarian public nonprofit company for regional development and town planning), 2006 (http://www.vati.hu).

competitiveness by generating development in the regions. See Figure 6.3 for the various poles and axes in the regional development plan.

The Pole Strategy of Competitiveness, designed in 2005 by a Pécs-based consortium consisting of the City of Pécs, the University of Pécs, the Pécs Chamber of Commerce and Industry and Baranya (Pécs Development Ltd, 2006) is also called 'the Pécs Pole of Quality of Life' (see Figure 6.4) and is built on the development of three services: health care, environment and culture. It aims to establish a network of services in the city and the region involving a broader perspective of human health (including physical, mental and social well-being), with a strong input from the economy and higher education. The main goal is to launch information technology development projects and training programmes through which Pécs and the surrounding region can become a more healthy and desirable place to live, while at the same time providing new stimulation to the regional economy.

As a result of the implementation of this Pole Strategy, the newly established infrastructure should attract more people from the country and overseas to settle in Pécs, in particular the elderly, and young adults. The former group may be attracted by, first, high-quality healthcare serving the needs of elderly people suffering from chronic diseases, secondly, good transport to hospice services and care and thirdly, by the natural endowments of the city and the region, including low housing costs. Young people may be attracted by the university and the high-quality cultural services which Pécs can offer.

The implementation of the Pole Strategy is also intended to encourage the growth of tourism in the region, primarily through the expansion of health care, heritage, culture and 'gastronomic tourism'. This strategic view is based partly on the principles of sustainable growth, ecological awareness, the social integration of people with disabilities, social solidarity and lifelong education, and partly on the evaluation of the social and economic conse-quences of a European demographic trend: life spans are longer, which means an increase in the proportion of elderly people in the region.

In accordance with these trends, the Pole Strategy marks a trajectory of development, including the development of health rehabilitation centres and sporting facilities, the establishment of residential parks for elderly people and the development of food products offering healthy nutrition. The strategy also proposes to establish an environmental research centre, to develop the technology of land rehabilitation, to introduce a regional system of ecological economy, to design environmental protection technologies and to develop

Figure 6.4: The Pécs Pole of Quality of Life

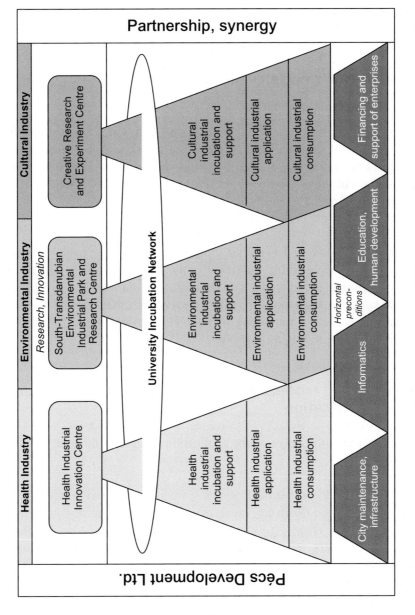

Source: Pécs Development Ltd., 2006 (www.pecspolus.hu).

urban rehabilitation, cultural tourism and digital television broadcasting.

The section of the Pole Strategy dealing with cultural industry directly refers to the European Capital of Culture application as one of its 'most important strategic elements' (Pécs Development Ltd, 2006).

Fundamental principles of the European Cultural Capital: Pécs, 2010

The Pécs application for the 2010 Cultural Capital of Europe was prepared with the aim of ensuring that development projects would provide the city with cultural and artistic spaces that would be sufficient in number, size and quality for the programmes of the European Capital of Culture year. The projects also needed to promote use of the city's economic potential and the development of the creative and (cultural) tourism industries.

It was clearly stated in the official application that cultural institutions in Pécs would be made compatible with those of the EU so that they would be able to fulfil international functions. The development plan had to provide funda-mental cultural experiences and aim to revive the urban character of the city to make it attractive for young people. This, it was hoped, would impact positively on the region as a whole.

Development models in the Pécs 2010 European Cultural Capital application

The development package of the application comprises three urban develop-ment models:

(1) Large-scale investment projects intended to revive underde-veloped, run-down city quarters with heterogeneous architectural elements. These projects are expected to raise the value of the environment, attract private investors and prepare the ground for a large-scale transformation of selected areas.
(2) The largest component of the development package involves the establishment of a cultural quarter in a former large industrial site, the monument buildings of the Zsolnay Porcelain Factory. The primary goal in establishing this cultural district is to create a dense, inner-city creative medium by making the district both a

scene of production and consumption and a mixture of different creative, entertaining and educational functions.

(3) The third model is a catalyst-like intervention through the renewal and transformation of public spaces to revive areas of the city. The renewal of a park, square or street may be a catalyst for development in a given neighbourhood; it may attract new residents, shops and investors (Takáts, 2005).

Education and training in 2007: preparing for the Pécs 2010 Cultural Capital Programme

The reason why the City of Pécs gave priority to education and learning in 2007 was that 2007 was the hundredth anniversary of the National Congress of Free Education held in Pécs in 1907, where the Hungarian intellectual elite discussed the role and tasks of, and programme for, intellectuals and intelligentsia in the twentieth century. The anniversary provides an opportunity to compare with the past the challenges facing the European and Hungarian educated classes (the social elite with the power of knowledge and information) in the twenty-first century. These include making the con-nections between globalisation and locality and the effects of the newly established information technology society. In addition, there will also be a chance to put the challenges that education and learning face into a local and regional context, and to consider the roles of local and regional stakeholders in education, training, culture and science. It will offer a challenge for Pécs to establish itself as a learning city for September 2007. There will be meetings to analyse the role of the university and how it can be changed in the future, the revival of art after the 'death of art history', and the role of tradition in the age of digital databases and digital media.

The 1907 congress was one of the programmes of the Pécs National Exhibition and Fair, which lasted for six months, and which, according to the local press, attracted one million visitors. One hundred years ago, a separate city quarter was created by setting up pavilions to display industrial, mining and artistic products, and wines. The main organiser of the event, Miklós Zsolnay, sought to open the doors towards the Balkans by means of this exhibition, and complement the system of relations between industry and trade in South Transdanubia. For the 2007 events an exhibition and fair are planned to display the newest technology in culture and education.

However, 2007 is not centred only on teaching – that is, on knowledge and the mediation of culture – but also on the problems of learning and the reception of knowledge. The EU document, *Education and Training 2010* (EC, 2003), had as its main goal establishing cooperative relations between culture, education, science and economy, ensuring the necessary conditions for lifelong education and learning, and giving priority to the role of the university in its endeavour to create a Europe of Knowledge in local and regional partnership models.

The programmes organised in the preparatory years leading up to 2010 could be devoted to discussing how these goals have been achieved in the country, while in 2010 Pécs could host an international conference to review the European lessons of the programme. In 2007, the primary emphasis is on the University of Pécs. For the university, the year 2007 and subsequently the year 2010 may involve a year of conferences where it can establish co-operation with various partners through which its innovative power can be channelled into the local economy.

Conclusion

There are trajectories indicating that higher education institutions will rapidly change and try to meet the needs of the outside world. They will – as Jarvis points out – involve many forms of higher learning but in different organisational structures and with different educational methodology and content. It will, therefore, reflect the fragmentation of society (Jarvis, 2001, p. 35).

At the same time, universities should increasingly be demonstrating their new local and regional roles in economic development through educational and research partnerships, and their innovatory capacity through cooperating with stakeholders such as local councils, chambers of commerce and industry, trade unions and businesses.

A very significant role of the university in local and regional context, it has been argued here, is the promotion of critical thinking and active citizenship. In 2001, UNESCO connected lifelong learning and active citizenship to higher education. In addition to disseminating knowledge for lifelong learning, the learning city and region model needs to characterise universities as promoting broader social objectives. Duke (2002) refers to the community service of universities as the 'third leg'. This chapter has argued that the co-operative approach in local and regional revival should be the 'fourth leg'.

Note

[1] The Open Method of Coordination (OMC) was introduced by the European Council of Lisbon in March 2000. It was a method designed to help member states progress jointly in the reforms they needed to undertake in order to reach the Lisbon goals. The method included the following elements:

- fixing *guidelines and timetables* for achieving short-, medium- and long-term goals;
- establishing quantitative and qualitative *indicators and benchmarks*, tailored to the needs of Member States and sectors involved, as a means of comparing best practices;
- translating European guidelines into *national and regional policies*, by setting specific measures and targets; and
- periodic *monitoring* of the progress achieved in order to put in place *mutual learning* processes between Member States.

For more on this see http://ec.europa.eu/invest-in-research/coordination/coordination01_en.htm (accessed August 2007).

References

Bologna Declaration (1999) In *The Bologna Process: Towards the European Higher Education Area* (http://ec.europa.eu/education/policies/educ/bologna/bologna_en.html).

Duke, C. (2002) 'The morning after the millennium: building the long-haul learning university', *International Journal of Lifelong Education*, 21(1): 24–36.

European Commission (1993) White Paper on Growth, Competitiveness and Employability. Brussels and Luxembourg: EC-EUROP.

European Commission (1995) White Paper on Education and Training: Teaching and Learning. Towards the Learning Society. Brussels and Luxemburg: EC-EUROP.

European Commission (2000) The Lisbon Special European Council (March 2000): Towards a Europe of Innovation and Knowledge (http://europa.eu/scadplus/leg/en/cha/c10241.htm).

European Commission (2003) Education and Training 2010. The Success of the Lisbon Strategy Hinges on Urgent Reforms. Brussels: EC-EUROP.

European Commission (2005) Working together for growth and jobs. A new start for the Lisbon strategy. Communication from President Barroso in agreement with Vice-President Verheugen. EC. COM 24 final – not published in the official journal.

European Thematic Network of University Lifelong Learning (EULLearN) (2007) (http://www.eullearn.net/), accessed August 2007.

European Universities Association (2003) *Trends 2003*. Geneva and Brussels: EUA.

European Universities Association (2005a) *Trends IV: European Universities Implementing Bologna. An EUA Report*. Brussels: EUA.

European Universities Association (2005b) *Glasgow Declaration*. Brussels: EUA.

European Universities Association (2007) *Trends V: Universities Reshaping the European Higher Education Area. An EUA Report*. Brussels: EUA.

Hungarian Ministry of Education (2005) (http://www.okm.gov.hu/doc/upload/200602/kiadvany_hungarian_strategy.pdf), accessed August 2007.

Jarvis, P. (2001) 'Universities as institutions of lifelong learning', *Journal of Higher Education Outreach and Engagement*, 6(3): 23–39.

Jarvis, P. (2007) *Globalisation, Lifelong Learning and Learning Societies*, Part 2. London: Routledge.

Learning in Local and Regional Authorities (LILARA) (2007) (http://www.lilaraproject.com) *and* lilara in the media (http://www.cor.europa.eu/cms/pages/documents/educ/pecs_rev.doc), accessed August 2007.

Longworth, N. (2006) *Learning Cities, Learning Regions, Learning Communities*. London: Routledge.

MELLearN (2007) Hungarian Universities Lifelong Learning Network (http://www.mellearn.hu), accessed August 2007.

Osborne, M. (2003) 'University continuing education – international understandings', in M. Osborne and E. Thomas, *Lifelong Learning in a Changing Continent: Continuing Education in the Universities of Europe*. Leicester: NIACE.

Pécs Development Ltd (2006) Strategy for the Development of the City of Pécs (http://www.pecs2010.hu/eng/main.php?include=vednokeink&abra=6), accessed August 2007.

Reichert, S. (2006) *The Rise of Knowledge Regions: Emerging Opportunities and Challenges for Universities*. Brussels: EUA.

Szilágyi, A. (2005) 'Learning through Life (TÉT)'. In József Mayer (ed), *3L Academy 2004. Gyula. Innováció–Integráció–Inklúzió/Innovation-Integration-Inclusion*. Budapest: OKI.

Takáts, J. (2005) *Borderless City: European Capital of Culture – Pécs, 2010*. Pécs: Pécs Direkt.

UNESCO (2001) *Cape Town Statement on Characteristics Elements of a Lifelong Learning Higher Education Institution*. Hamburg: UNESCO-UIE.

van der Hijden, P. (2007) *From Bergen to London*. The Commission Contribution to the Bologna Process. Paper presented at the 33rd UUCEN Conference, Ljubljana, 15–17 March. (Original paper, 22 December 2006, Brussels: EC.)

Zachár, L. (2004) 'Directions of Lifelong Learning'. In Roland Soós, László Fedor and Tamás Balázs (eds), *A felnöttképzés módszertana IV. A nonformális tanulás térhódítása*. Budapest–Miskolc: ÉRÁK-NFI.

Websites

www.pecspolus.hu

www.vati.hu

www.okm.gov.hu

Chapter 7

Community education, learning communities and national skill policy in Australia: is there light at the end of the tunnel?

Peter Kearns and Denise Reghenzani

While declared learning communities exist across Australia, progress has been slow, and there is no comprehensive national policy for lifelong learning. At the national level, skill policy has been driven up to now by an industry-led, competency-based training paradigm in which community education and learning communities have been marginalised. Moreover, government funding of adult and community education has declined in most states in recent years.

Although this situation would seem bleak for the roles of community education and learning communities, there are nevertheless some early signs of possible change driven by key mega-trends that are coming centre stage on the national policy agenda. In this context, this chapter discusses whether there is light at the end of the tunnel.

Central to policy shifts that are starting to emerge in this context is concern at the implications of demographic change with the ageing of the Australian population and workforce, recognition of the need with intensified international competition to raise the skill level of the Australian workforce, and concern at potential long-term skills shortages. The longer-term implications of these drivers for learning in communities, and the sustainability of many communities, merit careful consideration.

Emerging policy responses include a new collaborative Commonwealth/State

National Reform Agenda which includes a human capital strand, an Australian Government Skills for the Future package, and a discussion paper on *Community Education and National Reform*. Whether these emerging policy shifts may lead to a more strategic and collaborative approach to fostering lifelong learning in Australia, and harnessing the learning resources of communities in support of national economic and social objectives, is discussed in this chapter.

The current pattern of development

While various government policies at both state and Commonwealth level may be seen as contributing to the capacity of Australians to continue learning throughout life, Australia has no comprehensive and coherent national policy for lifelong learning, and there has been no systematic discussion of the concept and its implications at the national level.

This situation was reviewed in a 2006 report by one of the authors of this chapter for Adult Learning Australia on future directions for lifelong learning in Australia. This report concluded that overall lifelong learning was poorly understood in Australia and had not received the attention the concept deserved (Kearns, 2006).[1] This situation was seen as a barrier to Australia's development as an inclusive and successful society under twenty-first-century conditions.

In the absence of comprehensive national policy for lifelong learning and mobilising the resources of communities for learning in strategic ways, there has been an ad hoc pattern of development in building learning communities which has varied from state to state, with progress largely driven by individual initiatives. A consequence has been that the national skills agenda up to now has not been underpinned by community and regional learning strategies, except in a few isolated cases.

The first declared learning community in Australia, Albury Wodonga, dates from initiatives taken in 1998. Most development since that year has occurred in Victoria, supported by the strong Victorian system of adult and community education. The Victorian government funded a network of ten Learning Towns from 2000 to 2006, while other learning community initiatives emerged in Victoria during this period as a result of individual initiatives. No other state has funded learning community initiatives, so that development across Australia has been slow.[2]

Learning Towns in Victoria

The Learning Towns funded by the Victorian Government from 2000 to 2006 were all, with one exception, located in regional areas of the state. These were mostly significant regional centres such as Ballarat, Bendigo, Geelong, and Albury Wodonga. Funding was provided through the Adult and Community Education Board, with programmes administered through adult and community education providers in these locations.

Government support over this period enabled learning community initiatives to be sustained in these communities, although it did not serve to extend similar initiatives in other communities.

It was decided that funding would be discontinued at the end of 2006 with a programme of community learning partnerships providing more general support for community learning across the state. During 2005 and 2006, 46 initiatives were funded under this programme, enabling a broader support of learning partnerships across Victoria.

The Australian Learning Community Network was an offshoot of initiatives taken in Victoria. By 2007, 40 communities were members of the Network. National conferences were held in 2000, 2002, 2004 and 2006 to disseminate information on good practice.

While the Victorian Learning Towns did not have a direct influence on similar initiatives across the state, a few other learning communities have emerged in Victoria in different ways, in addition to the initiatives now being supported under the community learning partnerships programme. The Hume Global Learning Village in northern Melbourne and the Yarra Ranges Learning Communities in the outer eastern area of Melbourne illustrate a different pattern of development with local government councils playing a key role.

The Hume Global Learning Village

The origins of the Hume Global Learning Village lay in initiatives taken by the Chair of the Social Justice Committee of the Council, Frank McGuire, to secure a library for Broadmeadows. Strong corporate support was found for this initiative, leading to a shift in the objective from securing a library for Broadmeadows to building a Global Learning Village. What's in a name? A good deal in this case, and the vision of a Global Learning Village has become the focus for a distributed pattern of leadership in which the Hume City Council has been supported by leadership from the Hume community and from elsewhere.

The concept of the Global Learning Village was given visible shape and form in a Global Learning Centre built in Broadmeadows. The centre incorporates a large library, computer and training rooms, and community space for a range of activities. A key feature was the establishment of an advisory board, chaired by a former Premier of Victoria, John Cain, with strong community membership supported by a number of outside appointments.

In 2006 the Global Learning Village won a National Local Government award for excellence in community/industry partnership, and has been a pacesetter in progressing the frontier of learning community development in Australia. A key feature has been the strong support given to the initiative by Hume City Council, and the blend of local and external leadership which has kept a flow of new ideas into the development of the initiative.

Community learning in South Australia

While lifelong learning and building learning communities have not been seen as priorities in most states and the Commonwealth in recent years, with the exception of Victoria and Tasmania,[3] a development of some significance was the release by the Government of South Australia in late 2006 of a policy statement and strategy on Community Learning (Training and Skills Commission, 2006).

This statement provides a broad approach to the role of community learning in the development of the state and affirms the goal to develop South Australia as a learning state. The four goals of the policy include the goal of 'learning and growing together', with the following objective: 'Offer learning opportunities in all communities so that the whole State becomes a network of Learning Communities.'

South Australia has a rich heritage of innovation in education and human resource development and the outcomes of the policy could have national significance. Whether active support is obtained from local government will be a key issue.

National action

While there has been no consistent comprehensive national action to promote lifelong learning and learning communities across Australia, some ad hoc initiatives have been taken from time to time, and there have been developments both in the school sector and vocational education and training to foster the capacity of Australians to continue learning throughout life.

In the case of schooling, these have included initiatives to strengthen literacy and basic skills as outcomes of schooling to be achieved for all, while in the vocational education and training (VET) sector a significant development has been the promotion of the so-called employability skills to enable Australians to maintain skills and employability throughout life.[4]

However, the focus of national action in preparing young people for working life has been a training approach through a National Training Reform Agenda which evolved from the late 1980s. From 1992 to 2005 this agenda was driven by a collaborative Commonwealth/State Australian National Training Authority (ANTA), with a small board comprising mainly leading industry representatives. While ANTA touched on broader aspects of learning from time to time, its main focus was strongly on training to meet the skills needs of industry in an industry-led, competency-based system.

An exception was, however, in 2001, when ANTA sponsored a National Learning Community Project which was managed by one of the authors of this chapter. Ten communities across Australia, involving all states, participated in this project. This was a limited time project which focused on each community conducting a learning audit. While interesting learning audit reports were obtained, the project was not evaluated and a number of the initiatives have been discontinued.

With the abolition of ANTA in 2005, the Commonwealth Department of Education, Science, and Training has assumed direct responsibility for national training reform and there are some indications that training reform in Australia may be moving to a new stage of development in which learning throughout life and community contexts for learning will become more important in national policy than they have been up to now.

Some drivers of change

A set of key mega-trends are starting to influence national policy and are likely to have a growing influence on policy. These include:

1 demographic change and the ageing of the Australian population and workforce
2 the ongoing impact of globalisation and increasing international competition in higher-skill occupations
3 persisting skill shortages in certain occupations
4 concerns at the sustainability of many 'bush' communities
5 recognition of the extent of adult literacy deficiencies in Australia
6 research evidence that future demand for VET skills is likely to evolve in two major ways: towards higher-level skills and VET qualifications and towards more interactive and cognitive skills as distinct from motor skills.

While the implications of these drivers are likely to take some time to work through current policy frameworks and approaches, there are grounds for believing that lifelong learning objectives, equity and inclusion strategies and community learning strategies will become more significant in national and state policy. Some changes have already occurred and collaborative Commonwealth/state partnership is intensifying under the influence of the agreed National Reform Agenda.

1 Demographic change and an ageing population
Like other OECD countries, Australia faces the challenge of demographic change with an ageing population and workforce. The financial, economic and other costs have been examined in a series of reports, including a 2005 Productivity Commission report (Productivity Commission, 2005). This mega-trend interacts with concern at persistent skill shortages in certain key areas, and has been a key influence on policy.

2 International competition and higher skill requirements
A key influence of growing significance in government education and skills policy is the recognition that intensified international competition is requiring higher skill levels for a country to be competitive. This recognition is reflected in the Australian government's *Skills for the Future* package, released in late 2006, which is discussed below.

3 Skill shortages

Persistent skill shortages have attracted considerable attention in Australia and have led to a good deal of research to clarify the nature, causes and responses (Bureau of Transport and Regional Economics, 2006; NSW Legislative Council, 2006). A particular concern has been skill shortages in regional areas, with a new Australian government initiative directed at responses to skill needs in regional areas. Concern at skill shortages interacts with the impact of demographic change and the influence of global competition, and will be a key driver of policy shifts.

4 Sustainability of rural communities

Many rural communities are faced with loss of wealth from traditional sources, the impact of policies driven by economic rationalism with a loss of services, an ageing population, and the loss of young people to the cities and larger regional centres. In many of these communities a limited range of jobs is available to retain young people.

These problems have been recognised in a series of research reports (Plowman *et al.*, 2003), while governments have sought to respond with initiatives such as the Queensland Blueprint for the Bush and the Victorian Small Towns programme. However, such government responses seldom include community learning initiatives as key aspects of such policy responses directed at sustainable development.

5 The challenge of adult literacy

Australian participation in the 1994–96 OECD International Adult Literacy Survey (IALS) pointed to a significant adult literacy challenge. The Survey of Aspects of Literacy (SAL) conducted by the Australian Bureau of Statistics (ABS) showed that some 40 per cent of the Australian adult population were at the bottom two levels in a five-level scale (ABS, 1996). This involved about 2.6 million adults at Level 1, 3.6 million at Level 2, and about 7.1 million at Levels 3–5 compared to the 6.2 million at Levels 1 and 2.

Australia is now participating in the follow-up OECD Adult Literacy and Life Skills survey, with Australian results likely to be available in about a year. There are grounds for believing that Australia will follow Canada in showing little progress in adult literacy in the decade since 1996. If this is the case, the need to raise adult literacy levels is likely to become a key driver in policy shifts.

6 Shifts in demand for VET skills

A recent major study on tailoring VET to the emerging labour market, involving a consortium comprising the National Institute of Labour Studies and the Centre for Post-compulsory Education and Lifelong Learning at Melbourne University, concluded that the demand for vocational skills would evolve in two ways: (1) towards higher-based VET qualifications; and (2) towards more interactive and cognitive skills as distinct from motor skills (Richardson and Teese, 2006, p. 1).

This will require a considerable shift in the focus of the VET system in Australia which, up to now, has been oriented towards low-level VET Australian Qualifications Framework (AQF) qualifications and with considerable priority for motor skills.

While it is policy to build the so-called employability skills into training packages, a shift towards more interactive and cognitive skills would require strengthening the educational component of VET, and revisiting VET learning strategies. This may see, over time, a shift from the current training paradigm that drives VET policy to a learning paradigm more attuned to the challenge of encouraging and supporting individuals in learning and maintaining skills and employability throughout life.

The role of local government

While a few local government councils such as Hume, Marion, Salisbury, Yarra Ranges, Thuringowa and Lithgow have given active support to local learning community initiatives, overall local government has not been an active initiator or supporter of learning community initiatives. However, drivers such as demographic change and an ageing population, and possibly the impact of the COAG National Reform Agenda, are likely to lead to change. A good test will be in South Australia with the new Community Learning Policy, which includes the objective of the whole state becoming a network of learning communities. Discussions with councils are being initiated to stimulate consideration of the council role.

The COAG National Reform Agenda

A development of considerable significance for the workings of the

Australian federal system occurred in February 2006 when the Australian and state/territory governments agreed through the Council of Australian Governments (COAG) to initiate a collaborative National Reform Agenda which would include human capital as one of the main streams. This National Reform Agenda will focus on human capital, competition, and regulatory reform (COAG, 2006a).

The human capital strand is at present focused on a limited number of objectives and outcomes. Initial priority is being given to early childhood development, literacy and numeracy in schools, childcare, and a health objective (COAG, 2006b, p. 2).

Eleven high-level outcomes have been agreed as a framework for the human capital agenda to improve participation and productivity. These include the following:

- to improve significantly the proportion of children acquiring the basic skills for life and learning; and
- to increase the proportion of adults who have the skills and qualifications needed to enjoy active and productive working lives (COAG, 2006b, p. 2).

While the human capital strand of the COAG National Reform Agenda is currently focused on a few priorities, it may also be seen as involving some necessary steps towards a more comprehensive lifelong learning set of policies for Australia. The initial priorities given to early childhood development and basic school achievement for all could be significant aspects of such a framework. The involvement of local government in the COAG process may also be significant in the longer term.

For the time being, economic and skill objectives are likely to be the key drivers. Concern at the long-term impact of an ageing population on the workforce and supply of skills has already led to a shift in skills policy, aligned with discussion of the contribution of community education to the National Reform Agenda.

These initiatives have involved:

- the release by the Australian government in late 2006 of a major package of skills initiatives titled *Skills for the Future* (Australian Government, 2006); and

- the release, also in late 2006, of a discussion paper on *Community Education and National Reform* (DEST, 2006).

Skills for the Future

The Australian Government's *Skills for the Future* package of initiatives worth AUS $857 million over five years was released in late 2006, focused on providing opportunities for more Australians to gain and maintain skills while at the same time building a more entrepreneurial workforce. A lifelong approach to skilling is recognised in the package with its reference to the need for continuous upgrading of skills over the course of an individual's working life.

The package addresses these objectives through the following programmes:

- Work Skills Vouchers: AUS $408 million (€290,000 million)
- Support for Mid-Career Opportunities: AUS $307 million (€185 million)
- Business Skills Vouchers for Opportunities: AUS $12 million (€7 million)
- More Engineering Places in University: AUS $56 million (€33 million)
- Incentives for Higher Technical Skills: AUS $54 million (€32 million)

The Work Skills Vouchers provide up to AUS $3,000 (€1,800) to assist people who do not have Year 12 or equivalent qualifications acquire the qualification or equivalent VET qualifications at Certificate II level. Support for Mid-Career Opportunities introduces more flexibility into apprenticeship training for older people.

The government statement also includes the objective to 'assist adults to gain literacy and numeracy skills that are basic requirements in the workplace'. It is not yet clear whether this objective will only be addressed under the Work Skills Vouchers.

Community education and national reform

The objective identified under the National Reform Agenda and the *Skills for the Future* package of bringing excluded adults lacking qualifications and skills into the workforce is also reflected in the discussion paper, *Community*

Education and Model Reform, released by the Department of Education, Training and the Arts in late 2006 (DEST, 2006). This may be seen as the first real attempt to identify the role of community education in a reformed and enlarged VET market, and in the context of the COAG National Reform Agenda.

The paper adopts a forward-looking orientation in pointing to the multiple challenges facing VET in Australia with an ageing population and increasing international competition in higher skill occupations that will shift the industrial and occupational compositions of the workforce. A key aspect of the necessary response is seen as finding ways to engage people who are marginally attached to the labour force and to provide them with the skills and qualifications to secure and retain full-time employment. Community education, with over 1,200 organisations across Australia, is seen as having a key role in addressing this challenge.

The paper also argues for a concept of community education as the outreach arm of the VET market using its community linkages and many points of presence to engage and re-engage adults into the VET system (DEST, 2006, p. 14). This role is seen as providing value for money because of its low-cost community infrastructure.

While the DEST discussion paper opens up basic issues for the role of community education in Australia that will require considerable debate and analysis, it at least recognises a national role for the sector that is related to policy directions for national VET reform, and the broader COAG National Reform Agenda.

Is there light at the end of the tunnel?

The policy developments discussed above can be seen as a recognition of the need for a broader and more collaborative and coherent approach to meeting Australia's human capital and skill requirements in the context of an ageing population and workforce, and increased international competition requiring higher skills levels. The COAG National Reform Agenda, the Skills for the Future package and the DEST Community Education and National Reform discussion paper can be seen as steps in this process of moving towards an enhanced understanding and recognition of the need for learning throughout life in many contexts.

Although the drivers of policy shifts are still focused on skill and economic objectives, aspects of the human capital strand of the COAG National Reform Agenda bring a broader social and educational thrust in such areas as the priority given to early childhood development and school achievement in basic skills.

While in this context there would seem to be opportunities for a revitalised articulation of the case for lifelong learning and harnessing the resources of communities for learning in strategic ways that connect to national reform objectives, a necessary requirement would also seem to be a clear demonstration of what community learning strategies can contribute. There is a significant role for research in meeting this challenge. Policy frameworks for community learning, such as the enlightened South Australian Com-munity Learning policy, should be seen as a necessary component in this process of finding better co-ordinated and integrated responses to the human resource challenge confronting Australia. While there is a need for much innovation and creativity in local initiatives, supported by a strong research agenda, there is considerable light at the end of the tunnel.

Notes

[1] The report recognised that there had been relevant development in several states, with Tasmania, in particular, having developed comprehensive policies for lifelong learning in the state.

[2] There is also an interesting South Australian Community Learning Policy which was released in late 2006, which is discussed below.

[3] Tasmania has developed comprehensive policies for lifelong learning and in 2005 convened a *Lifelong Learning: International Education* conference. The role of technology has been a particular interest, with a Tasmanian Communities Online program directed at harnessing technology for learning in communities.

[4] These skills include communication, teamwork and problem solving.

References

Australian Bureau of Statistics (ABS) (1996) *Aspects of Literacy: Assessed Skill Levels, Australia, 1996*. Canberra: ABS.

Australian Government (2006) *Skills for the Future*. Canberra.

Bureau of Transport and Regional Economies (2006) *Skill Shortages in*

Australia's Regions. Canberra: Department of Transport and Regional Services (DOTARS).

COAG (Council of Australian Governments) (2006a) Consequence of 10 February 2006 Meeting. Canberra: COAG.

COAG (Council of Australian Governments) (2006b) Communiqué of 14 July 2006 meeting.

Department of Education, Training and Youth Affairs (DEST) (2006) *Community Education and Model Reform*. Canberra: DEST.

Kearns P. (2006) *Achieving Australia as an Inclusive Learning Society*. Camberra: Adult Learning Australia.

NSW Legislative Council Standing Committee on State Development (2006) *Inquiry into Skills Shortages in Rural and Regional NSW*. Sydney: Legislative Assembly.

Plowman, I., Ashkanasy, N., Gardner, J. and Letts, M. (2003) *Innovation in Rural Queensland: Why Some Towns Thrive while Others Languish*. Brisbane: Department of Primary Industries.

Productivity Commission (2005) *Policy Implications of the Ageing of Australia's Workforce*. Canberra: Productivity Commission.

Richardson, S. and Teese, R. (2006) *A Well-skilled Future*. Adelaide: National Centre for Vocational Educational Research (CVER).

Training and Skills Commission South Australia (2006) *Community Learning*. Adelaide: Department of Further Education, Employment, Science and Technology (DFEEST).

Chapter 8

Issues and challenges for sustainable regeneration: a reflection on regeneration policy in Scotland

John Tibbitt

Introduction

The Scottish Executive published its current policy statement on regeneration in February 2006 (Scottish Executive, 2006). The strategy document builds on the experience and lessons learned from previous regeneration programmes in Scotland and elsewhere in the UK over the past 30 years or so, and sets out some key features which will guide the new strategy. The purpose of this chapter is to reflect on this strategy in order to highlight a number of issues and challenges which the strategy will need to address if it is to achieve its objective of sustainable regeneration of disadvantaged communities in Scotland.

The chapter will consider in turn the lessons which the strategy has identified from previous policies and the policy foundations on which the new strategy is based, and will note the main actions which are now being implemented to take the strategy forward. But as the strategy document itself makes clear, there are a number of wider issues and challenges which will have to be addressed to improve the chances of the strategy delivering sustainable change. One such is the role of the Executive itself, and the ways in which local communities engage with the strategy and in which local voices are heard. In commenting on these last issues, the chapter identifies continuing dilemmas over issues of governance, understanding and managing the links between economic and social drivers of sustainable regeneration, and the role of research in informing policy and bridging government and local action.

Regeneration experience in Scotland

Over the last several decades, the Scottish Executive and, prior to devolution in 1999, the Scottish Office supported some significant regeneration programmes, including most notably Glasgow Eastern Area Renewal (GEAR) launched in 1976 (Scottish Development Agency, 1980), New Life for Urban Scotland from 1989 (Scottish Executive, 1999), Social Inclusion Partnerships in 1999 and the Better Neighbourhoods Support Fund (BNSF) in 2000. These successive programmes illustrate the development of different approaches in the light of growing experience and research.

The GEAR programme was an ambitious strategy which concentrated mainly on the renewal and replacement of poor-quality housing provision and the built environment in the run-down east end of Glasgow. It was followed a decade or so later with the New Life for Urban Scotland programme, which addressed similar issues but focused on peripheral housing estates in Glasgow and also in other major Scottish cities, especially Edinburgh and Dundee.

In the late 1990s, the then Conservative government developed an approach to regeneration based on a partnership approach and the designation of Priority Partnership Areas and Regeneration Programme Areas. Some 21 Priority Partnership Areas were designated in Scotland through the then favoured process of 'challenge funding' in which local authorities bid for funds for relevant projects in their areas. Following a change of government, the Scottish Office developed Social Inclusion Partnerships (SIPs), a remodelled and extended version of these partnership initiatives, launched in 1998 with a focus more clearly on promoting social inclusion in communities, and the prevention of the development of social exclusion. The SIP programme eventually included 48 areas, spread across parts of 25 of the 32 local authorities in Scotland. The majority of SIPs were area-based, while some (14) were thematically or issue-based, most commonly focusing on young people. Funding for the programme rose from £46 million initially to £60 million in 2003.

Another initiative, the Better Neighbourhood Services Fund, provided £121 million to 12 'Pathfinder' councils during the period 2001–5 in a further attempt to improve services for people living in disadvantaged areas. Funds were allocated to many different kinds of local initiatives, aimed among other things at reducing crime and fear of crime, reducing vandalism, and improving education, training and employment opportunities for people living in these areas.

116

These specifically Scottish initiatives were developed and implemented in the context of both learning from direct experience and evaluation of Scottish programmes, but also against the emerging research and policy thinking being undertaken elsewhere in the UK, particularly from the UK Government Social Exclusion Unit and the Neighbourhood Renewal Unit in the Office of the Deputy Prime Minister. Increasingly, this thinking was placing the task of renewing physical provision in the context of wider policy objectives of social inclusion, which in turn required a range of social and economic interventions both to provide opportunity and facilitate access to such opportunity.

An additional strand of policy development of relevance here is that relating to community involvement. It was increasingly recognised that there was a need for greater efficiency in the planning and delivery of public services, and that there were benefits for the achievement of this objective arising from partnership between services and community involvement. Community planning initiatives were taken in a number of local authorities, and given statutory force in the Local Government in Scotland Act 2003.

Key lessons learned

This evolving understanding of the nature and complexity of regeneration, and the emergence of a wider set of policy drivers, have been reflected in two strategy papers published by the Scottish Executive. The first, *Better Communities in Scotland: Closing the Gap*, published in 2002, set out an approach to promoting social inclusion and reducing the opportunity gap between the most deprived areas and Scotland as a whole. The second, the current regeneration statement *People and Place*, published in 2006, sought to define new thinking on achieving sustainable economic and social regeneration in areas of deprivation. So what is the key learning which has informed these policy statements?

Learning has derived from a number of sources, including directly commissioned evaluations of previous policy initiatives, consultations with agencies and the practice community, and consideration of accumulating research on aspects of community development and neighbourhood change.

Evaluations of each of the policy initiatives outlined above have been commissioned by the Scottish Executive or Communities Scotland. For example, attempts were made to evaluate the progress made by individual SIPs, and these have been incorporated into an overview commissioned from independent consultants and published by Communities Scotland in 2006. It is the case, however, that the rigour of such evaluations has been hampered by a lack of data and of robust indicators closely linked to programme objectives. Overall, it seems that progress on many of these programmes has been patchy, incorporating, as they do, many different kinds of local initiatives within the overall programme rubric. Nevertheless, each can point to examples of successful provision and aspects where progress has been seen, and also identifies shortcomings.

The SIP overview is typical. While it is able to point to progress in diverse ways, it identifies a number of general problems across the programme, including problems with clearly defining objectives and targets, difficulties in engaging with mainstream funders in 'bending the spend' towards SIP areas and priorities, problems with maintaining a strategic focus as opposed to being project-focused and overly concerned with the distribution of available funds, and difficulties arising from only devoting limited resources to monitoring and performance measurement. The most positive outcome from the SIP programme identified by the overview report is the success of partnership working. It notes that many SIPs were successful in engaging a variety of service providers and community groups which, in many cases, improved the coherence of local service provision.

In addition to the messages to be drawn from these programme evaluations, recent years have seen a number of attempts to draw together the lessons from practical experience and from accumulations of research. Important examples relevant here are the review of evidence on community regeneration and neighbourhood renewal by Carley (2002) for Communities Scotland, prepared for the *Better Communities* strategy mentioned above, and a series of reports from the Office of the Deputy Prime Minister (e.g. ODPM 2005a, 2005b) on aspects of neighbourhood renewal. A number of themes consistently emerge from these appraisals concerning the need to integrate 'people' policies with 'place' policies, the role of community participation, the improvement of partnership working and the delivery of joined-up services at local level, and, crucially, the recognition that neighbourhood renewal and the social inclusion of deprived households is dependent also on the achievement of economic regeneration at higher spatial levels of local authority, travel-to-work, or regional geographies.

These themes find expression in the *People and Place* regeneration policy in five broad 'key lessons' identified in the policy's statement. These are:

1 Physical investment is important but not enough

It has been long recognised that poor-quality housing, a lack of local community facilities and problems of vandalism, crime and the quality of the local environment compound the problems of the most disadvantaged neighbourhoods. Earlier regeneration initiatives in Scotland, such as the GEAR project and New Life for Urban Scotland, delivered significant improvements to the quality of local housing and the physical environment, while other more recent initiatives such as the Better Neighbourhood Services Fund, like the neighbourhood renewal programme in England, have also placed emphasis on tackling these issues. However, none of these programmes addressed underlying problems of economic and social decline in these local areas or the wider areas in which they were situated.

Other kinds of initiatives have focused on creating conditions to attract people and investors to particular locations. The Scottish Enterprise programme for the creation of competitive places and the Cities Growth Fund have helped deliver significant physical and environmental improvements, as evident in Glasgow's digital media park, the medi-park campus in Dundee and the waterfront project in Edinburgh. In England, Urban Development Companies (UDCs) have transformed large areas of vacant, derelict or underused land into viable commercial centres. However, it is apparent that such schemes, whether in disadvantaged neighbourhoods, city-centre locations or on unused tracts of land, have not always captured the economic benefits for local communities.

It has been concluded that while investment in physical renewal is likely to be a crucial aspect of regeneration, and can be the trigger for it, it will not, on its own, deliver the combination of outcomes that make for sustainable regeneration.

2 There is a need to make investment work for people, linking opportunity and need

Other programmes have taken a different tack, by attempting to improve access to available labour-market opportunities through emphasis on skill development and improving employability. In Scotland, the SIPs and BNSF have helped people into work through employment and training programmes and by addressing barriers to work arising from transport or childcare. Similarly, at the UK level, programmes such as the New Deal for Communities and the Neighbourhood Renewal Fund made progress in the areas of health, education, housing and unemployment. However these programmes highlighted the need for more to be done to address the larger-scale economic and social processes which lie behind the persistent concentrations of unemployment and lack of local economic activity. It is apparent that stimulating economic growth, while at the same time assisting people, especially those in the most disadvantaged neighbourhoods, to access employment opportunities arising from such growth is a key challenge for delivering sustainable regeneration.

3 An integrated approach is necessary

If the foregoing sections emphasise the multifaceted nature of regeneration, so that changes are mutually reinforcing, the need immediately arises for the 'joined-up' planning and delivery of change on these different aspects. There is evidence that some SIPs were able to develop an integrated approach at local level, but the overall assessment of the programme was that it was less successful in integrating local approaches into the wider strategic planning and delivery of services, and broader economic and housing issues. Integration of this kind must embrace the wider geography of regeneration at the local authority, city and regional levels, and take into account planning of land use, transport and housing.

4 Leadership and clarity of purpose are required

Sustainable regeneration is therefore a complex process requiring integration horizontally across a number of strands of social and economic activity in specific areas, but also vertically over different geographies. Regeneration also takes time and sustained commitment.

The importance of clarity about aims and objectives of programmes, a clear commitment from key decision-makers and efficient use of public money to kick-start initiatives can raise investor confidence and help regeneration to become self-sustaining (OPPM, 2003a). The more easily objectives are understood, the more credibility schemes are likely to have in the eyes of potential investors.

5 Partnership working is vital

No single agency can deliver the range of outcomes required for successful regeneration. It is a recurring theme of the literature reviewed above that regeneration must involve a range of participants from the public, private and voluntary sectors and from the communities themselves. Establishing and maintaining strong and effective partnerships between agencies and sectors is vital.

While there is no single 'right' model for neighbourhood renewal, a key requirement is that community organisations must be empowered to work on a level playing field with institutional partners. There is evidence that good partnerships can foster integration between physical and economic development, time-limited initiatives with mainstream provision, and local neighbourhood initiatives with more strategic initiatives at higher spatial levels.

Involving communities

Carley (2002) found that, with some exceptions, good community participation was yet to be embedded in partnership or governance arrangements. Without it, residents could feel disenfranchised, having little influence over renewal or service delivery. His review also cites evidence of the need for social and community capacity-building to enable deprived neighbourhoods to better help themselves in a process of self-development. It is recognised that regeneration mistakes in the past can be attributed to the imposition of particular approaches to regeneration on communities, or to spending inadequate time building local capacity to be fully involved in the design and implementation of regeneration plans. Studies point to the benefits from involving communities in service delivery in terms of better knowledge about needs, greater potential for joined-up solutions and enhanced motivation of frontline staff to innovation in service delivery.

Policy foundations for new strategy

In the light of these key lessons, the 2006 *People and Place* policy statement establishes a number of principles on which the new strategies are founded. These involve a focus on achieving outcomes rather than defining programmes of activities, using economic growth to help people out of poverty, levering private-sector investment, providing a tighter geographical focus, tackling land issues which can inhibit regeneration, and creating mixed and vibrant communities.

Central to the strategy is a stress on partnership working, and boosting economic activity in a limited number of defined geographical areas. The principal vehicle for achieving this is through the establishment of Urban Regeneration Companies (URCs). A URC is a formal partnership of key representatives from the public and private sectors who operate at arm's length to deliver physical and economic regeneration in specified areas. They provide a strategic overview of an area which guides investment decisions by both public and private sectors toward an agreed set of objectives and outcomes. Involving stakeholders and engaging and communicating closely with local businesses and with residents are seen as vital elements to bring success, reflecting the importance of developing the perception of a well-managed area, and a clear commitment to take publicly funded early actions to set favourable conditions for growth.

The creation of 'mixed and vibrant communities' is also an important foundation for the new strategy. The intention is to create communities where, among other things, there is a mix of incomes and sufficient range of affordable and accessible housing. Such changes stem from the recognition that Scotland's most deprived areas are characterised by high concentrations of rented social housing. The achievement of tenure mix is seen as a way of meeting the aspirations of those who move up in income terms to access housing locally rather than move out. Such changes are to be supported also by improvements to the quality of services such as schools, leisure and retail facilities in order to provide more attractive places for people to develop their lives and lifestyle.

Initiatives at the local level

The *People and Place* statement also envisages a change in role for the Scottish Executive, one which is more concerned to provide resources and frameworks to enable actions to be taken forward by more locally focused agencies. Central actions include modernising the planning system, and working to remove barriers which have inhibited progress in previous initiatives by developing a one-stop shop for facilitating discussion and securing co-ordinated actions by relevant agencies. Once these frameworks are in place and commitment is demonstrated through the provision of resources, it is essentially up to local agencies to proceed in accordance with their understanding of local priorities. There are a number of strands of action to facilitate this local focus.

Community Planning Partnerships

Community planning is about the structures, processes and behaviours necessary to ensure that agencies work together and with communities to improve the quality of people's lives through more effective joined-up approaches to service planning and delivery. Although not a new concept, its legislative basis was established in the Local Government in Scotland Act 2003, which placed a statutory duty on local authorities and other 'core' public agencies such as enterprise networks, health services, police, fire and transport partnerships to engage in community planning. The Act is not prescriptive about how community planning should be carried out, recognising that structures and processes will depend on local circumstances. Community Planning Partnerships are operating in all 32 local authority areas, with a range of partners in addition to those with a duty to participate. Agencies such as employment and environmental agencies, further and higher education institutions, business representatives and the voluntary sector are represented in various combinations in a significant number of partnerships.

As has already been pointed out, *Better Communities in Scotland: Closing the Gap*, published in 2002, set out the Scottish Executive's strategy for closing the opportunity gap between disadvantaged communities and the rest of Scotland. The strategy included a commitment to integrate SIPs within the strategic framework of Community Planning Partnerships, which was also given statutory force in the 2003 Local Government Act. The integration aims to address a number of the issues identified in the assessment of previous programmes outlined above. In particular, it sought to ensure that local regeneration takes place within the wider context of community planning, to allow decision making on regeneration to be taken at local level within a national framework, to enhance the focus on disadvantaged communities who most need assistance, to link up physical, social and economic regeneration more effectively, and build on the successes of SIPs with the full engagement of communities.

The Community Regeneration Fund
In 2004, the Scottish Executive announced the creation of the Community Regeneration Fund (CRF) to run for three years from 2005 to 2008. The Fund was established by bringing together funds previously allocated to SIPs and the Better Neighbourhood Services programmes which it replaces. The CRF is distributed through Communities Scotland, and is targeted on the support of activities in the 15 per cent most deprived neighbourhoods as identified by the Scottish Index of Multiple Deprivation. The principal purpose of the CRF is to achieve one of the objectives of the Closing the Opportunity Gap programme of 'regenerating the most disadvantaged neighbourhoods, so that people living there can take advantage of job opportunities and improve their quality of life'. Community Planning Partnerships propose how they will use CRF funding alongside their own resources, to deliver specified regeneration outcomes set out in three-year Regeneration Outcome Agreements.

Regeneration Outcome Agreements

The three-year Regeneration Outcome Agreements (ROAs) are intended to provide the strategic and operational framework for Community Planning Partnerships to deliver the Closing the Gap objective above. ROAs set the course for the ongoing planning and delivery of services to achieve better and additional outcomes for disadvantaged communities.

Guidance has been issued on the form ROAs should take. They include sections on the strategic objectives of the Community Planning Partnerships, an analysis of need and targeting, a statement of outputs and outcomes, steps to be taken to secure community engagement, and the planned expenditure, including the CRF. Importantly, the guidance describes national priorities for community regeneration and provides a menu of indicators and data sources which are to be used to define baselines and against which to set targets and assess progress.

Giving voice to communities

As is recognised in the key lessons summarised above, important strands of regeneration strategy relate to community capacity-building, and enabling the articulation of the community 'voice' within partnership planning and delivery processes. These objectives are being pursued in a number of ways, and some key initiatives are described below.

The Scottish Centre for Regeneration

The Scottish Centre for Regeneration was established within Communities Scotland to help build skills and expertise and share knowledge among those working in community regeneration. The Centre is staffed by teams focusing on research and evaluation, knowledge and practice and skills and learning. These teams indicate the variety of ways in which the Centre pursues its objectives. A key one is through the publication of learning materials, such as 'how-to' guides on topics such as developing community engagement, partnership working, the identification and measurement of regeneration outcomes and 'Learning Points' and 'Perspectives' papers on issues such as schools and regeneration. The Centre also provides practice events, master classes and awards schemes to promote awareness and recognition of good practice and holds a database of project profiles for reference purposes.

The Scottish Community Action Research Fund (SCARF)

SCARF aims to enable communities to carry out their own research, develop their knowledge about their community, improve skills and help build community capacity. It does so by providing funds to community-led groups to undertake small-scale research projects that meet the needs of geographical communities or communities of interest. Established in 2002 as an experimental, demand-led programme, it is managed by Communities Scotland in partnership with the Scottish Community Development Centre. Demand for funds has outstripped supply, to the extent that in its third year (2004–5) funds had to be capped at £160,000 per annum.

An evaluation carried out after two years of operation was published in 2006. In all the cases examined research has been conducted in a highly participative manner, with a range of opportunities available for local people to become involved as volunteer co-researchers and through consultation. The emphasis of such community research has been on collaboration, the research being conducted by, with and for people rather than on people. The role of the researcher has become that of a mentor or facilitator, assisting communities to take forward their research in a systematic way. The evaluators comment that participative research of this kind is still not firmly embedded in mainstream agency practice. It is identified that a challenge for the research groups is to produce research outputs that are capable of generating sufficient interest and credibility to bring about change. While research reports seemed to be generally well received by interested parties, the continuing importance of balancing professional input, community ownership and the external validation of such research if change is to be effected, is highlighted.

'Rural Voices'

Scotland is, of course, a diverse country of not only predominantly urban environments, but also large tracts of rural and remote areas containing small, scattered communities. 'Rural Voices' was a two-year pilot capacity-building programme aimed at enabling rural communities to consult on aspects of local services of particular concern to them. Communities received financial and professional help from the Scottish Executive in order to identify their own needs and become skilled at undertaking their own consultations. Financial support was available for community action research projects lasting for a period of up to nine months. In the event 11 communities in the first year and 12 in the second accepted an offer of funding, covering a range of topics including wind farms, the viability of a local learning centre, special housing for older people and support for friends and relatives of drug abusers.

An evaluation of the programme and its impact has been commissioned, but is yet to be published.

Ongoing challenges

The account above has tried to demonstrate how policy initiatives in the field of regeneration in Scotland have evolved in recent years. It has been shown that policy objectives for regeneration have themselves evolved from a primary concern with the renewal of the built environment to an appreciation of area regeneration as an important means of achieving wider policy objectives of addressing poverty and social inclusion. Regeneration has come to mean place-based community development. Both policy and the measures adopted to achieve policy outcomes have been based on assimilation in a more or less systematic way of experience in the practice community, of project appraisals, and the synthesis of more systematic research into the social and economic processes which produce the spatial distribution of disadvantage.

It is possible to connect the initiatives described above with strands within this evidence, and see them as policy responses which attempt to deal with the issues identified, but for all the more sophisticated appreciation both of the policy objectives and the nature of the multifaceted responses which are required, the achievement of sustainable regeneration will only be possible if solutions to other problems are found. In this concluding section, three such issues are identified.

1 Making underperforming markets work as a basis for sustainable regeneration

The solutions proposed for sustaining the kind of changes which will promote social inclusion rely to a considerable extent on improving the way a number of markets work, principally the labour market and the housing market. Berube (2005) has argued that among other things, neighbourhoods with concentrations of deprivation reduce private-sector activity, limit job networks and employment ambitions and raise prices for the poor. The conditions which are likely to make activity in regeneration areas more attractive are becoming better understood, and require ways to be found to increase expectations and confidence in the sector that help produce certainty and minimise risk for sustained investment. It is increasingly recognised that underpriced markets can present both developers and investors with significant opportunities. Information, place marketing, the effective use of public funds to improve the access to under-utilised land and long-term commitment are all factors which will help in this regard.

Again, the commitment to mixed-tenure, mixed-income communities and the development of affordable accessible housing to those with rising incomes implies an intervention in the housing market which can alter present patterns of residential segregation. A recent review of research into mixed communities (Joseph Rowntree Foundation, 2006) does present a generally positive picture. The mixed-income communities studied were not characterised by the problems often linked with exclusively low-income areas, and developers engaged in mixing tenures reported no major problems (Rowlands *et al.*, 2005), but it is also clear that planning tenure mix is only part of the problem. Other dimensions of mix, income, home type and size, and household type also have to be considered and will change over time. The implications still need to be thought through.

Analysis of factors which influence the housing market points to the particular significance of the economy and employment, both at the wider area level and at local neighbourhood level (Bramley *et al.*, 2007). Poverty was found to be very important for the market status of neighbourhoods.

2 Making 'trickle-down' work better to connect opportunity to need

Since the 1980s there has been a belief that the benefits and opportunities from 'big' regeneration, major investment to secure large-scale economic development at a sub-regional level, would somehow 'trickle down' to those in need in local areas of deprivation. Experience shows that this does not always happen as it was intended. Economic innovation and opportunity may attract new people to areas and bypass those already there. There is now awareness of a variety of barriers to accessing the new opportunities, especially for people in more disadvantaged areas. The potential barriers range from infrastructure provision and legal constraints on contracting, to human and social capital, and attitudes and aspiration.

It is becoming clearer, also, that different kinds of community require different kinds of economic innovation. Inner-city neighbourhoods, communities in declining industrial areas and rural and remote communities have all been identified as needing different kinds of response if the economic activity base of the community is to be sustained.

3 Better understanding the significance and impact of regeneration activity for and on people living in disadvantaged places

Much has been made of the importance of community involvement in influencing the form that regeneration activity in particular and community planning more generally may take. There are good examples of communities taking the lead in improving their neighbourhoods, and evidence that targeting of local interventions is effective when the needs of particular groups are addressed by tailor-made projects within the neighbourhood, often managed by residents (Carley, 2002). But at the same time other studies report that the tangible impact of community planning is hard to determine (Stevenson, 2002). There is still much to learn about how policies and provision impact on neighbourhoods and how neighbourhood change comes about, and how people come to perceive that they may now have a different opportunity structure within which to develop their lives.

In this regard, the role of research may be crucial. The SCARF and 'Rural Voices' programmes discussed above are examples of an extension of the realm of publicly funded research which will help articulate community views of priorities and their responses to policy initiatives. It is important that this kind of research activity is embedded in the complex pattern of mainstream research and policy making in order to refine further the subtleties of measures required to produce real and lasting neighbourhood change.

Glossary

Communities Scotland: a government agency for the delivery of housing and community programmes in Scotland (see www.communitiesscotland.gov.uk)

Scottish Enterprise: the government economic development agency in Scotland (the successor to the Scottish Development Agency)

Scottish Executive: the devolved government for Scotland (see www.scotland.gov.uk)

Scottish Office: the government department for Scottish affairs prior to devolution in 1999

References

Berube, Alan (2005) *Mixed Communities in England: A US Perspective on Evidence and Policy Prospects*. York: Joseph Rowntree Foundation.

Bramley, Glen *et al.* (2007) *Transforming Places: Housing Investment and*

Neighbourhood Market Change. York: Joseph Rowntree Foundation.

Carley, M. (2002) *Community Regeneration and Neighbourhood Renewal: A Review of the Evidence*. Edinburgh: Communities Scotland.

Ekos Ltd (2006) *Evaluation of the Scottish Community Action Research Fund (SCARF)*. Edinburgh: Communities Scotland.

Joseph Rowntree Foundation (2006) *Mixed Communities: Success and Sustainability*. York: Joseph Rowntree Foundation.

ODS Consulting (2006) *An Overview of the Social Inclusion Partnership (SIP) Programme*. Edinburgh: Communities Scotland.

Office of the Deputy Prime Minister (ODPM), Neighbourhood Renewal Unit (2005a) *Making it Happen in Neighbourhoods: The National Strategy for Neighbourhood Renewal – Four Years On*. London.

Office of the Deputy Prime Minister (ODPM), Neighbourhood Renewal Unit (2005b) *Improving the Delivery of Mainstream Services in Deprived Areas: The Role of Community Involvement*. London.

Rowlands, Rob, *et al.* (2005) *More than Tenure Mix: Developer and Purchaser Attitudes to New Housing Estates*. York: Chartered Institute for Housing/Joseph Rowntree Foundation.

Scottish Development Agency (1980) *Glasgow Eastern Area Renewal (GEAR): Strategy and Programme*. Glasgow: SDA.

Scottish Executive (1999) *An Evaluation of the New Life for Urban Scotland Initiative in Castlemilk, Ferguslie Park, Wester Hailes and Whitfield*. Edinburgh: SE Central Research Unit.

Scottish Executive (2002) *Better Communities in Scotland: Closing the Gap*. Edinburgh: SE.

Scottish Executive (2006) *People and Place: Regeneration Policy Statement*. Edinburgh: SE.

Stevenson, R. (2002) *Getting 'under the skin' of Community Planning* (http://www.scotland.gov.uk/Publications/2002).

Part 2

Regional/local networks

Chapter 9

Policy learning and transfer in regional lifelong learning policies

Paolo Federighi

Introduction

This chapter is concerned with the improvement of regional policy-making processes as they relate to training and lifelong learning. It sets out a framework through which it is possible to analyse processes of innovation in lifelong learning policy. It provides some illustrations of the utility of the framework in a research project which focused on this topic in a number of European regional governments. The research was concerned with important questions about how new measures at regional level for training at post-secondary level and for the unemployed are introduced. Key objectives of the research are the development of measures to support processes of change and innovation and how to ensure that the changes introduced are implemented within a framework of high-level management and effectiveness.

Regional policy making is the outcome of formalised standards and pro-cedures, and does not depend on legal, contextual or cultural variables, which differ considerably from context to context. The first requirement of regional policy making arises from the fact that it operates within the framework of the relative margins of autonomy deriving from the institutional architecture of the state. Clearly, these margins also differ enormously according to the degree of centralism or federalism of the state model. Whether regional governments create independent policy-making procedures, or merely implement national policies, depends on such characteristics and the term *regional government* itself may convey different meanings. (See Europäisches Zentrum für Föderalismus-Forschung, 2002, p. 17 ff.) In this chapter regional government is understood to mean the level of government controlled by bodies democratically elected by the people, immediately under the national government and relatively autonomous (as regards politics, legislation, administration and finance), and the context is lifelong learning policies.

From the point of view of the quality management of policy-making processes, there is a difference between the processes adopted for the mandatory transfer of policies established by the central government and the policies drawn up at regional level, both in terms of the framework of standards and national guidelines. For compulsory policy transfer, the quality models and the processes and procedures form part of the national policy norm and are imposed via incentives and disincentives normally of financial (rewards or penalties, etc.) and moral (fame and shame, etc.) types. This is all the more accentuated the smaller the degree of vertical governance and subsidiarity. In the case of autonomous policy making, the definition of the adopted method depends on the regional government itself.

The lifelong learning policy innovation procedures may be generated either locally (in an in-house fashion) or with regard to external innovation drivers. In both cases consideration must be paid to the network of relationships or dynamic learning behind the changes. This is because, first, the process of innovation is still influenced by external factors. Secondly, we can hypothesise that every innovation is a development or adaptation, albeit partial, of previous policies implemented by some government, in some part of the world, at some point in the past. In both cases, the quality of the actual process can be improved, because lessons can be learned from the implementation process, increasing the possibility of predicting the effects. This is the reason why this research has adopted cooperation between various regional governments as the field of study and the source of empirical material. The fact that these are spread out throughout different European countries will further enrich the study.

Since our area of study consists of regional autonomous policy making, we should concentrate above all on the progress of political understanding within the institutions. These produce innovative intentions and ideas which then generate, in turn, the processes of transfer, adaptation and absorption of the innovations themselves.

On that basis, this chapter posits that it is possible to work out a detailed model of the management of the innovation of training and lifelong learning policies in general based mainly on voluntary and self-governing methodologies. The methodologies can then be adapted to the institutional norms and procedures existing in each regional government. It is for this reason that a soft Open Method of Coordination (OMC) model between regional governments has been adopted.

Institutional policy learning

Definition of some key concepts

The first question to be tackled concerns the way in which the regional governments identify the need for policy changes and how they build them into their compendiums of knowledge, until a point is reached where the policies are adopted. We move on from this type of question, since the research carried out confirms the fact that institutional learning is not exclusively connected to the moment of policy transfer, but, particularly in the case of autonomous policy making, is comprised of different stages. From a linear perspective, the learning process begins a long time before the occurrence of the transfer with many different changes along the way.

The concept of policy learning requires more analysis in order to understand better the meaning applied to the specific context. The term 'learning' is not particularly clear when applied to the individual in a training situation.

One way in which this may be relevant to our area of study is in terms of the (substantive) learning acquired by the individuals and institutions involved in policy innovation learning processes. This is distinct from the learning achieved by the regional institutions which is only evident once translated into political decisions expressed in new instruments of various kinds.

The processes which lead to (or accompany) the attainment of these results are made up of a series of educational and training actions. These are aimed explicitly at and structured by the fulfilment of predetermined learning objectives, or of actions of an informal nature which have been entrusted to the dynamics of political interaction. As a consequence, the purpose of policy learning (and the detailed model to be constructed) does not comprise individual learning, but educational and training actions whereby the institutions acquire ideas while they are being translated into political action.

The actors

In terms of governance and, in particular, of horizontal subsidiarity, the actors involved in policy learning are identifiable with all the other players in civil society. Mulgan (2003) fairly points out that:

smaller entities are more attuned to their external environment, aware that it will shape them more than they will shape it, less attached to the illusions and complacency that scale breeds…they are closer to the fields where much of the best innovation is coming from: the non-profit movement, social entrepreneurs, and the businesses in the new economy. The conclusion is clear: in looking for promising approaches to social care, or housing policy, for transport, it is vital to look beyond the large western nations (p. 4).

At the institutional level the problem consists of involving both those driving the process of institutional innovation and those directly responsible for policy making in education and training policy. This solution makes it possible to overcome divisions between individuals and institutions, and hence the nexus between policy learning and policy transfer. The key players in a regional government who underpin this nexus are represented by those to whom the task and power of 'thinking the unthinkable' (Bernstein, 1990) has been entrusted, or rather by the institutional innovation operators. The nature of the individuals in question varies depending on the subject matter in hand, the level of transformative impact attained and those who are essential to the political heads and their first-level officials (directors general, advisers, etc.).

The transnational networks of dynamic learning

Policy learning and to an even greater extent the introduction of innovative elements is always the product of an action undertaken within a network of relationships. This does not mean solely the totality of entities obliged by law to participate in the decision-making processes (enterprise parties, associations, etc.), but rather the formal and non-formal networks of individuals, both inside and outside the institutions, which prepare the ground for the decisions. As far as the specifics of policy learning are concerned, the problem for regional governments consists of participation in the networks which produce 'political awareness' and which are able to energise joint action capable of producing innovation.

In regional policy learning, the networks consist of the players involved in the processes of institutional innovation being directly involved in policy making. They are networks of equals, with the membership varying according to the subject in hand, the level of technical detail attained and the time. These networks are not, in fact, permanent in nature. Their existence is related to the learning project and they remain so related, according to need, until the project is completed. This by no means implies that there are no useful institutional networks that are permanent in nature. On the contrary, they may provide the impetus for the creation of networks for policy learning (see Box 1).

Box 1 European Association of Regional and Local Authorities for Lifelong Learning (EARLALL)

The European Association of Regional and Local Authorities for Lifelong Learning (EARLALL) has developed a device that streamlines cooperation between regional governments aimed at policy learning and policy transfer in the field of lifelong learning. The service has been built and developed through an applied research initiative, which has directly involved the regional governments of Andalusia (Spain), Wales, the Basque Country, Southern Denmark, Tuscany, Västra Götaland (Sweden) and the Vidin District (Bulgaria). *Source*: SMOC. The Soft Open Method of Coordination between the Regions: Presentation (project information at http://www.mutual-learning.eu).

These, however, display other characteristics: they emerge among equals in response to a shared need to develop knowledge related to political action, and they last the length of time needed to complete the task of selecting the policies to be transferred. It is because of their tendency to support the dynamic of institutional learning and to be based on an exchange of knowledge that we define them as networks of dynamic learning (an expression already adopted from Reich, 1991).

Policy learning units

Two purposes

With regard to the processes governing policy learning of a voluntary nature, the choice of the subject of study is defined by criteria established by the 'importer' on the basis of assessments of necessity, possibility and the will of the actual institution.

There is nothing to say that such choices will not be influenced by references to external influences, such as a comparison with the performances of other regions. But benchmarking alone is not the central subject of the learning process; it can only be an additional motivation. Nor is the solution to be found in a collection of best practices: actions worthy of respect, but which are difficult to export, when they are not selected, because they are 'the ones with impressive public relations but which don't actually work' (Mulgan,

2003, p. 5). What is paramount in policy learning is neither benchmarking, nor best practices, but a 'complex mixture of ideas, issues, compromises and practices that go to make up "policy"' (Page, 2000, p. 4). Having stated the matter thus, the necessity still remains, however, to identify the formal components of policy learning.

The definition presented here reduces the components to two main categories: on the one hand are the ideas (the concepts, the ideologies, the policies), and on the other, examples of instruments (or rather the way they are applied) used to implement them and which we will call "measures".

The study of policy ideas is a process which depends on the ability of the institution to locate itself within the world of development and research, in our case into lifelong learning policies. The ability of an idea to travel (Rose, 1993) must be combined with the ability of an institution to find that idea. The history of the spread of the idea of 'lifelong learning' is worthy of attention, an idea which appeared in the first half of the 1990s, and then spread rapidly, at least at the level of an idea. This is a symbolic example of how the same concept appears to be present in all national and regional policies, but the application of which varied considerably from context to context, and not only because of matters concerned with political will but also because of the different historical stages of the development of education and training itself. There are further examples of the spread of an idea concerning adult education during the second half of the twentieth century. These examples help us to understand first and foremost how, when we consider the question of political ideas in movement, we should bear in mind that a twofold dimension applies: that of the history of the idea, and that of its semantic variation. In this field, the same meanings do not attach to the same terms, or where identical semantic content corresponds to different terms, or again where some ideas and some terms are completely absent. The study of 'measures' is the concrete area of comparison of the actions undertaken and the results achieved. It is therefore the area where analysis, comparison and assessment are more feasible and the subsequent transfer simpler.

The concept of measures
The concept of measures is widely used in the field of labour policy to identify the instruments by means of which actions are undertaken for the purpose of improving the flexibility of the labour market and maintaining the income of the unemployed, etc. It has only recently been adopted in the area of education and training. The term 'measure' is used here instead of its

possible synonyms such as 'provision' or 'stipulation' because it refers in a more explicit way to a particular action intended to achieve an effect and to the objective of ensuring that the results achieved are measurable.

Measures are seen here as the components of a policy through which the policy acts on a range of intended factors (the beneficiaries, the roles of the various players, the costs of the education and training initiatives, conditions of access thereto, the tasks involved in the systems concerned, the categories of activities accepted, content, instruments implemented, etc.). In this sense, the measures comprise an action model. The need to pursue more objectives gives rise to the addition of more measures. For example, a study grant is a simple measure, but grows when it is incorporated into a complex of coherent and related measures (study loans, accommodation, etc.) which together comprise the policy of the right to university study. The specific effects of a measure are determined by the relationship it has with other measures.

As suggested above, a measure is intended to determine the model of inter-action between the various components of a situation, such as the type of training designed for the top management of a company, the payment of the direct costs, the bodies authorised to provide it, the research and innovation plans of the company itself and career development (see http://www.mutual-learning.eu for around 200 examples of policy measures).

Assuming the measure as the minimum unit for the study of a policy helps to isolate the individual rules of the device of which the measure forms a part, and should facilitate for our benefit the assessment of the effects, both at the level of the specific measures and at that of the combination of measures.

The policy learning method
The policy learning method immediately reveals a twofold requirement: on the one hand, the need to adopt an open approach, and on the other the need to guarantee a device that permits the communication, collection and organisation of results of use for political action. The method is based on shared methods and instruments in the support of cooperative and trans-formational learning.

The starting point is the adoption of the Open Method of Coordination (OMC), launched with the Lisbon strategy: 'by avoiding centralised supranational governance, the OMC shall enable European politics to effectively deal with strong national diversity' (European Commission, 2005).

But at the same time, this search aims to define a 'soft' model, one which is capable of supporting the policy-learning and policy-transfer processes between the regions in a more effective way.

The adoption of the OMC model in intra-regional cooperation cannot be reduced to mere transposition. The initial problem derives from the fact that the way it is currently being developed is connected to experiments, mainly at national level, excluding in particular regional governments from the lifelong learning field, and only in rare cases including actual decision makers. This has certainly pushed it further in a technicistic direction (Delbridge, Lowe and Oliver, 1995; Tronti, 1998; Schmid, Schütz and Speckesser, 1999; Arrow-smith, Sisson and Marginson, 2004) and has not improved its relationship with policy transfer. Some authors have even described the phenomenon in terms of the development of 'audit cultures' (Strathern, 2000) or even an 'audit society' (Power, 1997).

The research here has aimed at the identification of the substantial elements of the OMC, that is, those which are essential for achieving the objective of voluntary policy transfer. This choice does not exclude the study of best practices – including the contribution of ethnographic methods – and does not even exclude recourse to the most refined method of benchmarking based on historical series of data. OMC is not an end in itself and needs to be simplified to increase its functionality.

The essential components of OMC in the policy learning phase may be identified thus:
- Regulatory mechanisms related to knowledge and meaning-making (Jacobsson, 2004, p. 14).
- The identification of some key steps. In the case of policy learning, we can hypothesise that the essential phases correspond to those appropriate for the political response to a social demand for education and training (Federighi, 2006).
- The availability of instruments which can be used to orientate and organise one's own course of knowledge and action. This is the weakest aspect particularly in the field of training and lifelong learning in general, because of the low level of invest-ment into specialised research on policies in the sector (see Box 2).

Box 2 Services provided by EARLALL supporting the SMOC Soft Open Method of Coordination

Networking support whereby they can express their benchmarking interests in:

- the matter of lifelong learning and identify institutional partners who are interested and available;
- a database of policy measures via which they can collect detailed information on the individual provisions adopted by the various regional governments which are involved in the SMOC;
- support service for building contacts with the political and institutional heads involved in lifelong learning policies from other regions, with a view to organising study visits;
- a dedicated search engine to facilitate searches within the websites of the regions themselves;
- a consultancy service to lay down bilateral or multilateral agreements in support of policy transfer actions.

Source: SMOC. The Soft Open Method of Coordination between the Regions: Presentation (Project information at www.mutual-learning.eu).

Policy transfer between institutions

Two complementary definitions of voluntary policy transfer

The scientific literature contains a number of terms referring to policy transfer, such as 'band-wagoning' (Ikenberry, 1990), 'policy borrowing' (Cox, 1999) or 'policy shopping' (Freeman, 1999) and 'systematically pinching ideas' (Schneider and Ingram, 1988), or 'rational shopping', among which everybody chooses that which best meets their needs (Bennett, 1991; Westney, 1987). From a historical perspective, policy transfer accompanies all the actions of colonial expansion or the widening of the borders of a country; this was what powered the spread of Roman law throughout all the cities taken over by ancient Rome and which made it possible for an Iberian or a Celt to declare *Civis romanus sum* ('I am a Roman citizen').

On this subject the present research has shown how policy transfer undertaken in a cooperative way, carried out via the shared creation of policies and measures so far not in existence within any of the partner governments may constitute the most effective and rapid form of transfer (see Box 3).

Box 3 Effectiveness of the SMOC Soft Open Method of Coordination service

SMOC has already demonstrated its effectiveness through its support for policy learning and policy transfer processes.

Examples of initial experiences are:

- the joint construction of cooperation models between the regions supporting mobility for students and young graduates (trainees);
- the establishment of bilateral agreements for the development of shared and coordinated investment plans in the area of e-learning;
- the transfer of innovative services for active ageing (Project Senior at Work);
- the harmonisation of measures aimed at trans-regional cooperation in the framework of the Regional Operational Programmes of the European Social Fund.

Source: Federighi, Abreu and Nuissl, 2007.

For this purpose, the definition adopted in this research makes reference to two types of voluntary policy transfer. The first relates to 'the transposition of policies and/or practices *already in operation* in one jurisdiction to another' (Page, 2000, p. 2). The second is understood as *cooperative policy transfer*, connected to the introduction of innovation in the policies and measures of a regional government, with a view to their total or partial incorporation, carried out by means of joint planning and implementation, peer monitoring and the harmonisation of the progressively introduced changes.

The specific components of policy transfer

The components of policy transfer, in theory, are the same as policy learning: on the one hand the ideas (the concepts, ideologies and policies), on the other, the measures (how they are implemented, the instruments used in that implementation). In actual fact, however, we should bear in mind the fact that these components change their connotations the moment they come into play and move towards the innovation of a political system.

As Page (2000) notes: 'In the study of transfer, ascertaining precisely what was borrowed is far more difficult to determine ... *we are again faced with a* complex mixture of ideas, issues, compromises and practices that go to make up *policy*' (p. 4; original emphasis). Even in the simple case of the transfer of a policy from one country to another, the imported object loses many of its original characteristics because of the way it is slotted into another economic and social context. An example is the conflicting functions which the introduction of a measure such as the training voucher may assume depending on the context, democratisation of individual rights of access to training, or abandonment of the citizen to the dynamics of the free market in education and training. The object (the voucher) is only formally the same. In reality it has changed. In policy transfer, the real object consists of the policies and measures of lifelong learning of the country into which the innovations are being introduced. The idea and the original measure disappear and are replaced by the policy decisions, the institutional, managerial and administrative decisions, the ideologies and constructed justifications, the attitudes and ideas that accompany the introduction of innovation in the regional and local context.

This consideration also has consequences for the identification of the subjects of policy transfer. Here the main players change and go back to being those of regional governance, the management of the systems and of the services which may come to be incorporated, if and when necessary, by the trans-national partners. The main policy transfer players are those who need to share and participate in the choices to be made regarding the adoption of the new policies and measures (local governments, business partners, regional institutions) and those who need to acquire the skills required by the implementation of the innovation introduced.

The process and the instruments

The process of policy transfer is essentially one whereby an innovation is introduced into a political system. It is only in compulsory policy transfer situations that this does not occur. In the present research, the original, predefined object loses its centrality and attention comes to focus on the process of regional policy making.

In this respect Rose (1993, p. 30) proposes a categorisation of five different types of learning: at the one extreme is direct copying, where the programme or policy is transferred lock, stock and barrel from one jurisdiction to another (see Box 4 for a suggested example of this) and at the other extreme is 'inspiration' according to which a policy in one jurisdiction is based on an idea identified in another.

In between these two extremes come 'adaptation' (see Box 5), 'creating a hybrid' and 'synthesis'. The concept of 'hybrid' implies that the innovation is preceded by aspects of policy or pre-existing measures; 'synthesis' that the

---

Box 4 Report from a visit in Wales by the Region of Southern Denmark

We have much to learn in the Region of Southern Denmark as far as this is concerned. Maybe a regional 'copy' of an organisation like NIACE Dysgu Cymru would be very effectual in promoting regional growth in a learner-centred way, so the unique combination of a bottom-up and top-down approach could be transferred to a Danish regional context.

Marianne Horsdal, in Prevalet, 2007.

---

question is partly of copying, partly adapting policies or measures, and 'inspiration' where some suggestions have simply been garnered from the experiences of others, with policies or measures created without further interrelationships.

Box 5 Policy transfer analysis: from the Basque Country to Andalusia

- Title of measure: Project for Establishing a Registered Quality Management System
- What kind of official document from your Regional Government gave legitimacy to the measure?
- Policy that has been transferred
- Inspiring policy
- Description of the institutional process that followed how information and data about the inspiring policy have been treated and used, for which purpose, etc.
- Involvement of other national/local institutional actor in the policy transfer process and promotion of synergies among different actors.
- Which kind of changes the inspiring policy had after the policy transfer process was implemented and the contribution it made to quality in the educational system.
- Whom and how the measure has been implemented.
- Results obtained after the policy transfer and impact analysis on the policies involved.
- Sources (internet, websites, bibliography).

Source: Prevalet, 2007.

To these five types the author adds *cooperative policy transfer* (see Box 6), in which the governments involved cooperate in the synchronised introduction of a new policy or measure into their respective systems.

Box 6 Mobility of students, trainees, researchers and workers: policy paper

Instruments for the support and implementation of the mobility

Three essential instruments can be identified to support the implementation and generalisation of the mobility projects aimed at VET students and apprentices:
- participation in European Programmes, mainly LLP, and in the activities covered by the ESF and ERDF transnational cooperation lines;
- participation in regional administrations networks on VET subjects;
- establishment of bilateral cooperation agreements between regional administrations for the enhancement of mobility.

Organisation and management of the mobility

For the regional administrations to be in a position to carry out such functions of support and encourage the mobility, the necessary instruments must be at their disposal:
- legal instruments: basic competencies in the management and organisation of VET in their territories;
- economic instruments: specific budgetary items for the funding of mobility;
- technical instruments: human support teams for the promotion and development of the mobility projects in the training centres.

Source: Xavier Farriols, in Prevalet, 2007.

As previously stated, in all these cases the process is identified with that of normal policy making, with the sole difference that in cooperative policy transfer direct participation of the partners from outside the region must occur at some stage in the procedure.

For successful policy learning and transfer in regional lifelong learning policies *the following components of the transfer process* are highlighted as being essential:

- creation of institutional conditions for transfer;
- choice of the process for the transfer (copying, adaptation, creating a hybrid, synthesis, cooperative model);
- decision-making process of the transfer;
- implementation of the transfer;
- institutionalisation and follow-up.

For the duration of the process it is important to consider that 'policy transfer may take place over more extended time periods. One of the most significant instances of transfer for the modern European state, the "reception" of Roman law, took centuries' (Koschaker, 1966). More recently, the adoption of trends such as liberalisation and *new public management* are observed over many years rather than a single point in time (Lawton, 1999; Wright, 1995). In this respect, Page notes that 'the shorter the time period, the more likely an innovation is likely to appear as an alien import; over a longer time period the innovations become domesticated as the relationship between established institutions and policies shapes their development' (Page, 2000, p. 5).

Obviously, all this depends on the complexity of the innovation introduced and the stage of development of the context in which it will operate (e.g. demand policy or one of its measures may be imported only if there exists a sufficiently developed supply policy). In the model presented in this chapter, regional policy making is entrusted with the function of protecting the local system from unsuitable transfers, and at the same time, policy learning is entrusted with the task of 'understanding the conditions under which policies or practices operate in exporter jurisdictions and whether and how the conditions which might make them work in a similar way can be created in importer jurisdictions' (Page, 2000, p. 2).

Conclusions

Methodological improvement in the field of policy learning and policy transfer is significant at a time when European countries and the European Union are prioritising activities designed to help local and regional governments achieve agreed European benchmarks in the field of education and training, for example, the assessment of performance.

It is possible to speed up the process of modernising and upgrading the quality of education and training systems if incentives are put in place to encourage cooperation and coordination between local and regional governments (mutual learning, the development of common instruments, etc). As the Helsinki Council of Ministers' communiqué stresses: 'A more systematic approach is needed to strengthen mutual learning, cooperative work and the sharing of experience and know-how. This should be facilitated by (among other things) a systematic and flexible framework to support peer learning activities in the field of VET. The framework should also support decentralised peer learning' (European Council, 2006). Our optimism is based also on the fact that the new ESF regulation (which is scheduled to stay live until 2014) will make it possible to fulfil this requirement through the transregional cooperation measure.[1]

The objective is to help all the regional and sub-regional territories satisfy the European benchmarks set by Lisbon and subsequent agreements. Cutting dropout numbers, raising lifelong learning participation, improving reading skills, and so on, are relevant objectives at more than just the European or national level. Each individual territory should be able to make a self-assessment as regards the challenges raised by the Lisbon strategy. Regional and local governments should be able to define its own objectives regarding each of the benchmarks, be in a position to take on increased responsibility and understand how to implement effective regional and local policies in their areas.

Advances are needed on a broad front, otherwise there is the danger that we will only fulfil the Lisbon objectives by favouring some areas to the detriment of others. The solution to the problem does not lie in rendering all the European regions uniform (equality is not the same thing as uniformity). Nor is it to be found in centralising responsibility or generalising uniform solutions. Rather, it is to be found in establishing responsibility at the regional and local level.

Notes

This article emanates from an empirical research project on regional policy making (PREVALET) carried out by the European Association of Regional and Local Authorities for Lifelong Learning (EARLALL) involving six regional governments (Andalusia (Spain), Wales, the Basque Country, Southern Denmark, Tuscany, Västra Götaland (Sweden) and the Vidin District (Bulgaria)), financed by the EU Leonardo Program 2005–07.

[1] Council Regulation (EC) No *1083/2006* of 11 July 2006 laying down general provisions on the European Regional Development Fund, the European Social Fund and the Cohesion Fund and repealing Regulation (EC) No 1260/199.

References

Arrowsmith, J. and Sisson, K. (2001) 'International competition and pay, working time and employment: exploring the processes of adjustment', *Industrial Relations Journal* 32(2): 136–53.

Arrowsmith, J., Sisson, K. and Marginson, P. (2004) 'What can "benchmarking" offer the open method of co-ordination?', *Journal of European Public Policy*, 11(2): 311–328.

Bennett, Colin. J. (1991) 'Review article: what is policy convergence and what causes it?' *British Journal of Political Science* 21: 215–33.

Bernstein, B. (1990) *The Structuring of Pedagogic Discourse*. London and New York: Routledge

Cox, Robert (1999) Paper presented to the conference on 'Global Trajectories: Ideas, International Policy Transfer and "Models" of Welfare Reform', Robert Schuman Centre, European University Institute, Florence, Italy 25–26 March.

Delbridge, R., Lowe, J. and Oliver, N. (1995) 'The process of benchmarking. A study from the automotive industry', *International Journal of Operations and Production Management* 15(4): 50–62.

European Council (EC) (2006) *The Helsinki Communiqué on Enhanced European Cooperation in Vocational Education and Training*, Communiqué of the European Ministers of Vocational Education and Training, European Social Partners and the European Commission, convened in Helsinki on 5 December to review the priorities and strategies of the Copenhagen Process (http://ec.europa.eu/education/policies/2010/doc/helsinkicom_en.pdf), accessed July 2007.

Europäisches Zentrum für Föderalismus-Forschung, Università di Tubinga (2002) *Poteri regionali e locali in Europa. Istruzione e gioventù, cultura, sanità pubblica, reti transeuropee, politica regionale e strutturale*. Brussels: Unione Europea, Comitato delle Regioni.

European Commission, Directorate-General Education and Culture (2005) *Implementation of 'Education and Training 2010.' Work Programme Working Group E 'Making the Best Use of Resources.' A European Toolbox of Policy Measures*. Brussels: European Commission.

Federighi, P. (2006) *Liberare la domanda di formazione*. Rome: Edup.

Abreu, C. and Nuissl, E. in P Federighi (ed) (2007) *Learning among Regional*

Governments: Quality of Policy Learning and Policy Transfer in Regional Lifelong Learning Policies. Bonn: Bertelsmann.

Freeman, Richard (1999) 'Policy transfer in the health sector', working paper (http://www.pol.ed.ac.uk/research/working_paper1.html).

Ikenberry, G. John (1990) 'The international spread of privatization policies: inducements, learning and "policy band wagoning"' in E. Suleiman and J. Waterbury (eds), *The Political Economy of Public Sector Reform and Privatization*. Boulder: Westview Press.

Jacobsson, K. (2004) 'Soft regulation and the subtle transformation of states: the case of EU employment policy', *Journal of European Social Policy* 14(4): 355–70.

Koschaker, P. (1966) *Europa und das römische Recht*. Munich: Biederstein.

Lawton, Thomas C. (1999) 'Governing the skies: conditions for the Europeanisation of airline policy', *Journal of Public Policy* 19(1): 91–112.

Mulgan, G. (2003) *Global comparisons in policy-making: the view from the centre* (http://www.opendemocracy.net/democracy-think_tank/debate.jsp).

Page, E.C. (2000) *Future Governance and the Literature on Policy Transfer and Lesson Drawing*. ESRC Future Governance Programme Workshop on Policy Transfer, Britannia House, London, 28 January.

Power, M. (1997) *The Audit Society: Rituals of Verification*. Oxford: Oxford University Press.

Prevalet (2007) *Tools for Policy Learning and Policy Transfer*. Bonn: Bertelsmann.

Reich, R.B. (1991) *The Work of Nations: Preparing Ourselves for 21st-Century Capitalism*. New York: Knopf.

Rose, R. (1993) *Lesson Drawing in Public Policy*. Chatham, NJ: Chatham House.

Schmid, G., Schütz, H. and Speckesser, S. (1999) 'Broadening the scope of benchmarking: radar charts and employment systems', *Labour*, 13(4): 879–99.

Schneider, Anne and Ingram, Helen (1988) 'Systematically pinching ideas: a comparative approach to policy design', *Journal of Public Policy* 8(1): 61–80.

Strathern, M. (2000) *Audit Cultures: Anthropological Studies in Accountability, Ethics and Academy*. London and New York: Routledge.

Tronti, L. (1998) 'Benchmarking labour market performances and practices', *Labour*, 12(3): 489–513.

Westney, D.E. (1987) *Imitation and Innovation. The Transfer of Western Organizational Patterns to Meiki Japan.* Cambridge MA: Harvard University Press. Cited in E.C. Page (2000) *Future Governance and the Literature on Policy Transfer and Lesson Drawing.* ESRC Future Governance Programme Workshop on Policy Transfer, Britannia House, London, 28 January.

Wright, Vincent (1995) 'Privatizations in Western Europe: paradoxes and implications for institutions', paper presented at the annual conference of the Netherlands Institute of Government, Oosterbeek, 9–10 November.

Chapter 10

Higher education and regional development

Jaana Puukka

Introduction

Following decades of expansion in higher education, policy attention in OECD countries has begun to focus on the outcomes of higher education, such as quality, impact and equity. Consequently, there is also stronger interest in how higher education contributes to regional development. With the processes of globalisation and localisation, the local availability of knowledge and skills and the transfer of technology and innovation to SMEs and industry in general are becoming more and more important. In recent years there have been many initiatives across OECD countries to mobilise higher education in support of regional economic, social and cultural development. The key questions in this context include the following: What is higher education's regional engagement all about? What are its drivers and barriers? What does it mean to the governance and management of higher education institutions? And how does regional engagement fit with the pursuit of world-class academic excellence?

This chapter attempts to draw lessons from the OECD study, 'Supporting the Contribution of Higher Education Institutions to Regional Development'. This thematic review project was managed by the OECD Programme on Institutional Management in Higher Education (IMHE). It engaged 14 regions across 12 countries in 2005–06. The review sought information on institutional, regional and national strategies, policies and activities in order to understand the rationales, stages of development and drivers and barriers to higher education institutions' regional engagement. This chapter outlines the IMHE project and highlights some of the key conclusions. It also draws attention to the management and institutional capacity of higher education institutions through case examples.

The OECD project

Universities and other higher education institutions can make a significant contribution to regional development. The IMHE project, in collaboration with the OECD Public Governance and Territorial Development Committee, conducted a comparative thematic review of how issues relating to higher education institutions and their regional engagement were addressed in the OECD area.

Following the publication by the OECD in 1999 of a report entitled *The Response of Higher Education Institutions to Regional Needs*, the OECD project, 'Supporting the Contribution of Higher Education Institutions to Regional Development', was launched in 2004 as a response to a wide range of initiatives across OECD countries to mobilise higher education in support of regional development (OECD, 2007a). There was a perceived need to synthesise this experience into a coherent body of policy and practice that could guide institutional reforms and relevant policy measures, including investment decisions seeking to enhance the connection of higher education institutions to regional communities. Current practice needed to be analysed and evaluated in a way that was sensitive to the varying national and regional contexts within which higher education institutions operate.

The methodology chosen for the project was a thematic review which was influenced not only by other OECD peer reviews, but also the developmentally oriented evaluation projects commissioned by the Finnish Higher Education Evaluation Council. The methodology of the project consisted of the following elements: (1) a common framework for regional self-evaluation developed by the OECD task group; (2) a self-evaluation report by the regional consortium using OECD guidelines; (3) a site visit by an international peer review team: (4) a peer review report and a response from the region; and finally (5) analysis and synthesis by OECD task group drawing upon regional case studies (OECD, 2007b, forthcoming). There was also a commissioned literature review (Arbo and Benneworth, 2006).

There was no predetermined selection, instead 12 regions from ten OECD countries opted into the project which, in practice, started in early 2005. The regions were: Busan Metropolitan City (Korea), the Canary Islands (Spain), Jutland-Funen (Denmark), the Jyväskylä region (Finland), the north-east of England, the State of Nuévo León (Mexico), the Øresund Region (Denmark/Sweden), the Sunshine-Fraser Coast Region (Australia), Trøndelag (Norway), Twente (the Netherlands), the Autonomous Region of Valencia

(Spain) and Värmland (Sweden). By the end of 2005, two new regions had joined the project: Atlantic Canada and northern Paraná in Brazil, thus extending the review outside the OECD area.

There were essentially two main criteria for accepting a region in the project. First, it needed to have a recognisable regional identity (whether as a formally constituted administrative region or in some other way), with some history of working with higher education institutions; and second, all higher education institutions operating in the region were required to be engaged in the review in order to identify the impact of the entire higher education sector as well as the division of tasks and key partners.

These criteria and the selection process resulted in a wide variety of participating regions with different regional and national contexts and different types of higher education institutions. The participating regions thus ranged from rural to metropolitan and from peripheral to central. The participating higher education institutions, on the other hand, included not only research-intensive, but also vocational and professionally oriented institutions. At national level, the review embraced highly centralised as well as devolved governance systems.

Developmental focus: seeking to empower the regions

The focus of the IMHE project was on collaborative working between higher education institutions and their regional partners. It sought to establish a regional learning and capacity-building process: the participants were not only higher education institutions, but also the regions with which they shared a history of joint working, as well as public authorities which were responsible for territorial and higher education development at national and regional levels. The fundamental aim of the project was to reinforce the partnerships between higher education institutions and the regions through the learning process triggered by the OECD project.

Unlike most thematic reviews, this OECD exercise sought to make an active intervention in the participating regions. Therefore, as a way to enforce the partnership-building process, the OECD guidelines asked the participating regions to build up regional steering committees with representation from the key stakeholders in the public, private and nonprofit sectors. The steering committees were charged with the role of driving the process of self-evaluation and partnership building.

In practice, the regions were at different stages of maturity in capacity building. While for some regions the OECD project was the first opportunity to bring together the higher education institutions and stakeholders to discuss the development of the region, some already had – to a larger or smaller extent – operational mechanisms in place for that purpose. For example, in the north-east of England the existing higher education regional association (HERA), known as Universities for the North East or Unis4NE, took the responsibility for coordinating the exercise. In Busan, Korea, the Regional Innovation System (RIS) Committee assumed the role of the Regional Steering Committee.

The self-evaluation process was followed by a site visit by a peer review team. Each team comprised two international experts as well as a national expert and a team coordinator, usually from the OECD secretariat. Based on the review visit, the self-evaluation report and other information, each peer review team prepared a report analysing the situation and providing policy and practice advice to higher education institutions and the regional and national governments. The final synthesis report drawing from the 14 reviews will follow in 2007.

What is regional development of higher education institutions all about? A broader interpretation of development

Regional development is often thought of in economic terms only. The OECD project briefing notes, however, suggested a wider interpretation. The OECD template guiding the self-evaluation process asked higher education institutions to critically evaluate, with their regional partners and in the context of national higher education and regional policies, how effective they were in contributing to the development of their regions. The key aspects of the self-evaluation related not only to the contribution of research to regional innovation, but also to the role of teaching and learning in the development of human capital, the contribution to social, cultural and environmental development; and the role of higher education institutions in building regional capacity to act in an increasingly competitive global economy.

Hence, the regional engagement of higher education institutions has a number of dimensions, including (1) knowledge creation through research and its exploitation via technology transfer (spin-out, IPR and consultancy); (2) knowledge transfer through human resources development, education, localising the learning process by work-based learning, graduate employment in the region, continuing education and professional development; (3) cultural and community development creating the milieu, social cohesion and sustainable development on which innovation depends. Higher education institutions can play a key role in the region and its civil society by joining up the different elements of national policy on learning and skills, research and innovation, culture and social inclusion.

Regional engagement: a challenge to the management of higher education institutions

Based on the multiple dimensions of regional engagement and many roles of higher education institutions, it is evident that the regional engagement agenda requires an institutional-level response with coordination and transversal mechanisms. Figure 10.1, developed by Goddard and Chatterton (2003), aims to describe this perspective. While the left-hand part of the diagram refers to the three roles of the higher education institutions, namely

Figure 10.1: HEI/region dynamic interface

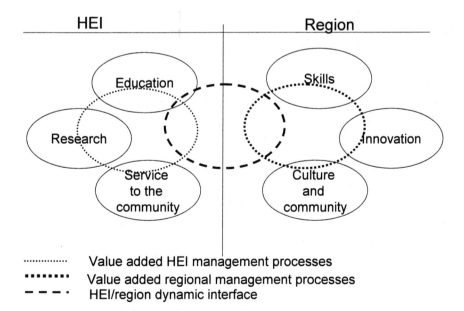

Source: Goddard and Chatterton, 2003; adapted by the author.

education, research and the third mission, the right-hand part symbolises the key dimensions to regional development, such as innovation, skills and cultural and community cohesion. In order to serve the region in the best possible way, the higher education institution needs to bring together its three tasks to the community in a consistent and systematic way. At the same time, systematic mechanisms for bridging the boundary between the higher education institutions and the region need to be put in place.

The enhanced regional role poses challenges for higher education institutions. If an institution intends to play an active role in regional development, it must initiate a process of institutional adjustment. In order to be able not only to respond to, but also to shape the development of the wider society, it needs to transform itself into an entrepreneurial university with a strengthened management core and fully operational professional management systems, for example in knowledge transfer, human resources management, financial management and information systems management. It may also need to set up a single access point for stakeholders, for example, from industry. The more professional management style may induce opposition within the academia. We shall return to this issue in the next section.

Drivers and barriers

The second part of the twentieth century witnessed a massive expansion of public investment in research and development and higher education in OECD countries. The expansion of higher education typically took place outside the established universities which were perceived to be too inflexible to meet the demands for new skills emerging in the workplace and from communities. The higher education map in most countries has thus been filled with a diverse set of institutions. Many of the new institutions have been built on previous foundations, typically with limited research traditions, but with strong regional links.

In the knowledge economy, economic development focuses on core regions and major cities. The leading higher education institutions in these regions generate and transfer new knowledge as global players. The emerging hierarchy of higher education institutions thus underpins the hierarchy of cities and regions. The key challenge is to establish regionally engaged higher education institutions with global standing to counter the polarisation in the knowledge economy. There is a need to combine the pipelines of higher education institution innovation with the development of the region in which it is located. The mobilisation of large, research-intensive universities in support of regional development has proved a particularly challenging task.

Regions can, with the help of higher education institutions, play a key role in making OECD countries globally competitive. There is ample evidence of a positive link between economic competitiveness and investments in regional innovation systems which link higher education institutions, public authorities and business and industry. In practice there are, however, external and internal barriers for higher education institutions to become more regionally engaged.

The national systems may impose regulations that reduce the capacity of higher education institutions to engage regionally and limit their institutional autonomy and flexibility. Although the higher education legislation may have an explicit requirement for regional engagement or third-role activities, there are usually no major incentives or funding streams to support this goal and no set of indicators or active monitoring of the outcomes. Furthermore, a strong emphasis on excellence in allocating research budgets may result in over-concentration in advanced regions. Funding for teaching is weakly oriented towards building human capital in deprived regions and, in general, higher education institutions' role in aiding community development is not system-atically funded. In addition, the related metrics are underdeveloped, retro-spective and do not take account of the developmental work that may lead to future income or services in the public interest. Regional development itself remains a contested terrain, with the involvement of many ministries, often working in isolation and sometimes sending mixed messages.

Regional engagement strategies of higher education institutions depend on the role the institution chooses for itself and the leadership role it adopts. In many cases, there are perceived tensions between the pursuit of world-class research and enhanced regional engagement. Case studies from the regions that participated in the OECD study suggest that there has been, and continues to be, resistance in the research community against enhanced attention to regional engagement at the expense of national and international engagement. The main argument is that a higher education institution does not have the capacity to engage in regional development but must give priority to research collaboration at the national and international levels. Regional engagement which diverts the attention from international quality development could, in the longer run, weaken the university.

Evidence shows that academic excellence and regional engagement can be, and in many regions are, complementary activities, with the one reinforcing the other. There are numerous cases across OECD regions where a world-class university or its departments gain an international profile acting in concert with regional actors. Institutional adjustment can also help in creating mechanisms linking the locality to the global body of scientific and cultural knowledge.

To institutionalise the third mission, there is a need to find a balance between allowing and encouraging individual initiatives and introducing a strengthened management core. The introduction of a regionally engaged institution may be met with objection by the academia. The strong management and the professional management systems supporting the new focus may be perceived as a threat to academic autonomy, both at the individual and institutional level. Regional engagement can be seen as subordination to external expectations, threatening the pursuit of knowledge *per se*.

What do the outcomes of the OECD review tell us? How has the regional engagement agenda been taken on board in different regions and at the level of individual institutions? We shall address this with reference to the Jyväskylä region in central Finland, which has two higher education institutions, the University of Jyväskylä and the Jyväskylä University of Applied Sciences, formerly known as the Jyväskylä Polytechnic.

The Jyväskylä region: traditional university and new university

In the 1980s, the Jyväskylä region was one of the most affluent regions in Finland. At the start of the next decade, the region experienced a deep recession followed by business closures, the disappearance of thousands of jobs, cuts in local government spending and an unemployment rate of 25 per cent. As a result of collective efforts from the local authorities, the higher education institutions and the business sector, a regional knowledge economy emerged through a series of steps, including a science park, EU-funded university master's programmes, high-technology companies and the establishment of a multidisciplinary polytechnic. Today, the Jyväskylä region is one of the fastest growing city regions in the country.

The expansion of higher education has been a key factor in the growth of the regional economy, with students accounting for one-third of the population of the city of Jyväskylä. The two higher education institutions, the University of

Jyväskylä and the Jyväskylä University of Applied Sciences, are very different institutions, reflecting the Finnish binary system of higher education. They have a distinct history, missions, governance structures and funding systems. While they both articulate a desire to implement regional engagement strategies, there is diversity in implementation and emphasis: the University of Jyväskylä is geared towards research connecting the locality with the international knowledge base, whereas the Jyväskylä University of Applied Sciences is concerned with the development of well-being and working life here and now.

During the review, the OECD peer review team became acutely aware that few mechanisms were in place within the University of Jyväskylä to establish institution-wide systems and procedures to link the university with business and regional economy. The number of success stories, including the establishment of the ICT Faculty and the launch of a number of master's programmes geared towards enhancing the growth of the knowledge-based economy in the region, were largely down to the drive of individual academics partnering with external agents. University leadership, elected and based on broad consensus, was unlikely to take action until either a new consensus was reached internally or it was explicitly tasked by national policy. A new vice-rector's position with responsibility for this area had been established, but it was acknowledged that the position would have 'no mandate' until a new university law on intellectual property was passed. Within the academic hierarchy responsibility for engagement with business and working life in general was left by deans, many of them in part-time positions, to individual departments and research groups and centres where external funds could be utilised. The university had a limited technology-transfer capacity with its Research Services Unit and innovation manager, but no organisational capability for searching internally for technology with economic potential and arranging for its utilisation. Nor did the university have a formal incubator facility to mentor and otherwise assist the firm-formation process. The university's academic strengths as recorded by Centres of Excellence in research designated by the Academy of Finland did not map well on to the regional economy.

The limited central capacity to manage engagement with business in the University of Jyväskylä stood in strong contrast to the situation in the Jyväskylä University of Applied Sciences. Formerly focused on skills training and the provision of human capital relevant to local industry, the Jyväskylä University of Applied Sciences had expanded its remit to provide R&D support to local industry and working life. It was closely related to the interests of local companies and equipped to work with the SMEs which form the backbone of the regional economy. It had a board with strong regional representation and nine multi-disciplinary Centres of Expertise to respond to regional needs. They were not separate parts of the institution but formed co-operative groups which were supported and marketed centrally. Most significantly, the institution also maintained a sophisticated management information system which tracked the performance of each individual school. Of 29 Balanced Scorecard performance indicators, eight were specifically linked to regional engagement. These school-based indicators were regularly monitored by the central management team. Finally, and unlike the University of Jyväskylä, it also ran an entrepreneurs development programme. This three-year undergraduate programme was generating graduates able to hit the deck running in the SME sector. In short, the institution attempted to make up for its limited research resources by maximising the effective use of these resources.

The above case example describing the differences in institutional capacity between a traditional university and a new university is by no means unique to Finland. It is evident that the regional engagement agenda poses particular challenges for the profile and management of traditional research-intensive universities. They have often grown incrementally with gaps in key areas relevant to regional development opportunities. Their governance structures support dispersal of responsibility and heterogeneity of substance. The emphasis is on producer-led research and teaching. If external engagement is taking place, the academic heartland is often protected by specialist units.

Finland has arguably one of the most sophisticated and well-funded national innovation policies amongst OECD countries. The regional dimension to this policy is only just beginning to emerge, promoted by the success of the lightly funded Centres of Expertise programmes and science parks. Higher education institutions can play a major role in driving the internationally competitive hubs in the global knowledge economy. But for this to happen, the higher education institutions themselves must change. This requires a fundamental transformation of the funding mechanisms for higher education institutions to give greater financial rewards for external engagement and more autonomy to institutions working with their regional partners. It also requires greater institutional autonomy. The journey down the road of linking academic excellence and regional opportunities could be a long one, especially if there are limited financial incentives to work regionally.

Building innovation-led growth

Innovation is a key catalyst for productivity and economic growth in the knowledge-based economies. For example, between 1970 and 1995 more than half of all total growth in output across the developed world resulted from innovation and the proportion is increasing (Simmie *et al.*, 2002). As a consequence, OECD countries are increasingly investing in the science base in order to enhance innovation. A considerable part of this investment finds its way into higher education institutions which are expected to contribute not only to knowledge creation, but also to knowledge exploitation. At the same time, matching the supply of skills and services with the demand of local and regional firms is becoming an increasingly important part of regional policy, given its growing orientation towards competitiveness, innovation capacity and skill enhancement (OECD, 2007b).

The Local Innovation System project (Lester, 2005) identified four local pathways of innovation-led growth. These are (1) indigenous creation of new industry; (2) exogenous creation of new industry; (3) diversification of existing industry into new; and (4) upgrading of existing, mature industry. What type of contribution do these pathways require from higher education institutions? And how do they fit into the regions that participated in the OECD review? We shall briefly address these questions with reference to the case studies in the OECD project, particularly that of the north-east of England.

Indigenous creation of new industry refers to the local creation of an entirely new industry that has no technological antecedent in the regional economy. This is the kind of process that tends to be associated with higher education institutions, particularly research-intensive universities. Across OECD countries, we see examples of Silicon Valley-type activities with a focus on nanotechnology, biotechnology and ICT and, to a lesser extent, to health and culture industries. For indigenous creation of new firms, the regions need to provide space for R&D-intensive companies, adequate sources of finance for new ventures, critical mass and highly skilled labour.

While it is clear that higher education institutions have become more active and have established infrastructures for commercialisation of research results and ideas, the role and success they have had as sources of indigenous creation of new industry is not yet clearly recorded. Government interest in the indigenous creation of industry is, however, evident. For example, recently, Newcastle, the largest city in the north-east of England, received science city status among five other cities, which means that it is earmarked for support to develop science and technology facilities (see Figure 10.2).

Figure 10.2: Newcastle Science City

The Science City Newcastle project is a response to the government's decision in 2004 to designate Newcastle, together with five other cities in the UK, as a Science City. This multi-million pound project aims to develop both pioneering scientific research and knowledge-based businesses in areas such as nanotechnology, bioscience and molecular engineering at a number of sites in the city, among others, the former Scottish & Newcastle Breweries site. Within five years it is estimated that up to 100 new companies could be set up and up to 5,000 new jobs will be created. Three organisations, Newcastle University, Newcastle City Council and One NorthEast, have formed the Newcastle Science City partnership, which leads the initiative. The project also aims to involve other universities, such as the University of Durham and the University of Northumbria.

Source: Duke *et al.*, 2006.

Exogenous creation of new industry in the region refers to the development of an industry that is also new to the region, but in this case it is imported from elsewhere. Hence, it represents a foreign investment-led industrial development. This strategy has implications on policy areas under national control. Therefore, the negotiating power of the region in the national arena becomes a key factor for success. In the case of the north-east of England, foreign direct investments have gradually increased but remain on a modest scale, with the manufacturing sector showing comparative advantages when compared with other regions. The scale of investment has fallen since 2001 and some investors have withdrawn and redirected investments to other countries, notably in Central and Eastern Europe. The attraction of foreign direct investments has been boosted by investment in automotive industry and technology-intensive areas such as biotechnology and chemicals (see also Figure 10.3).

Diversification of existing industry into new refers to transitions in which the existing industry goes into decline, but its core technologies are redeployed and provide the basis for the emergence of a related new industry. In non-metropolitan regions, there is often a limited presence of knowledge-based industries which provides limited base for diversification.

Upgrading an existing mature industry entails the infusion of new production technologies or the introduction of product or service enhancements. The NEPA project from the north-east of England demonstrates a case study of this type of activity. It also gives evidence that the existence of at least one large enterprise can have a beneficial effect on university–industry relations (see Figure 10.3).

Figure 10.3: University-led regeneration through the North–East Productivity Alliance: the NEPA Project

NEPA is a regional alliance of industrialists, academics and government agencies. Established in 2001, it aims to take forward the North-East region's manufacturing strategy by improving productivity and competitiveness. The NEPA programme covers four projects, including NVQ Workforce Development, Best Practice Improvement Engineering (supported by Industry Forum), Digital Factory and Engineering Fellows. NEPA is based on the principle of responding to the needs of industry. It has delivered improvements to over 300 firms in the North-East. Agreement from Nissan Motor Manufacturing UK Ltd to champion NEPA has been critical to its success. The opportunity for other north-east firms to benefit from the collective experience of Nissan and others has proved compelling. Nissan, on the other hand, benefits indirectly from upgrading of its supplier firms in the region.

The University of Sunderland delivers 50 per cent of NEPA's programmes with participating firms. It has gained recognition for its role in helping to facilitate NEPA by seconding and/or recruiting experienced staff in collaboration with industry. The outcomes of NEPA include 5,000 Level 2 engineering-based NVQs gained by manufacturing staff, 2,500 design engineers trained in digital factory tools and techniques and eight industry-led research projects.

Source: Duke *et al.*, 2006.

While the last strategy appears to gain less focus in most regional development strategies, it may provide a sustainable solution for most non-metropolitan regions. Discovering the genuine competitive assets of the region and building on existing strengths can make a difference. For example, in the Province of Castellón in the Spanish Autonomous Region of Valencia, the research institute of the local university, Jaume I, has helped to transform the existing traditional tile industry into a global leader with the help of technology transfer, spin-outs and work-based learning, improving the overall absorptive capacity of the industry (OECD, 2007b).

Most regions participating in the OECD project had a diversified industrial and economic base with SMEs as major employers. There were usually only few big industrial firms and little R&D-intensive industry. The international marketing and commercialisation competences of the firms in the regions were also weakly developed. For example, in Trøndelag in Norway, 84 per cent of the enterprises have fewer than five employees and only few companies are internationally oriented. In the Canary Islands, 94 per cent of business enterprises employ fewer than ten people and most of them none. The dominating tourism sector has limited cooperation with higher education institutions. Central Finland as a whole suffers from low productivity within the existing business base, which is predominantly SMEs with low levels of R&D investment.

The predominance of the SMEs suggests that future economic growth will depend not only on fostering the growth in new knowledge-intensive sectors but also on the continued upgrading and strengthening of the current industry strengths and technical capabilities of the manufacturing sectors. Thus, the appropriate strategy for many non-metropolitan regions appears to be a mixed strategy which allows for incremental change. Therefore, in addition to measures supporting the type I pathway, regions need concerted measures to support the upgrading of existing firms. While this provides higher education institutions with a number of opportunities, it also requires enhanced co-operation and more systematic, co-ordinated efforts to serve industry. One way of doing this is by introducing a single access point in higher education institutions to serve regional needs. Knowledge House in the north-east of England provides a model for other regions with its significant impact on the regional economy, high engagement of academics, and profitability and long-term sustainability (see Figure 10.4).

Figure 10.4: Knowledge House

Established in 1995, Knowledge House is a joint effort of the north-east universities through the higher education regional association known as Unis4NE to help companies access university skills, expertise and specialist resources. Working together across a wide range of disciplines including industrial design, IT, manufacturing, marketing, life sciences and environmental issues, Knowledge House offers expert solutions for developing ideas and solving problems through collaboration, consultancy, training and research. Originally planned to provide a service to local SMEs, the project has grown to include large companies, and multinationals from all over the country.

Knowledge House has a central headquarters and staff distributed at the partner sites. The network and its operations are supported by a web-based enquiry-handling/project-management and client relationship-management system (KHIS). Knowledge House receives over a thousand enquiries from client companies and delivers almost two hundred client contracts on an annual basis. Business growth averages 25 per cent.

In contrast to networks providing signposting services, Knowledge House offers a 'cradle to grave' service, stretching from the receipt and circulation of enquiries through project management and delivery to post-completion evaluation. This contributes to improved customer experience, but also to higher operational costs.

Source: Duke *et al.*, 2006.

Conclusions

Regions with the help of higher education institutions can play a key role in making OECD countries globally competitive. There is ample evidence of a positive link between investments in regional innovation systems and economic competitiveness and numerous cases that show that academic excellence and regional engagement can be complementary activities, with the one reinforcing the other. In practice there are, however, internal and external barriers for higher education institutions to become more regionally engaged.

The national systems may reduce the capacity of the higher education institutions to engage regionally and limit their institutional autonomy to decide on their inputs and outputs. In general, regional engagement is not supported by major incentives or active monitoring of the outcomes.

The regional engagement agenda is a challenging task, particularly to traditional research-intensive universities, which often have limited management capacity and experience tension between regional engagement and the pursuit of national and international excellence in teaching and research.

References

Arbo, P. and Benneworth, P. (2006) *Understanding the Regional Contribution of Higher Education Institutions: A Literature Review*. Paris: OECD (http://www.oecd.org/dataoecd/55/7/37006775.pdf).

Duke, C., Hassink, R., Powell, J. and Puukka, J. (2006) *Supporting the Contribution of Higher Education Institutions to Regional Development, Peer Review Report: North East of England* (http://www.oecd.org/dataoecd/16/54/35889695.pdf).

Finnish Higher Education Evaluation Council (2006) www.kka.fi/english (accessed 3 January 2006).

Goddard, J.B. and Chatterton, P. (2003) 'The response of universities to regional needs'. In F. Boekama, E. Kuypers and R. Rutten (eds), *Economic Geography of Higher Education: Knowledge, Infrastructure and Learning Regions*. London: Routledge.

Goddard, J., Etzkowitz, H., Puukka, J. and Virtanen, I. (2006) *OECD/IME – Supporting the Contribution of Higher Education Institutions to Regional Development: Peer Review Report, the Jyväskylä Region of Finland* (http://www.oecd.org/dataoecd/27/24/36809119.pdf).

Lester, Richard K. (2005) *Universities, Innovation, and the Competitiveness of Local Economies: A Summary Report from the Local Innovation Systems Project – Phase I* (MIT IPC Local Innovation Systems Working Paper 05-005 | IPC Working Paper 05-010, http://web.edu/lis/papers/LIS05.010.pdf).

Mukkala, K., Ritsilä, J. and Suosara, E. (2006) *OECD/IME – Supporting the Contribution of Higher Education Institutions to Regional Development: Self-Evaluation Report for the Jyväskylä Region in Finland*. University of Jyväskylä/Jyväskylä Polytechnic (http://www.oecd.org/dataoecd/16/9/36175211.pdf).

OECD/IMHE (1999) *The Response of Higher Education Institutions to Regional Needs*. Paris: OECD.

OECD (2007a) *Supporting the Contribution of Higher Education Institutions to Regional Development* (http://www.oecd.org/edu/higher/regional development).

OECD (2007b) *Globally Competitive, Locally Engaged: Higher Education and Regions*. Paris: OECD.

Simmie, J., Sennett, J., Wood, P. and Hart, D. (2002) 'Innovation in Europe, a tale of networks, knowledge and trade in five cities', *Regional Studies*, 36: 47–64.

Chapter 11

Commitment, research, connection and community: learning in networks in regional development

Anne Badenhorst

This chapter uses an exemplar project, the Whittlesea Youth Commitment, to demonstrate how success is built on research, collaboration and the inter-section of policy development and practice. The aim of the project was to assist young people at risk in schools into pathways into further education, training or employment. The project is located in the northern metropolitan region of Melbourne, Australia. It did not develop in isolation but arose from the efforts of a number of people and organisations committed to supporting the economic development effort in the region, where there is considerable history of collaboration and leadership at the local level, and where the university has taken a key role. The issue was prominent in national and state government concerns, and the project influenced and was influenced by policy and programme development.

The northern metropolitan region

The northern metropolitan region of Melbourne, as defined by the regional agencies and organisations, consists of the following local government areas: the Cities of Whittlesea, Hume, Nilumbik, Banyule, Darebin, Moreland and Yarra. It has a population of approximately 750,000 and is a culturally diverse region with areas of dramatic socioeconomic contrast ranging from very prosperous to severely disadvantaged, also with areas ranging from inner city to suburban and rural interface and rural areas. The City of Whittlesea is the largest local government area in the region. It has a population of 132,000, with rapid growth and a high proportion of new families and young people.

There have been significant and continual changes in industry in the region including the ongoing loss of larger companies, the demise of the textile, clothing and footwear industry and increasing relocation of manufacturing offshore. Many of the companies are small to medium enterprises and the current environment brings increasing pressures to operate differently in a more competitive and international environment. Manufacturing employs 16.5 per cent of the residents and the value of the output represents 19.5 per cent of manufacturing in Victoria and 7.8 per cent in Australia (Shepherd, 2003).

Building from a manufacturing base, there are very real questions about ways to develop the region and particularly to grow employment in the business and service sectors and in advanced manufacturing, in the 'new' knowledge economy. Selby Smith *et al.* (2001) undertook a study of the Australian labour market based on the classification of workers as 'symbolic analysts, routine production workers and in person service workers' (Reich, 1992), which found that Australia has among the highest rates of part-time and casual work of all OECD nations. This is very much a feature of many of the local government areas in the northern metropolitan region, with very high rates of un/underemployment in some areas. Also there is a high exposure to low-skilled and unskilled residents in these areas – a remnant of the former manufacturing economy (Shepherd, 2003), yet some of these areas are also the location for new and expanding enterprises requiring workers with different, knowledge-economy skills.

Also very noticeable in the region are increasing polarisation and pockets of severe socioeconomic disadvantage. Parts of the region rate well against measures of employment, levels of education, innovation measures such as patents and research and development, and creativity (Florida, 2000), but there are clearly serious issues of access, equity and social inclusion.

Policy context

The notion of a Youth Commitment was first proposed in Australia in the OECD *Thematic Review of the Transition from Initial Education to Working Life – Australia Country Note* (1997), which had been picked up by the Dusseldorp Skills Forum (DSF),[1] 'an independent, not-for-profit body with a mission to achieve changes needed to enable all Australians to reach their potential through the acquisition of productive skills.' The DSF is well respected for leadership in this area and is engaged with national policy debates. It published *Why Australia Needs a National Youth Commitment* in 2000 and this was cited in the report from the *Prime Minister's Youth Pathways and Action Plan Taskforce* in 2001. The task force's recommendation was a national commitment to youth, and it chose the Whittlesea Youth Commitment as an example of the key features of collaboration, and a 'classic example of a good action research project' (Australian Government, 2001: 199).

The issue of young people at risk of leaving school early without pathways into further education, training or employment was high on the agenda of both federal and state governments at this time. A number of Commonwealth programs were introduced to address the issue, which had been under discussion since the late 1980s, and by the late1990s there was still 'very little success, as the numbers of "at risk youth" had remained unchanged over this time', and Australia was 'one of the few OECD countries where school retention rates declined over the 1990s' (Spierings, 1999, 2000).

At this time the Victorian State government was also developing its policy to address issues for young people and transitions and pathways to education, vocational education and training and work. In 2000 the final report of the *Ministerial Review of Post Compulsory Education and Training Pathways in Victoria* was published. A key recommendation from this report was the establishment and phasing in of local planning networks for statewide coverage to:

- develop collaborative approaches towards planning and improved delivery of post compulsory education and training programmes and services; and
- instigate and trial key elements of regional coordination and delivery of programs (VDET, 2000, p. 19).

These were established as Llens, or Learning and Employment Networks. The report stated that they were directly influenced by the DSF and quoted Jack Dusseldorp. However, they did not cite any examples of this activity so as not to 'prejudice the decisions about the networks to be included in the first phase of the Llens implementation' (VDET, 2000, p. 117).

In the report *Setting the Pace*, prepared for the DSF, the Education Foundation and the Business Council of Australia, Victoria was identified as 'not just … a leader in terms of actual youth transitions from school … the state became the national youth transitions policy pathfinder during the early 2000s'

(VDET, 2005, p. 6). The Victorian Education and Training Department has since reviewed the Education and Training Act and made a number of changes, including the introduction of a youth guarantee which 'provides a guaranteed place in TAFE Institutions, the Centre for Adult Education, Adult Multicultural Education Services and participating adult community education providers, to young people who have not completed Year 12 or its equivalent' (VDET, 2006a).

Economic development in the northern metropolitan region

There has been some local effort in economic development since the late 1970s, beginning with the establishment of the Northern Region Commission, which involved local governments. This has grown into a commitment to a vision of an integrated economy in the northern metropolitan region. This is being led by two regional development agencies. One, the Northern Area Consultative Committee (NACC), is an agency funded by the Commonwealth government with a brief to support local partnerships in economic development, and the other is an industry education network established in the late 1980s and funded by its membership.

The NACC commissioned research to support the regional economic development project. The result, *Growing Melbourne's North – Developing an Integrated Economy* was launched in August 2003. The research concludes that 'the region has the potential to achieve significant economic and social benefits if stakeholders share resources and cooperate across local government boundaries to form a discrete economic zone', and that it includes 'benchmarks that will support growth and quality employment outcomes for the region' (Shepherd, 2003).

There is strong take-up of the recommendations and buy-in to the regional economic development 'project' that it proposes, by the local governments, by the CEOs, and particularly with the economic development groups from all councils and educational institutions in the region. A concerted effort has been made to involve the local members of parliament from both state and federal governments. This has led to biannual meetings which are now well attended and have successfully raised the profile of the regional development organisations and the local issues. There is an economic development working group with the directors from the local governments, also an education and training working group with key representatives from the four institutions, plus work under way with the Llens.

The industry education network was formed in response to a 'crisis' as the federal government introduced their policies to restructure Australian industry and reduce tariffs in the late 1980s. This was a direct threat to the manufacturing industry of the region. As skills improvement and training were also major platforms of the changes, it also raised concerns regarding the low retention rates in schools and low participation rates in higher education of young people in the region. The education providers and industry identified the importance of working together to support the measures needed to alleviate some of the impacts of the new policies including accessing government programmes. A concern about access and social inclusion and also an element of 'our fair share' which is contextualised in the politics of the region were also motivating factors. The region consists of 'safe seats', consistently supporting the Australian Labour Party and, as is demonstrated in the research in *Growing Melbourne's North*, it does not have a proportionate share of infrastructure and amenities compared with other regions of Melbourne (Shepherd, 2003).

The network

There has been a fairly robust network supporting the regional development project in the region. The two agencies, the NACC and the industry education network, have representatives from key organisations and increasing access to local members of parliament. Another key player is a group which was established at the same time as the industry education network (at the time called NIECAP),[2] to support science and technology education in schools and links between schools, education and training and industry. This group, now based in the university, has been instrumental in providing leadership, expertise and resources in this project and the wider regional development project.

The experience of the networks linked through the regional economic development work suggests that bridging networks and weak ties (Putnam, 2001; Granovetter, 1973) are important in the effort to have an impact in the region in both the economic and social spheres. Granovetter (1973, 1983, 2005) studied the 'strength of weak ties' and the flows of 'unique and non-redundant information' (2005, p. 35) which is more likely to transfer across weak ties to otherwise 'disconnected segments' of social networks. This is important in this project as it is from these 'weak ties' that the initial group who initiated the project were able to garner support, involve the range of players necessary, and disseminate the picture of the region they were developing.

A 'communities of practice' framework (Wenger, 1998) has assisted in understanding the groups and development of this work in the region. At the core of this network there is a 'community of practice' which has, over the years, influenced the regional activities, brought new members into the community, and played key roles in establishing the regional agencies, other 'communities of practice' or projects. This small 'community of practice' has provided leadership skills and development for a number of players who have influenced activity. This group displays characteristics of a 'community of practice' with:

- mutual engagement: sustained interpersonal engagement;
- joint enterprise: a collective process of negotiating the aims and a mutual obligation/accountability among participants; and
- shared repertoire: shared resources, documents, anecdotes, history and language.

This group developed a growing commitment and expertise in the development of programmes which address issues in the regional economic development project and link organisations. They have an explicit approach which aims to build social capital, the 'networks, together with the norms, values and understandings that facilitate cooperation with or among groups' (Healy et al., 2001). They are not, however, operating in an environment without politics, and have supported some projects over others. They have also been identified in a less positive light as an 'in-group' clearly influential in the politics in the early discussions and establishment of the Llen, insisting on space for the Whittlesea Youth Commitment. Against opposition, there were well-managed politics and the ability to draw on the number of people supportive of and engaged actively in the network. It was important to those engaged to have the Whittlesea Youth Commitment considered carefully in the establishment of the Llen to ensure the real outcomes and work already under way were not lost, and, more importantly, complemented the work of the Llen, which was logically seen as additional resource and support. The local government support was critical to this discussion.

The Whittlesea Youth Commitment (WYC)

The Whittlesea Youth Commitment (WYC) started in 1998. It grew from concerns which were constantly in the conversation of the 'community of practice' and the development was led by the university group who took an action-research approach.

They started with research to understand the situation locally, and a project which examined the impact on young people of changes to the Youth Allowance highlighted some significant issues. The changes to the Youth Allowance aimed to encourage young people to stay in school by making them ineligible for support unless they were in training or education. This research found that young people did not know they would be without assistance or what support would be available to them if they left school, and that in one year 450 young people left school in the City of Whittlesea and their whereabouts were unknown. They were not tracked, and it was not known whether they were not in training, education or employment (Kellock, 2001).

A solid body of local information was developed, not exclusively within this project but within the regional network, and this included:

- an environmental scan of youth participation in employment, education and training and the broader community services available to meet their needs;
- a destination survey of school leavers;
- an audit of career teaching and vocational guidance to the local public;
- secondary schools;
- a regional skills audit to identify skills strengths and weaknesses in local industry; and
- a funding map to chart the distribution of resources in employment, education and training from all sources, across the dimensions of school completers and early school leavers, which found:
- average per capita resources for school completers in Years 11 and 12, AUS$5,600 per annum (compares with Commonwealth estimate of AUS$8,300 per annum);
- average per capita resources to assist early school leavers total AUS$2,900 per annum to reach post-school employment, education and training destinations;
- average per capita resources to assist early school leavers in TAFE total AUS$4,200 per annum;
- average per capita resources to assist early school leavers in new apprenticeships total AUS$4,500 per annum; and
- average per capita resources to assist early school leavers in the Job Network totalled just AUS$760 in 1998–99. (Spierings, 2000, p. 9).

The 'community of practice' was looking for ways to address the issues specifically and locally, and was put in touch with the DSF. This connection was brokered by one of the new staff brought into the research project who had a contact there. The DSF was looking to develop a pilot Youth Commitment project and was interested in the already established network as a starting point. The intention to establish the WYC came out of a meeting which involved the DSF, the tertiary institute, the local government, schools, a job network provider, TAFE and employers.

Establishing the project was slow. Even with existing networks in place, it took two years to achieve meaningful collaboration and levels of trust (Spierings, 2000). Research outcomes were very critical to bringing people together around the issues. Data on school-leaver destinations was powerful, as it established that of those leaving school before Year 12 in the City of Whittlesea, one-third went to unknown destinations.

The DSF had also brought new and vital information from one of their pilot projects where they had trialled *transition officers* working in a community service organisation assisting young people at risk while they were still in school. They also brought information on general trends and issues for young people and their work in the formation of a Youth Commitment. This knowledge was shared and used to demonstrate the importance and relevance of the issues to the very different organisations which needed to engage.

The original aim of the WYC was to 'ensure that every young person leaving school in the City of Whittlesea, especially those who leave before completing VCE or its equivalent, makes a smooth transition to another education option or further training or employment or their desired goal' (WYC, 1998).

The community team is the collection of organisations which form the WYC. They have signed an agreement but made a very deliberate decision not to incorporate or enter into a formal arrangement, as they wanted to retain a collaboration built on trust and shared commitment as expressed in the 'Spirit of Cooperation' signed by all. These organisations include:

- nine industry partners;
- two industry associations;
- five job network providers;
- four government agencies, including the government social security agency, the local police, the Adult and Community Further Education Committee and the Area Consultative Committee;
- three tertiary providers;

- the eight secondary schools in the city; and
- two community agencies.

The WYC has one position, funded initially by the City of Whittlesea and now with costs shared by the Llen. It is housed by the university, which provides physical resources, but also colleagues working with related issues and programmes. The committee for management is a small group which brings the community team together and plans activities and programs. The key resource is in the schools where each school now has a transition broker. These positions were established initially with funds from the DSF, the City of Whittlesea, the TAFE and the university, and then funded under a government programme called Managed Individual Pathways (VDET, 2006b) which, rather fortunately, in terms of timing, came together well for the WYC. This was not just serendipity but rather evidence that the project was very much situated within the debates and the developments in national and state policy and programmes. It is a measure of the level of collaboration among schools that they pool the funding they receive, to resource brokers across schools and other organisations and agencies.

The transition brokers mentor and support individual students in schools, identifying students at risk in Years 7 and 8, working with them individually to establish potential pathways, setting up interviews and contacts, and monitoring progress. The WYC coordinator supports the committee for management, the community team and programmes which involve all the schools and stakeholders.

The outcomes and initiatives of the WYC include:

- the implementation of a common exiting procedure used across the secondary colleges;
- the development and publication of the School Leavers' Guide and the Education and Training Passport;
- the collection and sharing of data, agreement about benchmarks and a willingness to increase the complexity and breadth of indicators;
- the appointment of transition brokers jointly resourced by the secondary colleges to provide counselling, advice and support to young people leaving school before completing Year 12 and to track their destinations for at least 12 months;
- the establishment of the community team to develop cooperation and collaboration across agencies to facilitate tracking of young

people and, through consideration of anonymous case studies, to explore options and appropriate support for young people; and

- the implementation of an innovative mentoring pilot project to support young people who have left school before completing Year 12 and have not moved into other education or training options or employment. Participants will receive training access and appropriate support services, undertake paid work placements and be matched with a mentor (Edwards, 2002, p. 3).

The key area where the WYC acknowledges they have made little progress is in greater cooperation across the employment services organisations. This is a complex system in Australia since the disbanding of the Commonwealth Employment Services and the contracting out of different employment services and setting of targets and priorities to these companies. What has proven so successful with young people is the case-management approach. Early school leavers require support to build confidence, to create CVs and to identify opportunities, and encouragement to continue to search for opportunities when unsuccessful, and transition brokers have provided this. However job, apprenticeship and traineeship opportunities are available through the employment services organisations, so these connections are important. Employers are also difficult to keep engaged.

It has also been a somewhat fraught process establishing the Llen in this region in the first phase of implementation in 2001 with two cities – Hume and Whittlesea – covered by one Llen. The goals and the role of the Llen and the WYC were very close, which made the first two years of the Llen implementation very complex. The experience in this region was captured well in the Review of the Llen which suggested that considerable work was required to impose a coordinating structure in areas where other organisations and institutions were well established (VLESC, 2002, p. 19). As the Llen shared the main aim of the WYC this needed to be established as complementary, not competitive. In the words of one interviewee, 'the Llen stopped the momentum of the WYC and the WYC made it more difficult to establish the Llen'. There was also a feeling that because the WYC was not established and funded by the state government it was not valued as highly as a programme 'belonging' to the government. This is not entirely resolved. The Llen currently sees the WYC management committee as a local planning group, and have contributed funds to the project coordinator position in the WYC, but there are currently questions about the role of the WYC and how it needs to work within the Llen framework. The aims, and objectives and strategic and work planning are being reviewed.

Collaboration and learning

The WYC represents the community ownership of the issues of young people leaving school early or at risk of doing so (Kellock, 2001, p. 16). The agencies and organisations involved identify their part of the problem or the way they see/experience the issues, but through the WYC the issues are owned and worked on as a community. When the Llen was announced there was considerable concern that this 'imposed' framework would be a problem for the grass-roots-based development through the WYC.

There is a strong identification within this community as it is both 'place-based' and focused on very real and obvious issues of relevance and importance to the stakeholders. Also the attention to research and indicators which support the understanding of impact and changes has provided local data and concrete goals. Considerable trust was developed through the process of collecting data on individual organisations and aggregating it, and considerable care has been taken to keep the bigger-picture approach, addressing issues to develop solutions across the Commitment.

Collaboration is fundamental to this project. It has always been identified as a community partnership, and much was invested by the signatories to the 'Spirit of Cooperation' in ensuring this remained a priority. The executive support provided by the funded project officer position is identified as very critical in keeping the team approach alive and allowing people to participate without increasing workloads.

A number of examples of learning were cited by interviewees. Key to many was the development of indicators and the ongoing research which provided real data and formal approaches to solving problems. The WYC, according to a number of those involved, and supported by the review undertaken in 2001, grew from good relationships across organisations and good research. The results from the small research projects provided specific local knowledge and data. This brought people together because they could see how their organisation could play a part in addressing the problems represented by those statistics.

Clearly a dynamic environment was created in the early stages of the WYC and there was excitement and sometimes tension in the development of the project. People felt they were learning and involved in something new and innovative which would really make a difference. A technique identified which supported learning was the use of anonymous profiles for community case management used in discussions involving the participating agencies who work with young people, e.g. youth workers, job network providers, education providers, police, and so on, at their meetings which were held approximately six to eight times per year. One interviewee suggested that a key learning might be 'that it is possible for the community to learn, to change what they are doing ... it was a special project and we all learned from each other and now even though it is not so exciting we all can take that belief and that experience and make it happen again when we see an opportunity'.

There is evidence and thorough documentation of the learning available from the Dusseldorp Skills Forum Tools and Resources website. These include a Youth Commitment resource kit and self-assessment kit to enable practitioners to assess best practice (DSF, 2007).

There were also a few pointed comments about the ability of the Victorian government to take the lessons from the project and incorporate them, but to ignore the project itself because it was not 'owned or invented' by them.

Those involved in the Llen have great respect for the work that has happened in the WYC, and believe a great deal has been accomplished. They are aware of some of the issues faced by the WYC, and of course members of WYC are now on the Llen, so learning is transferred. The role of the WYC in relation to the Llen is being clarified. There is a very obvious fit of the work of the WYC with the objectives and strategies of the Llen, and clearly scope for the work to continue. There is a sense among some that the Llen could subsume the WYC, with responsibility transferred, and given work pressures on most members, an acceptance of less involvement if someone else will take on the activities. This is doubted by others who have retained the close connections, regular involvement and sense of community or a place in the 'community of practice', so it is likely there will be another push to ignite greater identification and engagement to build further, as a very key success factor is the very local and specific nature of the project.

Conclusion

The 'Spirit of Cooperation' agreement is just being reviewed. Logically, the future of the WYC is dependent on the way the role is determined within the framework of the Llen.

The Review of the Llen undertaken in 2004 raised very pertinent issues. It acknowledged how long partnerships take to develop and to deliver gains to the community, and it listed barriers to improving outcomes for those at risk of not succeeding as:

- achieving the cross-government collaboration on which solutions depend;
- building genuine local community accountability;
- accepting the resource intensive nature of assisting those missing out; and
- dealing effectively with the factors leading to poor engagement with schooling in the years prior to the post-compulsory levels (VDET, 2005, p. 22).

The Whittlesea Youth Commitment grew from local collaboration and commitment. It reflects approaches in the northern metropolitan region; it is not the only project to achieve outstanding results locally. Potentially the Llen, rather than being competition, could become a vital lever in the critical area of joining up government programmes and responses. In the Review of the Llen, the Northern Area Consultative Committee, well experienced with these issues in this region, asked the question: 'Can you reasonably ask Llens for a whole of community approach without government providing a whole of government response?' (VDET, 2005, p. 50).

The WYC grew from local issues with organisations who, when faced with the facts, were committed to being part of the solution. This has been high-lighted as a strength of the project but was not the approach in the imple-mentation of the Llen. The Llens were imposed in areas by government with standard requirements and funding accountabilities, and it would be very challenging to government to manage any other way. Membership was also contested as it is 'drawn from any individual or organisation with an interest in post compulsory education, training and employment within the area covered by that Llen' (Selby Smith *et al.*, 2001).

The aims and objectives of the Llen programme are clear, but obviously have played out in different areas differently, depending on skills of the Chairs and executive officers, local priorities and conditions (VLESC, 2002). The WYC responded to a clearly defined problem and engaged the organisations who could see their obligation and a role in the solution. The world of the WYC is not without politics and agendas, but the responses are more clearly defined by the issues at hand than by the power and position of organisations, as many of the Llens have experienced. The WYC were fortunate in resourcing, but that has been a continuing concern. The Llens faced the challenge of being seen as additional funds to be used towards other agendas (VDET, 2004). The Llens however do have access to state government programmes and direct access to a state government committee with some progress in cross-departmental initiatives. This is identified as an area for the government to improve. This is far more than the WYC could achieve as a local entity.

The Whittlesea Youth Commitment is an example of the power of local collaboration, and ability to match and leapfrog the research and development of solutions by government. It is also an example of learning from local practitioners by government and researcher. It highlights the limits of the local without the matching programme and policy responses from government, but is hopeful in that lessons have been learnt and strengths acknowledged and therefore well documented. The outstanding outcomes are the local solutions and the barriers, often linked to structures and programs, beyond local control. The Llens have the potential to bridge this gap at the state level, and with the Llens coverage in the northern metropolitan region, perhaps also to complement the regional approach of the NACC.

It does beg the question, of course, why the Llen had to be imposed when the WYC was in place. In this lies a key challenge in policy and programmes, and in this context it perhaps opens an even wider debate about how different levels of government interact, how local is understood and accommodated in programmes, and how knowledge is gained and valued across organisations and the different worlds of government and community.

Notes

[1] Dusseldorp Skills Forum (http://www.dsf.org.au/index.php).
[2] The Northern Interactive Education Collaborative Area programme, initially located in the Phillip Institute of Technology, which became RMIT University. Currently named Community and Youth Partnerships.

References

Australian Government, Department of Education, Science and Training (2001) *Youth Pathways Action Plan Taskforce Report: Footprints to the Future* (http://www.dest.gov.au/sectors/career_development/publications_resources/profiles/footprints_to_the_future.htm).

Dusseldorp Skills Forum (2007) *Tools and Resources* (http://www.dsf.org.au/index.php).

Edwards, J. (2002) *Northern Partnerships*. OECD Victoria, Learning Cities and Regions Conference, Melbourne, Victoria.

Finn, B. (Chair) (1991) *Young People's Participation in Post Compulsory Education and Training*. Report to the Australian Education Council, Melbourne.

Florida, R. (2000) *Competing in the Age of Talent: Environment, Amenities and the New Economy*. Report prepared for the R K Mellon Foundation, Heinz Endowments and Sustainable Pittsburgh (http://www.heinz.cmu.edu).

Granovetter, M.S. (1973) 'The strength of weak ties,' *American Journal of Sociology*, 78(6): 1360–80.

Granovetter, M.S. (1983) 'The strength of the weak tie: revisited', *Sociological Theory*, 1: 203–33.

Granovetter, M.S. (2005) 'The impact of social structure on economic outcomes', *Journal of Economic Perspectives*, 19(1): 33–50.

Healy, T., Côté, S., Helliwell, J.F. and Field, S. (2001) *The Well-being of Nations: The Role of Human and Social Capital. Centre for Educational Research and Innovation*. Paris: OECD.

Kellock, P. (2001) *The Whittlesea Youth Commitment: A Review*. Melbourne: Asquith Group.

Long, M. (2005) *Setting the Pace* (http://www.dsf.org.au/papers/174.htm).

OECD (2000) *From Initial Education to Working Life: Transitions Work*. Paris: OECD.

Putnam, R. (2001) *Bowling Alone: The Collapse and Revival of American Community*. New York: Simon & Schuster.

Reich, R. (1992) *The Work of Nations: A Blueprint for the Future*. London: Simon & Schuster.

Selby Smith, C., Ferrier, F., Anderson, D., Burke, G., Hopkins, S., Long, M., Maglen, L., Malley, J., McKenzie, P. and Shah, C. (2001) *The Economics of Vocational Education and Training in Australia: CEET's Stocktake*. Leabrook, SA: National Centre for Vocational Education Research (NCVER) (http://www.ncver.edu/publications/585.html), accessed 13 July 2007.

Shepherd, C. (2003) *Growing Melbourne's North: Developing an Integrated*

Economy. National Institute of Economic and Industry Research (NIEIR), Northern Area Consultative Committee (http://www.northernacc.com/index.jsp), accessed 31 July 2006.

Spierings, J. (1999) 'Why Australia needs a national commitment', Dusseldorp Skills Forum (http://www.dsf.org.au/papers.php?s=1&s1=desc&page=6).

Spierings, J. (2000) 'Developing a new regional education, employment and training agenda: early lessons from Whittlesea' (http://www.dsf.org.au/papers.php?s=1&s1=desc&page=5).

Victorian Department of Education and Training (VDET) (2000) Kirby, P. (Chair), *Ministerial Review of Post Compulsory Education and Training Pathways in Victoria: Final Report*. Melbourne.

Victorian Department of Education and Training (VDET) (2005) *Evaluation of Local Learning and Employment Networks*. Post Compulsory Division, Victorian Department of Education and Training, for the Victorian Learning and Employment Skills Commission (also published on www.vlesc.vic.gov.au/vlesc/news_publications/publications.htm).

Victorian Department of Education and Training (VDET) (2006a) *The Education and Training Reform Act 2006*.

Victorian Department of Education and Training (VDET) (2006b) *Managed Individual Pathways* (MIPS) (http://www.education.vic.gov.au/student learning/careersandtransition/mips/).

Victorian Learning and Employment Skills Commission (VLESC) (2002) *Evaluation of Local Learning and Employment Networks*. Communications Division, Victorian Department of Education and Training, for the State of Victoria.

Wenger, E. (1998) *Communities of Practice. Learning, Meaning and Identity*. Cambridge: Cambridge University Press.

Whittlesea Youth Commitment (WYC) (1998) Whittlesea Youth Commitment, Information Paper. Melbourne: NIECAP, RMIT University.

Whittlesea Youth Commitment (2001) *Spirit of Cooperation Agreement* (http://www.dsf.org.au/nycarchive/whit.html).

Chapter 12

Connecting communities: an Indigenous education initiative in the Canberra region, Australia

Carolyn Broadbent

The role and function of universities are changing as they become more outward-looking and involved in building mutually reciprocal links to the wider educational community. This chapter examines the development and value of strong university–community partnerships that bring together universities, schools, families, cultural institutions and community organisations, in promoting the learning of the participants and in ensuring more equitable outcomes for all within our present-day diverse and inclusive society, particularly within the field of Indigenous education.

Members of the Australian Indigenous community are significantly under-represented at all levels of education, including within school communities, the teaching profession, administrative or learning support staff working in classrooms, and as school office assistants. There is potential for community-based projects to build a greater sense of connectedness throughout the Indigenous and wider education community.

A community-based initiative, the *Connecting Communities Project* in Canberra, Australia is discussed. This section outlines the context, project objectives and collaborative processes undertaken between government and non-government agencies, schools, teachers, university academics and members of the Indigenous community in the development of the project. It examines the way in which the project has assisted in building mutual trust and respect between the participants for the sharing of knowledge and expertise. The successful outcomes of earlier programmes are used to argue that deepening an understanding of, and respect for, Indigenous traditions and culture is essential to improving the achievement levels of Indigenous students and members of the wider Indigenous community. This section provides details of the learning programme and outcomes emanating from the *Connecting Communities Project*, reports on progress, and identifies some directions for the future.

Introduction

The increase in political and economic pressure by governments on universities has seen the development of new strategies aimed at reducing the reliance on government funding through external consultancies, increasing the impact and relevance of research, improving the quality of the teaching and learning process, and strengthening partnerships with the community (Broadbent, 1998, 2000; Sunderland *et al.*, 2004). Universities can no longer afford to exist in isolation and their changing role is reflected in the establishment of mutually reciprocal links and the development of new and innovative partnerships that bring together educational institutions, businesses, industry and members of the wider educational community (Bourner, Katz and Watson, 2000). Through meaningful engagement, these partnerships have the potential to build dynamic communities of practice (Wenger, McDermott and Snyder, 2002), where knowledge is shared and valued for the benefit of all participants.

The importance of creating learning partnerships in many forms and contexts and to be innovative in forging relationships between stakeholders has been highlighted (Kearns, 2005). Yet the establishment of collaborative partnerships is not an easy process and requires a significant investment of time and effort. Important elements and stages of the collaborative process have been identified. They include networking, cooperation, coordination, coalitions and multi-sector collaboration; this requires the development of a shared vision, risks and rewards, and highly developed forms of communication (Hogue, 1995). In determining the success of any collaborative initiative, the elements of trust, cooperation and mutual reciprocity are also significant. These require patience, a willingness to listen, and engagement in democratic decision-making.

Success is also related to the achievement of common goals established through an effective collaborative process and the dependency of the participants on the combined effort and resources of others to bring about the

184

achievement of meaningful and sustainable outcomes (Munt, 2003). Therefore collaboration, as well as process, constitutes an outcome in itself and forms a vital element in the development of social infrastructure that can be sustained long after the conclusion of the project (Munt, 2003). Schuller *et al*. (2004) argue that learning should be viewed as a process 'whereby people build up, consciously or not, their assets in the shape of human, social, or identity capital, and then benefit from the returns on the investment in the shape of better health, stronger social networks, enhanced family life, and so on' (Schuller *et al*., 2004, p. 12).

Knowledge, skills, self-concept, friends, networks, and qualifications are regarded as 'capabilities', which represent the freedom to achieve diverse outcomes ranging from basic health to complex activities, or states such as active engagement in community life. Specific learning outcomes refer back to or even constitute the capitals and thereby allow the capital to grow and be mobilised. In the absence of the capabilities, individuals will be deprived of the opportunity 'to accumulate the assets from which the benefits in turn flow' (Schuller *et al*., 2004, p. 13). Understandably, the relationship between learning outcomes and the impact these have on family, health and social capital has generated considerable research (Putman, Leonardi and Nanetti, 1993; Stone, 2001; Schuller *et al*., 2004). Of importance is the need for the development of sustainable outcomes. As Eva Cox (1995) highlights, social capital should be 'the pre-eminent and most valued form of any capital as it provides the basis on which we build a truly civil society'. Without our social bases, she argues, 'we cannot be fully human'. Sustaining individuals, especially those with disabilities, youth, and members of Indigenous communities, is therefore critical as it relates directly to factors such as identity definition, which includes increasing confidence and self-esteem.

Kearns (2005) argues that in order to build an inclusive Australian society, there is a need to:

> empower individuals as motivated and capable lifelong learners; sustain and transform communities through learning; use technology to extend learning environments and transform the way we learn; develop the workplace as a key learning environment to underpin economic objectives; and extend and connect partnerships and networks (p. 5).

The creation of learning partnerships in many differing contexts and forms can lead to enhanced creativity and personal fulfilment while also strengthening capacity for enterprise and innovation within the community (Kearns, 2005, p. 5). Facilitating learning that encourages the active engagement of individuals requires a clear focus on intrinsic motivators, the adoption of multi-modal forms of learning and participation in a wide range of learning experiences that cater for the specific needs of all learners, while promoting the value of learning throughout life (UNESCO, 1996; Vaill, 1996; Jackson, 2003; Chapman, Cartwright and McGilp, 2006).

School–community partnerships

Strong community-based initiatives and partnerships that connect schools, families, universities and the wider educational community have demonstrated their value in providing mutually beneficial outcomes for all participants (Epstein, 2001; Broadbent and Boyle, 2004; Widin *et al.*, 2004; Broadbent, Boyle and Carmody, 2006). Bushnell (2001, p. 140) identifies three common themes in the school–community literature: the development of a sense of community within schools; a perceived link between a sense of community and functional democracy; and the development of connections between families, schools and the wider community. The third theme offers the benefits of improved communication, cooperation and shared resources (Schwab and Sutherland, 2001, pp. 2–3).

It is well acknowledged that members of the Australian Indigenous community are significantly under-represented at all levels of education, including within school communities, the teaching profession, administrative or learning support staff working in classrooms, and as school office assistants. In addition, there are often few opportunities for Indigenous adults and students to meet together on an ongoing or regular basis so that they can build community and share their knowledge, expertise and experiences. Increased participation of Indigenous school staff and community members in school and classroom activities can work effectively to create connections and relationships that impact positively on the school ethos and thereby bring benefits to both Indigenous and non-Indigenous students (Wano, 2006, p. 7). Frigo *et al.* (2003) noted the importance of attendance, attentiveness in class, language background, region and school as factors influencing the achievement of Indigenous students (p. 11). Schools regarded as the most successful were recognisable by their good teaching, high attendance rates and strong links to the Indigenous community (p. 11).

For Bowes and Hayes (2004), the question is 'how might a balance be achieved in matching the challenges inevitably experienced in life with the resources to enable people to deal with those challenges in a way that has benefits, rather than negative consequences for individuals, families and communities' (p. 17). While some progress has occurred, there is still significant room for improvement. As Ken Henry (2006) highlights, while the overall standard of living had increased in Australia to a higher level than every G7 country, other than that of the USA, this masked the 'severe capability deprivation suffered by most Indigenous Australians' (p. 20). Although part of mainstream Australia, Indigenous communities 'had a dramatically lower life expectancy, 17 years less than the Australian average, dramatically lower rates of schooling and employment, and substantially higher rates of imprisonment' (p. 20). Indigenous disadvantage, it is argued, diminishes all of Australia, 'not only the dysfunctional and disintegrating communities in which it is most apparent' (p. 20). This is not due, he argues, to a lack of policy action; it is, unfortunately, 'that decades of policy action have failed' (p. 3).

Wano (2006) extends the discussion as he reflects on his work with Australian Indigenous communities:

> Since colonisation, Indigenous Australia has been confronted by cultural discontinuity and interruption. As with other Indigenous populations globally that have shared parallel cultural discontinuity, our communities share indicators that are detrimental and limiting in terms of health, education and employment outcomes. As our modern world moves rapidly from the information age to digital age, our Indigenous communities find ourselves constantly on the front foot in terms of cultural transitions after 218 years of cultural interruption, that can impact negatively on one's self identity, self worth and their sense of belonging (p. 6).

Schools that initiate opportunities to consult with their respective Indigenous community on school matters related to the curriculum, teaching and learning, the school ethos, partnerships and services, should be better placed to enhance resiliency in their young Indigenous students (Wano, 2006, p. 7). Unfortunately, many opportunities for school leaders and educators to meet with community leaders, elders, parents and families are often overlooked. Meetings held in community settings, rather than in schools, provide greater opportunities for educators to demonstrate their willingness to connect with their Indigenous communities and show their commitment to enhancing the well-being and abilities of their youth (p. 7). Further, when school activities and programmes are replicated in the Indigenous community, they become more authentic and meaningful to young learners. This can lead to an increase in positive self-identity and self-worth because the positive messages and language presented in the school programmes are able to be reinforced in the community after school hours (Wano, 2006, p. 7). Identification and incorporation of, for example, family literacy practices into the educational programmes offered in schools, places greater credence on home experiences as relevant to school learning and thereby is more responsive to community needs. The level of family support available to students has been linked to length of time remaining at school (Howard, 2002). Of course, there are many influences impacting on the low levels of educational achievement experienced by members of the Indigenous community.

Price (2001) also notes the potential benefits of accessing cultural and community resources to establish links between the Australian Indigenous students' learning and the home. Developing respect for, and understanding of, Indigenous cultures remained fundamental to improving the level of achievement of Indigenous students (McRae *et al.*, 2000). Success, it is argued, remains dependent on the recognition of the cultural factors which may impact on that success, and will only occur when there is the 'consent, approval and willing participation of those involved' (p. 16).

Schwab and Sutherland (2001, p. 4) argue that for many Indigenous adults, alienation from educational processes and institutions is linked to the negative experiences in their own schooling. This is compounded by the fact that many Indigenous parents are ill-equipped to provide assistance and direction in their children's education. Generally, Indigenous adults have low levels of formal education and poor literacy and numeracy skills. Perhaps more significant is their limited experience with and knowledge of the processes that underpin formal education; consequently, these factors combine to produce debilitating, low levels of self-esteem and little confidence in their ability to effect change (Schwab and Sutherland, 2001).

> For many Indigenous Australians, schools have not been open and welcoming of Indigenous participation. Indeed, for many, schools have been the agents of disempowerment, and dismant-lers of cultures and traditions. Indigenous participation is marred by experiences of alienation and exclusion that have been propa-gated by systematic and institutional bias (Schwab and Sutherland, 2001).

Effective programmes focused on addressing the specific learning needs of the Indigenous community, including both parents and students, are still not readily available. A series of Strategic Results Projects (SRPs) related to the education and training of Indigenous students was launched by the Australian government in December 1997. As outlined by McRae *et al.* (2000, p.14), the significant messages to emerge from the Strategic Results Projects were: that it is possible to significantly improve Indigenous student learning outcomes through concerted effort; that strategies often described as conventional good practice, and which are readily portable to other similar contexts, can lead to productive results if used more intensively; and that clear targets and monitoring processes, adequate resources, and a firm belief in the prospect of success and a will to make it occur, were important (McRae *et al.*, 2000, p. 13).

More recently, the Australian Capital Territory (ACT) Government has responded to the need to address the imbalance in the educational achievements of members of the Indigenous community. In its report, *Within Reach of Us All, Services to Indigenous People, Action Plan 2002–2004*, it outlines its commitment to:

- overcoming racism and valuing diversity;
- forming genuine and ongoing partnerships with Indigenous communities;
- creating safe, supportive, welcoming and culturally inclusive education and service environments; and
- Indigenous children and young people achieving outcome equitable to the total population.

The development of genuine and ongoing partnerships between the ACT Government and Indigenous communities focuses on enhancing the work of Indigenous home/school liaison officers with Indigenous families 'to address a range of issues, including achievements, study habits, absenteeism and peer group relationships or to directly discuss with families progress towards goals articulated in individual learning plans' (ACT Government, 2005, p. 5). The report highlights the importance of a concerted and collaborative approach to Indigenous issues as well as the need for positive models of affirmation that build confidence and increase the motivation of students.

Recognition of the potential for community-based projects to build a greater sense of connectedness throughout the Indigenous and wider education community provided the catalyst for the development of the *Connecting Communities Project* offered in Canberra.

The Connecting Communities Project

The *Connecting Communities Project* emanated from the strong networks established during the Adult and Community Education (ACE)-funded *Families Learning Together* Indigenous programmes (2003–05). These programmes resulted from extensive collaboration between government and non-government agencies, staff in ACT Government and Catholic schools, parents of Indigenous students, Indigenous students, and academics from the Australian Catholic University in Canberra. The *Families Learning Together* programmes, which became known locally as the What's Up? programmes, were offered over a nine to ten-week period and aimed to strengthen the participants' literacy and numeracy skills through engagement in learning experiences that promoted a deeper understanding of Australian Indigenous traditions and culture. In some localities, *Parent Power* workshops were offered to parents who had young children either attending, or about to attend, school. The workshops provided information relevant to the early years of schooling and focused on areas related to learning, motivation, beginning reading and writing, and the development of positive behaviours.

The aims of the *Families Learning Together* Programmes were:

- to support the learning needs of Indigenous families, both parents and children, through facilitating improved literacy and numeracy skills;
- to contextualise learning through the use of appropriate community and curriculum resources, such as the local schools, the youth centre and library, to strengthen the concept of a community of learners;
- to stimulate and strengthen interest in the learning process through the provision of appropriate resources that increase relevancy and create a positive learning environment; and
- to construct learning experiences that build confidence and assist in the achievement of productive learning outcomes.

The weekly workshops focused on specific themes including work, family, tradition, recreation and community. The workshop activities encouraged the participants to become actively involved in the learning process and the facilitators emphasised confidence building, the sharing of information and development of group cohesion. The learning approach adopted throughout the *Families Learning Together* programmes catered for the differing learning styles and intelligences (Gardner, 1997) of the participants, while also strengthening their literacy and numeracy skills. Participation in a variety of workshop activities, such as mural making, boomerang throwing, jewellery making and dance increased the relevancy of the learning process and led to a deeper understanding of Indigenous arts and culture. University staff worked in collaboration with the Wiradjuri performing artists to present the workshops. An indication of the success of the workshops was that the attendance of students and adults increased as the programme activities became more known throughout the community. University pre-service teachers and a number of high-school students contributed to the programme workshops and effectively scaffolded the learning process for the younger participants. All *Families Learning Together* programmes concluded with a celebration of achievement during which the participants shared their learning experiences and outcomes with the whole school community.

In 2006, funding was obtained through the ACT Government's Community Inclusion Fund to coordinate the *Connecting Communities Project*, which comprised two components including a similar programme to the successful *Families Learning Together* programme for children and adults and a new adult education course titled *The Three Cs (Culture, Communication and Connectedness)*. The project reflected and supported the priorities and goals articulated in the Canberra Social Plan, developed by the ACT Government, and explicitly focused on securing the active participation of all members of the community, including respected elders of the Indigenous community. The project aimed to create a vibrant community of learners, which comprised adults, children, school staff, parents and other family members, in a southern suburb of Canberra. University staff worked collaboratively with members of the Indigenous community to develop and implement the teaching and learning experiences. Active participation in the learning process and increased participation of Indigenous adults in the school community were also project priorities.

Project objectives

The specific objectives of the *Connecting Communities Project* were:

- to provide a supportive group learning environment for children, adolescents, and families who may be otherwise disadvantaged due to social, economic, or other reasons;
- to encourage positive attitudes towards learning, through the provision of friendly and secure learning spaces within community settings;

- to develop new skills, attitudes, and strategies that promote engagement, independence and confidence in learning;
- to provide specialist tuition to children and adolescents situated within the most disadvantaged areas where after-school literacy and numeracy assistance might not readily be available;
- to provide parents with strategies to improve their ability to assist their children's learning; and
- to improve the transition between primary and secondary schools for young people through the formation of extended networks and stronger relationships with members of the community, for example, youth workers and Indigenous education assistants.

Project outcomes

At the end of the project, it is expected the participants will have:

- improved literacy and numeracy skills;
- heightened awareness of the cultural diversity within their local community;
- greater self-esteem and pride in the uniqueness of their own culture, within the broader Australian culture;
- built stronger relationships across and between young and aged generations;
- strengthened bonds and goodwill within the community;
- built individual and group self confidence through traditional crafts and arts-related activities; and
- broadened opportunities and working life experiences for those who participate in the project.

The *Connecting Communities Project* sought to encourage an holistic approach to learning through an integrated approach to the development of teaching and learning strategies that strengthened the sense of connectedness between families and schools. A strong emphasis on the arts as a vehicle through which to further develop cultural awareness, literacy and numeracy skills, and social skills worked successfully to engage the participants in multi-modal learning experiences. Key learning areas, such as mathematics, science and technology, were introduced into the teaching and learning programme where appropriate. The increased awareness that arises through the development of strong links between schools, families and the Indigenous community enables schools and other educational providers to respond more effectively to community needs.

Evidence of the success of the project is provided through: observation records of the participants' achievements; the level of interest demonstrated during the workshop activities; the quality of the learning outcomes overall; and the support for the workshops as articulated by members of the Indigenous and wider community. Documented evidence of achievement includes students' learning portfolios and examples of artwork, photographs and video material, all of which has been displayed and well received. The enthusiasm expressed for a continuance of the project in the second half of 2006 and interest expressed in the adult education course augurs well for a strengthening of the sense of community that has begun to develop in Canberra.

The Three Cs (Culture, Communication, and Connectedness) adult education course

A major aim of this new course is to increase opportunities for adult members of the Indigenous and non-Indigenous community, to develop new knowledge and skills that will enable them to become more proactive and confident members of their communities, especially in their local school communities. The course emphasises the development of critical literacy and communi-cation skills through a focus on furthering an understanding of cultural diversity and the management of cross-cultural conflicts. Learning is supported through the introduction of a variety of teaching and learning approaches including group discussion, cooperative learning groups, structured learning methods where appropriate, and use of information and communication technologies to access information and encourage research. Visits to community learning spaces such as: the National Gallery of Australia, the Australian Institute of Aboriginal and Torres Strait Islanders (AIATSIS), and the National Botanic Gardens, extended the learning environ-ment, increased relevance and heightened interest in learning. The inclusion of visits to local schools in the Canberra region provided opportunities for the participants to learn from others, share their experiences and build effective community networks. These have proved helpful in assisting the participants to be more confident in supporting their children's learning and to take greater pride in their Aboriginal culture. Further, through the integration of local knowledge with personal knowledge, the participants have been able to reflect upon their own learning processes and gain a deeper appreciation of the educational resources available in the wider educational community.

The development of the participants' critical thinking skills remained important throughout the course. Many of the adults did very little reading at home, preferring to engage in visual learning activities such as viewing movies and television shows. Therefore, as texts, films such as the recently released *Ten Canoes* (2006) were used to stimulate thinking and critical reflection. The depth of thought and clarity of expression exceeded expectations, indicating a sound understanding of the genre of film criticism and ability to think critically while viewing a film. Scaffolding learning through participation in the critical analysis of two very short films before viewing the *Ten Canoes* worked effectively to establish a framework through which to interpret and gain meaning from the film.

Each participant on the course was interviewed to ascertain needs and expectations and from these preliminary discussions a formal course structure emerged. A high priority for the participants was the development of a deeper understanding of Indigenous history and culture. Throughout the programme, the learning facilitators engaged in discussion with the participants to ensure the course responded appropriately to their learning needs and expectations. Where appropriate, the teaching and learning approach was modified to more aptly reflect the participants' expectations and interests. Although time consuming, this learner-centred approach to course development is essential if the participants are to assume ownership of the course. Negotiation of the course content ensured active engagement in the learning process worked effectively to build a strong community of learners. Recognition that the teaching and learning strategies were well-grounded in theory related to literacy teaching, such as experienced-based learning (Andresen, Boud and Cohen, 2000), literacy and work (Luke, 1992) and the use of visual texts in the classroom (Callow, 2006) provided a sound base for learning.

Both formal and informal assessment was conducted during the course. Formal assessment tasks included written exercises, such as writing a short film review, completing a complex form, and in some instances, developing a job application. Informal assessment included participation in structured discussions about films or books, individual contributions to discussions on topics focused on personal learning experiences, or expression of ideas related to their children's learning. Opportunities to engage in question-and-answer sessions occurred while participating in visits to national institutions such as the National Gallery of Australia. Newspaper articles and books relating to aspects of Indigenous culture proved useful in building knowledge and extending discussion.

Conclusion

A strong feature of the *Connecting Communities Project* is that it actively promotes reconciliation between members of the Indigenous and non-Indigenous communities through promoting a greater awareness and understanding of Indigenous culture throughout the wider community. Recognition of the valuable contribution made by respected members of the Indigenous community in teaching and in the development of new knowledge, skills and understandings is of significance. Overall, the project has been successful in impacting on the learning outcomes of young people and their families while fostering an appreciation of learning that is contextual, cultural and sustainable across the life span.

The two components of the *Connecting Communities Project* offered throughout 2006 have provided a friendly and stimulating learning environment for adults, young people and their families to meet in schools and in a variety of other community educational settings. This has provided many opportunities for interaction, discussion and deep engagement in learning about Indigenous traditions and culture. Expressions of support from all involved in the project are a positive outcome from this collaborative and community building process. The increased confidence and self-esteem of the participants provides further evidence of its success.

References

ACT Government, *Building our community*. The Canberra Social Plan (www.cmd.act.gov.au/socialplan/documents/Social_Plan.pdf), accessed June 2006.

ACT Government, *Within reach of us all, Services to Indigenous people*, Action Plan 2002–2004 (http://www.det.act.gov.au/), accessed January 2007.

ACT Government, *Performance in Indigenous education*. Eleventh report covering calendar year 2005. *Report to the Legislative Assembly of the Australian Capital Territory*, accessed February 2007.

Andresen, L., Boud, D. and Cohen, R. (2000) 'Experience-based learning', in G. Foley (ed), *Understanding Adult Education and Training*, 2nd edn, pp. 225–39. Sydney: Allen & Unwin.

Bourner, T., Katz, T. and Watson, D. (eds) (2000) *New Directions in Professional Higher Education*. Buckingham, UK: SHRE and Open University Press.

Bowes, J. and Hayes, A. (2004) 'Impacts on children, families and communities', in J. Bowes, *Children, Families and Communities: Contexts and consequences*, 2nd edn. Melbourne: Oxford University Press.

Broadbent, C. (1998) 'Transforming the university: tensions and opportunities for academics in a time of change', paper presented at *Australian Association of Research in Education Annual Conference*, Adelaide, November.

Broadbent, C. (2000) 'New challenges for the management of organisational change', XXVII International Congress of Psychology, Stockholm, Sweden, 23–26 July, abstracts, *International Journal of Psychology*, 35: 3–4.

Broadbent, C., Boyle, M. and Carmody, M. (2006) *Culture, Communication and Connectedness: Building social capital within the Indigenous community*. 46th National Conference, Adult Learning Australia, Melbourne, November–December.

Broadbent, C. and Boyle, M. (2004) '"What's up?" Building effective learning communities for Indigenous families'. *44th Annual Conference Bridging Cultures, Adult Learning Australia*, Glenelg, Adelaide, 18–20 November.

Bushnell, M. (2001) '"This bed of roses has thorns": cultural assumptions and community in an elementary school', *Anthropology and Education Quarterly*, 32(2): 139–66.

Callow, J. (ed) (1999) *Image Matters: Visual Texts in the Classroom*. Sydney: Primary English Teaching Association.

Chapman, J. Cartwright, P. and McGilp, E.J. (2006) *Lifelong Learning, Participation and Equity*. Lifelong Learning Book Series 5. Dordrecht: Springer.

Cox, E. (1995) 'Raising social capital', the 1995 Boyer Lectures, A Truly Civil Society, ABC Radio National, broadcast Tuesday 14 November, 8.30 a.m. (http://www.abc.net.au/rn/boyers/boyer12.htm), accessed 10 September 2006.

Epstein, J. (2001) *School, Family and Community Partnerships: Preparing Educators and Improving Schools*. Boulder, CO: Westview Press.

Frigo, T., Corrigan, M., Adams, I., Hughes, P., Stevens, M. and Woods, D. (2003) *Supporting English Literacy and Learning for Indigenous Students in the Early Years*, ACER Research Monograph No. 57. Melbourne: ACER Press.

Gardner, H. (1997) 'Multiple intelligences as a partner in school improvement', *Educational Leadership*, 55(1): 20.

Henry, K. (2006) Quoted in P. Martin, 'Indigenous deprivation a major economic problem: Treasury chief', *Canberra Times*, 3 November.

Hogue, T. (1995) 'Community based collaboration: wellness multiplied, 1994'. Columbus, OH: Oregon Centre for Community Leadership.

Howard, D. (2002) 'Family, friends and teachers: Why Indigenous students stay at or leave school', *Australian Journal of Indigenous Education*, 30(2): 8–12.

Jackson, N. (2003) 'Nurturing creativity through an imaginative curriculum', *Herdsa News*, 25(3): 21–6.

Kearns, P. (2005) *Achieving Australia as an Inclusive Learning Society. A Report on Future Directions for Lifelong Learning in Australia*. Canberra: Adult Learning Australia.

Luke, A. (1992) 'Literacy and work in new times', *Open Letter*, 3(1).

McRae, D., Ainsworth, G., Cumming, J., Hughes, P., Mackay, A., Price, K., Rowland, M., Warhurst, J., Woods, D. and Zibas, V. (2000) *Education and Training for Indigenous Students. What Works: Explorations in Improving Outcomes for Indigenous Student*. Canberra: Australian Curriculum Studies Association and National Curriculum Services, Commonwealth of Australia.

Munt, R. (2003) 'Building collaboration', *Stronger Families Learning Exchange Bulletin*, 3: 6–8.

Price, K. (2001) 'Aboriginal studies and Torres Strait islander studies', in C. Marsh (ed), *Teaching Studies of Society and Environment*, 3rd edn., Frenchs Forest, NSW: Pearson Education, pp. 293–316.

Putnam, R.D., Leonardi, R. and Nanetti, Y.N. (1993) *Making Democracy Work: Civic Traditions in Modern Italy*. Princeton, NJ: Princeton University Press.

Schuller, T., Preston, J., Hammond, C., Brassett-Grundy, A. and Bynner, J. (2004) *The Benefits of Learning: The Impact of Education on Health, Family Life and Social Capital*. London: RoutledgeFalmer.

Schwab, R.G. and Sutherland D. (2001) 'Building Indigenous learning communities', *Discussion paper No. 225*, Canberra: Centre for Aboriginal Economic Policy Research, Australian National University.

Stone, W. (2001) 'Measuring social capital', Research Paper No. 24. Melbourne: Australian Institute of Family Studies.

Sunderland, N., Muirhead, B., Parsons, R. and Holtom, D. (2004) *The Australian Consortium on Higher Education, Community Engagement and Social Responsibility, Foundation Paper*. Brisbane: Australian Consortium Project Centre, Queensland 'Boilerhouse' Community Service and Research Centre.

Sydney Film Festival (2006) *Opening Night – Ten Canoes* (http://www. sydneyfilmfestival.org/plugins/filmmanager.cgi/main/view?id=220), accessed 3 October 2006.

UNESCO (1996) *Learning: The Treasure Within. Report of the Commission on Education for the 21st Century*. Paris: UNESCO.

Vaill, P. (1996) *Learning as a Way of Being*. San Francisco: Jossey-Bass.

Wano, K. (2006) 'Reaching out to Indigenous communities: a personal and professional perspective', *Education Connect*, 6: 6–7.

Wenger, E., McDermott, R. and Snyder, W. (2002) *Cultivating Communities of Practice: A Guide to Managing Knowledge*. Boston, MA: Harvard Business School Press.

Widin, J., Norman, H., Ndaba, A. and Yasukawa, K. (2004) 'An Indigenous community learning centre to promote a culture of learning', *Adult Learning Australia 44th Annual National Conference*, Glenelg, Adelaide, South Australia.

Chapter 13

Building virtual communities: 'Youthcentral' in Victoria, Australia

David Adams

This chapter analyses, through the lens of a case study from Victoria, Australia, how the idea of community strengthening has been embedded into the institutional apparatus of a regional government. This is largely an insider's account of the emergence of a community paradigm with a focus on use of new technologies and new governance. Indeed, part of the emerging theoretical debate is an increasing emphasis on the interdependence of community with ICT and governance.

The focus in this discussion is on describing the key themes and the policy apparatus that have emerged to give public administrative form to the idea of stronger communities. Throughout the chapter links are provided to the key documents which provide the technical discussions of how the public policy and public administration of community is playing out in the State of Victoria, Australia.

Secondly, the chapter canvasses some of the policy challenges associated with governments becoming involved in the business of 'creating' community. In particular the example of an 'e' community in Victoria is examined. This case is presented to illustrate the depth of penetration of the public policy idea of community leveraging new technologies and with an eye to new forms of governance.

Overall the primary purpose of the chapter is to illustrate real-world examples of what governments are doing in this policy field, the public policy and public administration of an idea, rather than to critique it. I leave the critique of the communities' agenda to a brief concluding comment, noting here that for many people the whole idea of governments engaging in the communities' agenda is problematic.

The chapter takes the form of a brief contextual discussion of the link between new ideas and research followed by a general consideration of communities and of the approach adopted in Victoria (Part 2), followed by an account of the new Victorian 'Youthcentral' networked community initiative (Part 3). Extracts from some of the relevant DVC documents to which this chapter refers are appended.

Setting the scene: new ideas at play

Reading the scholarly literature on new trends in public policy and administration, three common themes stand out: a focus on communities; a focus on new forms of local governance and a focus on new technologies (see, for example, McConkey and Dutil, 2006; Haque, 2007; Perry, 2007; OECD, 2007). While there is much academic debate about how these trends are shifting the focus away from the 'new public management' towards more 'communitarian' orientations there is a dearth of research about what these trends actually look like on the ground.

In relation to community, for example, there has been and remains considerable international interest in the idea of how to strengthen communities and, over the past decade, many new ideas and practices have emerged (DVC, 2004a; FaCS, 2004; Gilchrist, 2004). Indeed, around the world there are 'new' government departments popping up all over the place with the word 'community' somewhere in the title. In Australia since 2002 five such entities have emerged and only last July (2006) the UK established a Department for Community and Local Government.

In relation to new forms of governance the current debate has much more focus on new relations between the centre and the local and on the future role(s) for local government as stewards of communities rather than as regulators (see for example DEMOS, 2007; UK Government, 2006, 2007).

In relation to ICT there is now an almost frenetic interest in how so-called 'web 2.0' technologies (designed to be much more interactive and user controlled – e.g. 'YouTube' and 'MySpace') can be leveraged to increase participation and the co-production of democracy (see for example CISCO, 2007).

These ideas (new approaches to place-based policies) are at the heart of the PASCAL agenda and yet a gap remains between the literature and the crucial question of how the ideas play out in particular policy settings. The research from Victoria presented in Parts 1 and 2 is an attempt to test how these ideas can be applied to improve the well-being and prosperity of young people.

Part I

In 2002 the Government of Victoria created the first department in federal Australia with a specific brief to explore the nature of community in public policy, and how the levers of a regional government could be applied to extract public value from the idea. There were four main drivers for the creation of the department:

- a sense that government was out of touch with the public and needed new ways of 'reading the pulse' of Victorians and engaging with them;
- a growing interest in the reconstituted ideas about social capital emerging from the Putnam and Coleman literatures but also from the social epidemiological literature;
- a concern that governance through functional programs was creating fragmentation and so-called 'silo' approaches to community, and that organising around people and places could generate new ideas about how to organise the planning and delivery of public value;
- a desire by the incoming Labour Government to put greater emphasis on social well-being compared to the focus on economic growth of the previous Conservative government.

The department brought together a range of people- and place-based functions from across government (Blacher, 2005, 2006) based, not around functions (such as health and education), but around the core ideas of strengthening communities, primarily through place-based strategies that explored new ways of planning and delivering services.

After four years we are now seeing four important interrelated themes consistently emerging – themes which reflect our learning to date and which may constitute the building blocks of the body of knowledge around the public administration of building stronger communities.

Importantly, these themes are not based on some predetermined deductive model. Rather, they are being built up from reflecting on practice and experiences to date. Indeed, what makes this field so interesting is that there is no model or template from which to work. We are all still exploring and learning as we go, and in doing so, developing a *public policy* of community strengthening.

The four themes are:

1 Community strengthening – This is about building active, confident and resilient communities; that is, communities that have a sustainable mix of assets (economic, human, natural, cultural) *and* strong networks that maximise the use of those assets.

2 Governance – If there is one key insight from which we have learned over the past three years, it is that governance issues and community strengthening are intertwined – the way resources are organised and delivered shapes community strength. Communities can make decisions about their futures through participatory governance arrangements. Partnerships are more likely to be active, confident and resilient. Strong networks require sound governance. This includes all the decision-making processes, policies and practices that impact on a community. Strong governance is characterised by broad and inclusive networks of decision makers utilising processes which ensure that all the interests within communities have a voice in decision-making and problem solving.

3 Place and local communities – One of the most prevalent criticisms of the existing programmatic approach to policy and service delivery is the centralisation of government decision-making and the fragmentation of services delivered on the ground. Under current administrative arrangements it is often difficult to:

- coordinate investment and service delivery at the local level;
- understand the cumulative impact of government on communities;
- involve people in decisions that affect their lives, particularly government investment in local communities; and
- adopt place-based approach in government for some issues and to develop a strategy to address them.

4 Skills and culture – A focus on community strengthening and place challenges the orthodoxy of the programme format of the public sector and the role of the public servant as the implementer of government policy through agreed policy and service delivery guidelines.

In principle, the shift is from a traditional hierarchical model to one characterised by multi-sector partnerships through which local communities have an enhanced capacity to shape directions, set priorities and control resources. This necessarily involves greater use of team-based approaches to planning, funding and delivery of services, and bringing together locally (often literally in terms of co-location) officers from various government (state, local and perhaps commonwealth) agencies working on similar objectives.

Changes of this nature need to be supported by the development of skills and leadership cultures within the public sector that are comfortable working in this environment. Communities that are more active, confident and resilient are more likely to be able to take control of their futures.

Community strengthening
There is a growing body of national and international evidence (DVC, 2005a; Lin, 2001; OECD, 2001; Vinson, 2004) that successful community strengthening strategies correlate strongly to the creation of stronger social and civic institutions, improved well-being (lower imprisonment rates, higher levels of school completion) and increased social and economic opportunities.

If community strengthening activities can contribute to buffering the impact of poverty and disadvantage for many, then it is particularly interesting that some of the strategies needed to achieve improved outcomes may not be very complex. They involve things like encouraging volunteering, investing in social infrastructure, sport, recreation and community arts facilities, and even improved streetscapes and attention to local amenities.

What this research is beginning to suggest is that investing in communities is really no more or less than an approach to prevention or early intervention, with the potential over time to be a factor in reducing the rate of increase in the demand on some of the most resource-intensive services provided by state governments.

Recently the DVC released a report tracking a range of community strengthening indicators across each of the 79 local government areas in Victoria (DVC, 2005a). What was particularly striking was the variation of these indicators from one local government area to another. For example:

- the proportion of the population who feel safe on the street alone after dark ranges from 50 per cent to 89 per cent;
- those who feel there are opportunities to have a real say on issues ranges from 41 per cent to 71 per cent of the adult population;
- parental participation in schools ranges from 44 per cent to 81 per cent;
- volunteering on a regular basis ranges from 23 per cent to 64 per cent (DVC, 2005a).

These data, a first for any jurisdiction in Australia, will provide a basis over time for tracking change and making community strength more visible as part of a more comprehensive approach to a common set of state-wide indicators of well-being in communities. They can also provide a guide for government as to where to direct its investments. For example, using the indicators we can see which communities lack strong local governance structures, which communities need assistance in increasing participation and which communities need to build their stocks of volunteers.

This raises the question of governance. While it is one thing to recognise differences in community strength between localities, it is another to create partnerships and relationships which link government investment to encouraging more active participation by individuals in their communities.

Governance
The term governance is used here in its broadest meaning; to include all the decision-making policies, processes and practices that impact on a community. This includes the internal policies and practices of the three levels of government, as well as the myriad of management committees that are associated with public institutions such as community organisations, school boards, residents' groups and business boards.

Strong governance is built through connectedness. Network theorists such as Berkman and Glass (2000) and Lin (2001) argue that healthy communities require a balance of three types of social connection:

- close personal networks;
- broader associational ties and community networks; and
- governance networks.

These different network types generate different benefits for individuals and communities (not always positive), and each provides a foundation for building the other; strong networks can give people the skills and confidence needed to participate in broader associational and community activities. This observation provided the basis for the government's recognition of the need to reform the way government agencies work with local communities; finding better ways of helping people to help themselves.

There are six key design principles which underpin reforms in changing the way government agencies interact with communities. They are:

- viewing the world through the lens of the clients, be they individuals, families or communities (*client-focused principle*);
- developing a simpler or single face of government locally (*principle of place*);
- shifting from government controlling and directing the delivery of services to government playing the role of facilitator and enabler (*principle of enabling*);
- devolving service planning and delivery to the local level (*principle of subsidiarity*);
- developing cross-sector approaches to addressing social opportunities and problems through partnerships between governments, community agencies and the corporate sector (*principle of partnership*);
- harnessing the capacity of local leaders and entrepreneurs (*principle of local capacity and ownership*). This means not just the 'usual suspects', but hearing the voices of people in addition to the peak bodies and organisations which governments usually deal with.

These principles are central to thinking at a conceptual level in relation to the changing role of government agencies in the emerging environment. The principles are not new; many received an airing through the Council of Australian Governments in the 1980s and 1990s. But for those who are public administrators the job is to give practical effect to the theory. This is a more difficult task. Put simply, the question is: how can we reorganise our structural and operational arrangements to give effect to these principles? The initial Victorian attempt at answering this question has included:

The alignment of regional boundaries of state departments into eight administrative regions. Prior to this reform each department had a set of unique regional boundaries. While they were similar, small differences meant that departments were neither coterminous with each other, nor with local government boundaries. This lack of consistency caused difficulties in establishing regional discussions within and between governments, and acted as a brake on establishing stronger working relationships at the regional level. The benefit gained from aligning the boundaries was to establish a more geographically consistent set of regional interests held by government departments and their corresponding local governments, and the creation of a structural platform for joining up at local level.

The establishment of Regional Management Forums (RMFs). Building on the boundary alignment initiative the government introduced a new form of regional governance to Victoria; Regional Management Forums (RMFs). These forums, which meet quarterly, include state departmental managers and local government chief executive officers, along with a departmental secretary as regional champion. The role of the RMFs is to examine critical issues facing the region, and to encourage cooperation between departments, and with councils and statutory authorities. Although they have only been in operation for a short period of time RMFs have already commenced a range of place-based initiatives, as well as commencing strategic projects designed to improve information sharing and joint planning processes at the local level.

A commitment to the greater use of team-based approaches. A Fairer Victoria included a commitment to develop Community Project Teams; a new type of administrative arrangement designed to deliver policies in a local setting that require the involvement of more than one department or sector. Community Project Teams are about creating the administrative flexibility needed to engage communities on complex issues and work with them collaboratively, and achieving this aim within existing public sector management, administration and accountability frameworks.

Local presence staff where we are increasing numbers of staff located in local communities across Victoria to work face-to-face with communities.

A focus on broadly based community consultation, including groups often excluded, such as culturally and linguistically diverse communities. An example of how we do this is through 'In the Community' forums where senior staff from the DVC regularly visit communities to canvass priority issues. Over twenty forums have been held so far, resulting in significant investment through DVC grants.

Community-level planning and priority setting. This is a key role for local government, for example in developing community plans. The DVC is rationalising the range of planning requirements imposed on local councils, boosting the importance of community planning, and aligning councils' planning and reporting with that of state government departments.

Strategic grant-making. All grants are being reconfigured to provide three types of supports into local communities: planning, to form partnerships and develop good strategies; capacity building, such as leadership investments; and infrastructure investments, such as community facilities.

Direct community involvement in governance, for example in priority setting, in the design of investment strategies, in delivery, in managing, in reporting. This is happening in the community renewal strategies and in the approach to indigenous communities.

The key point here is that building stronger communities requires us to reorient our focus from state-level programs to local communities, and in doing so to give greater priority than in the past to developing the capacity of communities, creating more opportunities for them to participate in priority setting and shaping local investment in infrastructure and services. Together, these initiatives are establishing a platform for simplifying and strengthening governance arrangements for a range of significant public institutions, not least of all state and local government. They create the conditions for stronger communities and to focus the scale and scope of government activity towards local communities, a focus on people and places.

Place and local communities

The current approach to public administration is organised primarily around portfolios and programs, rather than people and communities (Adams and Hess, 2001). This makes government easy for those on the inside to operate, but hard for communities to understand and work with. Organising around communities requires a rethink of many traditional public policy and administration settings. Three observations can be made in this context.

First, it is important to focus on communities, because they are places and spaces where people create identity, trust and a sense of belonging; they are where people can turn to others for support; they are where people learn to make judgements about the world; they are where people work and play and live their lives. Putnam would say that they are places where people bond, bridge and link. Secondly, the scale at which community strengthening interventions appear to work best is relatively small, at the level of a neighbourhood, a suburb or a town. Thirdly, by communities we should include communities of interest and identity as well as traditional communities of place. For example, the SMS texting world of young people can be considered a community. Why? Because it is a space where young people form relations, make judgements about the world, and turn to others for support. Those in public administration with a long history of program thinking need to better understand these new communities in order to be able better to engage with them.

Skills and culture

Delivering these types of interventions requires a rethink of how we organise and operate as public-sector agencies. It also highlights the need to focus on the cultures of our organisations, and reflect on the skills and norms which are valued by the leaders and managers of our departments and agencies. Increasingly we need to reward the capacity to work collaboratively, both internally and with external partners, no less and perhaps even more than we reward the more explicit displays of expertise which often pass for high-quality policy advice.

We need to reward those who go the extra mile in assisting people to find their way through the incredibly opaque maze that is often the public face of government agencies. And we need to go out and listen to the views of people wanting to participate in public debate, using consultative processes which suit those people rather than those that are convenient to us. These characteristics are not evident in large complex organisations which comprise the public-sector agencies.

The DVC is attempting this change particularly in the way in which both managers and other staff have developed the roles of our local presence teams; those in the department who work actively with local communities.

Essentially these teams have four roles:

- *Navigating government.* This role includes assisting people and organisations to better understand how to access DVC and other government funding programmes; an orientation by staff to be door openers rather than gatekeepers.
- *Brokering.* Working with individuals and community organisations to facilitate solutions to problems by bringing together appropriate resources from across government.

- *Facilitating investment.* This involves working with both communities and departments to try to coordinate the flow of investments in ways that make sense from the perspective of the projects or activities being considered, rather than being stymied by the artificial silos created by different funding programmes, with differing closing dates for application and different criteria often for similar programmes.
- *Partnerships.* To undertake these activities through creating networks which encourage the development of sustained collaborations and partnerships in local communities.

Part II

While critics and scholars are still debating the merits of social capital and the efficacy of the communities agenda, governments are now moving rapidly in the space of virtual communities. To show what governments are doing to help facilitate community formation, especially in new suburbs, the *Youthcentral* project in Victoria illustrates how ICT can be used to 'create' a community, not just a website. Again, the policy implications of governments being in these spaces are, in my view, quite profound.

Youthcentral, in its most basic form, is a website for young people, but importantly, the DVC has supported young people in creating a more attractive community to them out of it. This is reflected in its exponential growth. It enables government to explore how technology can be shaped to strengthen communities and tackle the many issues associated with how IT can be a source of both inclusion and exclusion. *Youthcentral* is therefore also part of transforming the way government thinks and works. For many young people the role of traditional place-based communities is being replaced by virtual communities such as *Youthcentral* and the SMS text-messaging communities.

The important issue about communities is not to debate endlessly the many types of communities – place, interest, professional, transient, mobile, professional, virtual, etc. – but to look at what features we value in the notion of community and how the levers of government can support those features. Communities are valued because they are:

- shapers of identity, belonging, pride, and self-esteem;
- a reference point for judgements;
- a site for service provision and/access to other services;

- spaces in which we can turn to others for support;
- a source of innovation and creativity; and
- meeting places and spaces, especially for disengaged or excluded people.

Youthcentral was designed with these valued community features in mind. Of course, business astutely worked out some time ago that communities (including virtual communities) are also markets, so we can add this as another feature, and indeed one that young people value highly.

The DVC is particularly focused on promoting better associational networks – sport, recreation, arts, culture, etc. – as well as concentrating on new ways of connecting people to associations and connecting associations to the key institutions of society, such as civic participation. To use a UK phrase, *Youthcentral* is also a strategy aimed at 'renewing the civic realm', that is, encouraging young people to be more active in their local communities and creating the incentives and means of doing so. So *Youthcentral* is one strategy to help create an inclusive community for young people, and to create links to broader social and civic engagement.

Governments worldwide are seeking effective ways to engage the youth demographic in policy making and social participation.The United Nations World Youth Report (May 2005) states: 'one example that seems to reverse the decline in traditional participation and civic engagement by youth is Internet-based activities'.

The rise of the internet as a dominant medium and two-way communication channel for young people has presented particular challenges and opportunities for government in relating to young people as a unique cohort in the community. The *Youthcentral* story demonstrates that a shift in the traditional service-delivery business model has been necessary to attract and retain young people's interest and attention. There are two possible reasons for this: the internet is fast becoming the dominant medium of choice for young people; and there is a different form of community at work for young people – their sense of community is expressed differently and we have to understand it through their lens.

As a snapshot of characteristics and behaviours of the eGeneration in techno-literacy terms, we note the following with respect to young people:

- They are in their comfort zone online: arguably the most

confident, tech-savvy, marketing-wary audience on the net, but hard to capture.

- They are embracing new technologies with passion, but for what purpose? They are downloading, gaming, chatting, texting, streaming, blogging, vlogging, trading, and podcasting to communicate, create community and create and maintain social networks.
- 96 per cent of all 16–29-year-olds last year in Australia have used the internet.
- Most access it from home.
- There is almost equal subscription to broadband in Victoria for rural and regional (42 per cent) as metro (45 per cent) subscribers.
- Latest studies show that it is their favourite information source: young Australians aged 10–25 rank the internet highly as a primary source of information for general issues and concerns.
- Next to family and friends, research shows that young people turn to the Net as a major source of advice and support: it is immediate, accessible and anonymous.
- It is their preferred source for jobs in particular.
- They are more likely to use the internet to source information than are any other age group in the community.
- In 2006 a Nielsen Net ratings survey found that 75 per cent of 15–17-year-olds use the internet for 5–15 hours a week.
- The rise of the internet as a user-driven content distributor is replacing traditional distribution methods as broadcasting moves from mass to niche channel.
- Two massively successful phenomena demonstrate this:
- YouTube.com: one year ago the creators of this phenomenon were working in a shabby office above a pizza shop. Now they are billionaires, because they have offered people 15 seconds of fame. YouTube.com is one of the most popular sites on the Web.
- MySpace tells a similar story, with user-driven control of content.
- As noted earlier, young people are also increasingly seeing the web as a medium for civic engagement as eCitizens:
- Young people are using the internet to gather information, express themselves and exercise power as pre-voting and voting citizens.
- The internet is intrinsically democratic. It engenders new skills, habits, protocols and forms of participation. It is subversive and

non-linear, not top down. It can create community easily, and young people recognise this.

- The internet has created an experimental space in which elements of contemporary citizenship are being refreshed, reshaped and redefined, and where two-way communication is the norm.
- Young people are attracted to innovative networks of civic connection.
- Young people are the first to recognise that the internet provides new forms of civic communication that will be ubiquitous within a generation from now.
- Peer-to-peer networks are available where views can be exchanged.
- Also available are discussion opportunities where young people have evidence that other people are listening to what they say.
- The challenge for government is to appeal to them in this space. How have we sought to do that in Victoria? The framework involves:
  - emphasis on peer-based content;
  - the embedding of young people within the governance model;
  - commitment to train and develop the skill base of diverse young people to ensure that they can contribute;
  - being both intensely local and global at the same time;
  - making it an enjoyable experience.

Youthcentral is built on a solid platform of voluntary youth participation, with the direct involvement of over 3,000 young people to date from all over Victoria. The demand is rapidly growing. Young people carry both paid and voluntary roles as writers, editors, mentors, trainers, reporters, designers, consultants, testers and more.

Youthcentral's content and training-based model of youth participation was designed to support DVC's place-based community-strengthening agenda. We have discovered that *Youthcentral's* participation model maps very effectively onto this agenda, because the internet for this audience is an ideal place-based information and community-building tool.

In e-service delivery terms *Youthcentral* seeks to provide convenient information pathways to assist young people when faced with life issues such as accessing training and finding employment, moving away from home, health and lifestyle decisions, connecting to events and services, and networking in their communities. User surveys have shown that the website is assisting young people to build their personal capacity, and to address some of the key drivers that affect their life chances, such as

- exclusion from the job market;
- education and training issues;
- health and wellbeing-related enquiries; and
- social networking capacity and civic participation.

This is not the only reason why *Youthcentral* is attracting a user base of 28,000–30,000 unique users per month. We think that the model is working so far because *Youthcentral* has grown essentially two kinds of interconnecting communities that young people value:

- The virtual user community who read and comment on one another's contributions, and who regularly return to the site to source the pages.
- The real community of young people participating all over the state, who have signed up for the training and development programmes which lead them into paid positions as content producers and coordinators. These young people (editorial team members and roving reporters) meet regularly to discuss and make decisions about the site. They are the key governing body – they own the product to a large extent.

It is the integration of online technology and internet communications, coupled with offline training and skill development activities, that is, connecting young people to government, their communities and each other.

Conclusion

The communities agenda internationally continues to pick up pace, driven by the pragmatic objective of governments wanting better services on the one hand and a better ability to understand and shape communities on the other.

Governments internationally are increasingly exploring this new policy space around communities. This chapter presented the basic logic of how and why this is happening. My purpose has been to illustrate the breadth and pace of action that is under way, much of it hidden from view. For many governments this is still a social venture-capital experiment.

It is, however, important to acknowledge that the communities agenda internationally is hotly contested. I have not canvassed the many critiques in this chapter. There are five main lines of critique:

- It is all a scam, glossing over the evils of capitalism and oppression of the poor.
- Community might have agency but we cannot really understand it sufficiently to warrant investment of public resources.
- The debate is now so muddled and politically appropriated by the left and right that it no longer has any currency.
- Government has made and will continue to make a mess of it; community strengthening should be left to families/the market/NGOs/local government/all of the above.
- Community is often a site of oppression.
- It is a form of social engineering by stealth.
- Cause and effect are tenuous and diffuse; the evidence at best ambiguous.

These critiques all have some efficacy; many governments and scholars have over-enthused and over-promised about communities. As a rhetorical political construction of government the idea of community has been well used by all sides of politics, and is not a panacea for structural inequality in society.

The communities' agenda continues to grow heuristically and exponentially as a new policy field, and needs to be the subject of more rigorous analysis as there are many implications for governments in moving into the communities agenda. Five are of particular significance to the PASCAL focus on place governance, social capital and learning.

Functional vs. population organising
First, the agenda throws out a challenge to the dominance of the functional mode of organising. To date Western public administration based on the Weberian model of rationality has been spectacularly successful in supporting the rapid growth of liberal democratic capitalist states. The organisation of public policy and its administration into functions (such as health and education) has been an efficient form of administrations enabling the growth of specialist forms of organising and specialist bodies of expertise. But it has come at a cost. Population and place-based policies and outcomes are rarely the sum of their constituent parts. The communities' agenda provides an alternative way of organising many public services – for example a shift from functional output-based funding to place or issues-based outcomes funding.

It has always been a historical nuance that while democracy is organised around place (electorates and parliaments), public policy and its administration are primarily organised around functions. The complexity of coordinating multi-functional approaches may well be at a point where the disadvantages outweigh the advantages.

Community vs. professional knowledge

Second, the communities' agenda challenges the dominance of professional expertise and the simplistic notion that community knowledge can simply be 'tapped' through consultation and fed into centralist policy processes. The communities' agenda has much more of a constructivist epistemological underpinning, that values tacit and historical knowledge to a greater extent than the rationality of professional expertise. The communities' agenda posits, for example, the importance of co-production of knowledge and the importance of iterative and inductive forms of reasoning to informing policy and its administration (see for example Stilgoe, Irwin and Jones, 2006).

Public value

Third, the agenda helps redefine the important idea of public value. To date the idea of public value has tended to focus on functional outcomes (better health and education for example) rather than on broader outcomes such as trust, reciprocity, happiness and supportive networks. As Moore (1995) and others have argued, public value is about what the public value, not about outputs and bureaucratically defined outcomes. The agenda highlights the active role of governance. In much of the writing on public administration the focus has been on administration as a consequential organisational issue rather being central to the co-production of policy. The challenge is to embrace new forms of local governance that embed the value of community knowledge and which focus on the place/space-level outcomes rather than simply a multitude of functional outcomes. One of reasons that the recent outcomes focus in the public sector has failed to deliver significant public value is because of the mistaken assumption that the accumulated functional outcomes of government interventions will constitute societal-level outcomes.

Needs vs. assets

Fourthly, the agenda challenges the traditional public policy paradigm of needs and services. This paradigm, which is especially strong in social policy, contrasts with the communities agenda which has an assets and opportunities framework. Youthcentral emerged because ICT connectivity is a potential community asset that can be exploited by governments, communities and markets to create opportunities (e.g. access to skills) and mitigate risks (e.g.

social exclusion). The communities' agenda commences not with the individual or the family or with specific functions but with the individual and family in a context of institutions, networks and the relations that are formed.

The policy response to a public policy risk (such as security of energy supply) or an opportunity (such as social innovation through community enterprises) should begin with an understanding of the relative strength of the community and the potential for existing assets to be mobilised as a response. Those assets include both endogenous and exogenous resources with the public policy focus being on how governments can build and utilise community network capacity (as with *Youthcentral*) as a key strategy.

The future of local institutions
The logical extension of the communities' agenda is to privilege those local institutions that can be close to the people, democratically responsible, general purpose and responsive to local risks and opportunities. In principle this pushes towards a greater role for local governments; indeed they can and should be the stewards of communities. Increasingly we are also seeing the emergence of new hybrid social institutions which have both network and institutional characteristics. These include, for example, catchment management authorities; growth area authorities; and public—private hybrids and regional development bodies. Such entities tend to have a place/community focus and operate at the regional and sub-regional level. Precisely because they can be simultaneously institution-like (e.g. reproduce the conditions of their own existence) and network-like (nimble and able to change form quickly) they may become a preferred form of future organising. In doing so they can sit uncomfortably with the old command and control model of public administration while at the same time sit very neatly with network governance models and with the idea of partnership-based models of co-producing new forms of democratic engagement using new technologies.

Entities such as PASCAL have an important international role in observing and analysing these new developments around community, around governance and around new technologies – to build better theory and to understand better the policy implications.

References

ABS (Australian Bureau of Statistics) (2000) *Measuring Social Capital: Current Collections and Future Directions*, Discussion Paper, November.

Canberra (http://www.abs.gov.au/websitedbs/D3110122.NSF/0/6CD8B1F3F 270566ACA25699F0015A02A).

Adams D. and Hess M. (2001) 'Community in public policy: fad or foundation?', *Australian Journal of Public Administration*, 60 (2),13–24.

Adams, D. and Blacher, Y. (2007) 'Working together for stronger Victorian communities', in S. Parker and N. Gallagher (eds), *The Collaborative State*. London: DEMOS.

Berkman, L.F. and Glass, T. (2000) 'Social integration, social networks, social support, and health', in L. F. Berkman and I. Kawachi (eds), *Social Epidemiology*. Oxford: Oxford University Press.

Blacher, Y. (2005) 'Changing the way government works', speech given to Engaging Communities 2005. Brisbane: United Nations Conference.

Blacher, Y. (2006) 'Changing the way government works', *Public Administration Today*, January–March, 3: 8–42.

CISCO (2007) *The Connected Republic 2.0*. Sydney.

DEMOS (2007) *The Collaborative State*. London: DEMOS.

DVC (Department for Victorian Communities) (2004a) *Changing the Way Government Works: New Interests, New Arrangements*. Melbourne: Department for Victorian Communities.

DVC (2004b) *Indicators of Community Strengthening in Victoria*. Melbourne: Department for Victorian Communities (http://www.dvc.vic.gov.au/spar.htm).

DVC (2005a) *Indicators of Community Strength at Local Government Area Level in Victoria*. Melbourne: Department for Victorian Communities.

DVC (2005b) *Indicators of Community Strength in Melton: A Discussion Paper for the Caroline Springs Partnership*. Melbourne: Department for Victorian Communities.

FaCS (2004) *Stronger Families and Community Strategy, 2004–9*. Canberra: Department of Families and Community Services (http://www.facs.gov.au/internet/facsinternet.nsf/aboutfacs/programs/sfsc-sfcs.htm).

Geddes, M. and Benington, J. (eds) (2001) *Local Partnership and Social Exclusion in the European Union: New Forms of Social Governance?* London: Routledge.

Gilchrist, A. (2004) 'Developing the well-connected community', in H.

McCarthy, P. Miller and P. Skidmore, *Network Logic. Who Governs in an Interconnected World?* London: DEMOS (http://www.demos.co.uk/catalogue/networks/).

Haque, M. (2007) 'Revisiting the new public management', *Public Administration Review*, 67(2): 179–82.

Hess, M. (2003) 'Governance and knowledge in the post-market state', *Canberra Bulletin of Public Administration*, 109: 33–6.

Lin, N. (2001) *Social Capital: A Theory of Social Structure and Action*. Cambridge: Cambridge University Press.

McConkey, M. and Dutil, P. (2006) *New Directions: The Top Ten Topics in Public Administration Scholarship: An International Perspective*. Toronto: Institute of Public Administration of Canada.

Moore, M. (1995) *Creating Public Value: Strategic Management in Government*. New Haven, CT: Harvard University Press.

ODPM (Office of the Deputy Prime Minister) (2004) *2002/3 Progress Report on Local Strategic Partnerships in Neighbourhood Renewal*. London: ODPM.

ODPM (Office of the Deputy Prime Minister) (2005) *Local Strategic Partnerships: Shaping their Future*. London: ODPM.

OECD (Organisation for Economic Co-operation and Development) (2001) *The Well-being of Nations: The Role of Human and Social Capital*. Paris: OECD (http://www1.oecd.org/publications/e-book/9601011E.PDF).

OECD (Organisation for Economic Co-operation and Development) (2007) *Vienna Action Statement on Partnerships*. Paris: LEED Forum.

Perry, J. (2007) 'Democracy and the new public service', *American Review of Public Administration*, 37(1): 3–16.

Productivity Commission (2003) *Social Capital: Reviewing the Concept and Its Policy Implications*. Melbourne: Productivity Commission.

Stilgoe, J., Irwin, A. and Jones, K., (eds) (2006) *The Received Wisdom: Opening Up Expert Advice*. London: DEMOS.

UK Government (2006) *Strong and Prosperous Communities White Paper*. London, October.

UK Government (2007) *The Local Government White Paper: Making it Happen: The Implementation Plan*. London, January.

Victoria (2001) *Growing Victoria Together. Innovative State. Caring Communities*. Melbourne: Department of the Premier and Cabinet.

Victoria (2005) *A Fairer Victoria: Creating Opportunity and Addressing Disadvantage*. Melbourne: Victorian Government.

Vinson, T. (2004) *Community Adversity and Resilience: The Distribution of Social Disadvantage in Victoria and New South Wales and the Mediating Role of Social Cohesion*. Melbourne: Jesuit Social Services.

Chapter 14

Building capacity for rural health: the role of boundary crossers in coalition maturity for partnerships with external agents

Sue Kilpatrick, Stuart Auckland, Susan Johns and Jessica Whelan

Introduction

The concept of partnership has entered policy rhetoric and is urged as good practice in a variety of domains, including health. Rural communities tend to have fewer resources available for the provision of services such as health than their metropolitan counterparts, and so could be expected to benefit from partnerships with external agencies. Indicators of coalition maturity for working in partnership with external agents in order to build stronger communities are distilled from the group development and partnership research literature and considered in the light of the experiences of the University Department of Rural Health in community engagement. The chapter draws on experiences of two rural community coalitions working to plan and negotiate health service provision. The coalitions were analysed against the indicators. A key indicator of maturity and readiness for working in partnership with external agents is related to the behaviour of 'boundary crossers'. Boundary crossers are defined as people who move freely between two or more domains and who understand the values, cultures and language, and have the trust, of both. Domains can be within a community or be the community and an external sector. Community health professionals, especially those in senior positions, often act as boundary crossers between the community and broader domains such as regional/state health services or policy, although other community members can fill the role. Other key indicators of coalition maturity for working in partnership with external agents include local leadership that empowers the community, a willingness of community coalitions to take risks and mould opportunities to meet their vision, and a culture of critical reflection and evaluation of past actions.

This chapter analyses the impact of boundary-crossing behaviour on community readiness and partnerships with external agents that are intended to build rural community capacity to plan and negotiate health service provision. It is argued that the characteristics and modus operandi of boundary crossers who are members of rural community coalitions affect the level of maturity of the coalitions and community readiness to work with external agents. An understanding of the characteristics and modus operandi of boundary crossers provides valuable insights for external agents in designing their approach to partnerships that build rural community capacity for health.

Background

Community participation in rural health services in Tasmania is growing, driven by the community sector and emerging community engagement agendas of stakeholders such as governments and universities. Often evidence of partnership arrangements with both internal and external agencies are prerequisites of funding.

Rural health in Tasmania is dominated by state government-owned facilities providing a range of health services, supplemented by several services operated under agreements between the three tiers of government. The University Department of Rural Health, Tasmania (UDRH) conducts a variety of community engagement projects in collaboration with rural communities.

Much of the UDRH's rural community support activity involves direct engagement with volunteer-based community health advisory committees administered, in most cases, under the auspices of agencies such as local government. The aim of these committees is to formulate strategies to address community health and health service needs. The scope of their work varies, but virtually all committee constitutions, for example, have a collaboration clause. The UDRH provides support activities such as strategic planning exercises, mentorship for writing grant applications, community needs assessments and information brokerage. In the course of the UDRH's work, it has been noticed that some community members who also had roles in local health services and had good links to other internal and external groups/agencies influenced the way the organisation engaged with its communities, and arguably, the quality of the outcomes. These people were frequently health service managers, though some were teachers, private health professionals or local government representatives.

Community coalition maturity and partnerships with external agents

Effective partnership harnesses the contributions of local partners and external agencies (Billett, Clemans, and Seddon, 2005). Our previous research in non-health contexts in rural communities has demonstrated that for external agencies, 'the trick is to partner effectively with the communities to assist them to utilise and develop their social capital so they can respond to change' (Kilpatrick and Loechel, 2004: 15). Social capital is defined as 'a set of resources that resides in the relationships among people and allows them to share their knowledge and skills' (Kilpatrick and Falk, 2003: 499), that is simultaneously drawn on and reproduced in collaborative action.

Many frameworks for assessing community group/coalition efficacy, maturity or readiness for working in partnership draw on social capital. The frameworks apply to partnerships for a variety of purposes: education (Billett, Clemans, and Seddon, 2005; Kilpatrick et al., 2002), natural resource management (Pretty and Ward, 2001), participation in local governance (Cuthill and Fein, 2005) and health (Johns, Kilpatrick and Whelan, 2006). Social capital is a community asset that influences community well-being, along with natural, physical, financial and human capital (Pretty and Ward, 2001). These are 'transformed by policy, processes and institutions to give desirable outcomes such as...better health' (Pretty, 1999: 225). People and institutions are the means through which community assets are operationalised.

Indicators of coalition maturity for external partnerships

A framework for building the capacity of community coalitions which draws on an extensive review of the literature (Foster-Fishman et al., 2001) includes the creation of positive external relationships, but restricts this to relationships with other community sectors, and is silent on relationships with agencies outside the community. We have previously analysed the maturity of partnerships between rural institutions (schools) and their communities (Kilpatrick et al., 2002) and developed indicators of partnership maturity which we have applied to partnerships between rural health facilities and their communities (Johns, Kilpatrick, and Whelan, 2006). In that research, the outcome of a mature, effective partnership was found to be a sense of community ownership of the health service as a rural community hub, bringing together physical, human and social capital resources. Here, we take the indicators we developed and consider them alongside other frameworks and indicators of coalition maturity and/or community readiness. We develop a set of indicators for rural community coalition maturity to partner with external agents for the purpose of planning and negotiating health and wellbeing services. The indicators and their derivation from the various frameworks are shown in the Appendix.

Johns, Kilpatrick, and Whelan (2006) identified an additional indicator of effective partnerships between rural communities and health services in local health managers. They often empower the community by employing a community development approach, and actively foster integration between health services and community. Cuthill and Fein (2005) support an empowerment approach to collaboration that 'begins within the community itself' (p. 75); however, they point out that power imbalances mean that the community is rarely able to achieve this. Local health managers are very well placed to empower the community from the inside because they understand both the community and external agency domains; and can thus be seen as boundary crossers.

Boundary crossers

'Boundary crossers'[1] were key players in development and operation of internal–external partnerships in our previous research in rural communities (Kilpatrick *et al.*, 2002). There, boundary crossers were those who spoke the language of both institution and community cultures, had the trust of both, and provided a key link between them. The boundary crossers crossed internal community boundaries; some also crossed outside the boundaries of the community and assisted in bringing external resources to rural partnerships. Some, but not all, were employed by a local institution (school) which was part of a large multi-site agency.

Roles similar to our concept of boundary crossers have been described, and termed boundary spanners (e.g. Williams, 2002), community organisers (Sutherland *et al.*, 1998), brokers and mediators. The role of broker or mediator, identified for example by Taylor (2000) in government-facilitated community development, calls for individuals or institutions who stimulate the exchange of information and make connections across boundaries. The role of 'knowledge brokers' in public service agencies such as health is to bring together those involved in the sometimes culturally and philosophically disparate fields of theory and practice (Canadian Health Services Research Foundation, 2003). Boundary spanners in the organisational literature build bridges that link the organisation to its environment and 'serve critical communicative roles, such as bridges for bringing distinct discourses together, cultural guides to make discourses of the "other" more explicit, and change agents for potentially reshaping participants' discourses' (Buxton, Carlone, and Carlone, 2005).

Boundary crossers play a similar role by linking discourses, through an understanding of the language, values and culture of two 'domains'. They also build relationships and help find common ground. Where they differ from brokers or mediators is that boundary crossers are a part of two 'domains'; for example, in the context of this chapter, the community and the health service, or the local government and the community.

Rural health professionals as boundary crossers

Rural health professionals' lives have been observed to be integrated into rural society, making it difficult to separate the personal from the professional (Lauder et al., 2006). They are thus often 'boundary crossers'. Lauder and colleagues acknowledge the role of rural nurses as brokers within their communities in facilitating information flows, for example between the healthcare professions and patients.

Many health professionals in rural Australia are employed by government. Cavaye (1999) proposes a virtuous circle of contact between communities and public agencies to build community capacity. He argues that the role of government service delivery should be expanded to include community capacity building. Cuthill and Fein (2005) note that there is a role for local government in building capacity of citizens to undertake collaborative local action for a sustainable community. Combining rural health professionals' capacity and willingness to boundary-cross, and the urgings of Cavaye and others that public agencies engage in community capacity building, we asked: what is the role of rural health professionals in spanning the discourse boundary between the community and external agencies, and in brokering relationships and finding common ground between communities and external agencies?

THE DATA

Our data come from a pilot project that used multi-method, multi-site techniques to investigate effective health service–community partnerships in rural Australia. The methodology comprised case studies of good practice in two small Tasmanian rural communities, Deloraine and Southern Midlands, centred on the Oatlands township, and input from stakeholders through a project reference group. The two sites were selected to represent differences in terms of community characteristics (composition of the community, history of partnerships); however, both feature a health facility operated by the state government, each servicing about 5,500 people. Deloraine has a district hospital which recently underwent a major redevelopment, as well as the Meander Valley Centre for Health and Wellbeing, located on the hospital site. In Oatlands, the Midlands Multi-Purpose Health Centre was established through the efforts of a local Council-driven steering committee in response to increasing aged care needs within the municipality and an ongoing threat of hospital closure.

Data were collected from three sources: individual and group interviews with relevant health service staff and community representatives, written documentation, and observation. Interviews were audiotaped and later transcribed. Transcripts were analysed manually for themes and two in-depth case studies were prepared.[2]

Characteristics and modus operandi of boundary crossers

Each community had several people or organisations with the ability to cross boundaries between community and external agencies. These people were current or former employees of local and/or state government agencies. In Deloraine, the hospital's Director of Nursing (DON) links the two levels of government, because he is also an elected councillor. The Chair of the community-driven Meander Valley Centre for Health and Wellbeing committee is another boundary crosser, employed by the state education department. In Oatlands, a former local council employee played a key boundary-crossing role in establishing the Midlands Multi Purpose Health Centre (MMPHC), while the current council General Manager played a hands-on role in negotiating a partnership between the council and the state health service (Tas Ambulance and the MMPHC) to enhance ambulance services in the region.

The skills, knowledge and networks of these people in drawing on and building community resources and facilitating interaction with external agencies are important in helping to secure resources for their communities. These boundary crossers all live in the community and see themselves first as community members, in addition to their professional roles. They are actively involved in the social and economic life of the community, have the ability to see and appreciate multiple perspectives because of their involvement in multiple groups and agencies and are committed to working in partnership.

In terms of their modus operandi, the boundary crossers identified in our research were deliberate and strategic in the way they operated, consciously building bridges within the local community, and between the local community and external agents. They used their formal position as government employees in multiple ways to facilitate greater community ownership of its health needs:

> So I don't see myself as the council representative I see myself as a community player who can tap into council resources for good and ... *that's* how I see *the DON* ... and I don't think that we would say sorry this has gone beyond my brief because that's not the way that we operate. (Community Development worker employed by Meander Valley council)

Utilising a community development approach, boundary crossers have the ability to recognise the capacity of the community in terms of partnership readiness, and to build on that: 'so it's all about finding that structure and how the groups work'. Boundary crossers work with community groups to identify and articulate needs and issues for which joint solutions can be developed, and gradually upskill and empower others, rather than doing it for them. Using their informal and formal networks, boundary crossers help to match solutions to community health and wellbeing needs to available funding sources, helping the community to change or shift focus as necessary in order to meet funding criteria.

Boundary-crossing behaviour impacts on community readiness through most or all of the indicators identified earlier, and particularly through empowering leadership, risk taking and moulding opportunities, and evaluation and reflective learning.

Empowering leadership

The ability and confidence of community members to leverage health services for their communities is an overarching capacity-building strategy. It is underpinned by the need to 'get your facts straight – know what's going on'. In both sites boundary crossers assist community groups to identify and analyse health needs, and plan initiatives to meet them. While they coordinate data collection and write funding submissions, a key priority for effective boundary crossing is to skill others to undertake these roles and give them confidence to use new skills.

Working with the Meander Valley Centre for Health and Wellbeing committee, the Deloraine Hospital DON was firmly committed to skilling others to undertake leadership roles:

> How about we encourage other people here to have a go at this … I can help you identify the grants, I'll help you write the submissions, but you work with me and eventually you'll get up some skills, I'm sure, and you're all smart people.

This developed a community leadership culture, while also contributing towards sustainability of the committee and increased capacity to engage with external agents, because there are multiple drivers.

Boundary crossers have the ability to see the bigger picture, and assist communities to align their initiatives with existing or proposed government services or external sources of funding. However, they are not always directly involved in these negotiations because of their role as government employees. Instead they assist community groups by identifying which bureaucrats to target and how to present their proposal in order to ensure a positive outcome:

> I certainly assisted the committee on who to speak to and what to ask and what sort of information to provide … What we wanted to do was say to the *state health* department, and this was being a bit strategic, is we've got money, we've got plans, we've actually come up with a design for a facility and we want to build it on the hospital site to complement the services that you are doing. *(Deloraine Hospital DON, regarding the location of the Centre for Health and Wellbeing)*

Negotiations were facilitated because of the skills, knowledge and external networks of the Chair of the Centre for Health and Wellbeing committee, herself a state government employee.

Partnerships mandated by external agencies may develop more slowly as they try to find a balance between meeting pre-established terms of reference and playing a meaningful and purposeful role in community health and wellbeing. In Oatlands, the site manager of the MMPHC assisted members of the mandated community advisory committee to explore new roles and alternative sources of power which saw them lobbying government ministers about a range of issues, including staffing, and the development of a new laundry for the MMPHC:

> The community advisory committee made some strong approaches to the minister and other people and now we have our laundry, but many hospitals don't have that. *(hospital business support manager)*

Buoyed by this success, a member of the community advisory committee noted that:

> When you are tied to the council or the state government it makes decisions hard, so we went to both of them for help but we could make our own decisions…

Risk taking and moulding opportunities

Effective boundary crossers build trust through their own engagement with the community, both personally and professionally. At the same time, their high level of trust in others (staff as well as other community members) encourages these people to seek and develop opportunities for the benefit of the community. A Deloraine Hospital employee, who has developed partnerships with external funding and service delivery bodies to address mental health issues, describes how:

> I'm trusted to do what I'm employed to do and there isn't that checking, it's very positive, and I was welcomed, and just to be trusted to do what I'm employed to do and given that autonomy and freedom to do, that is – look, I can excel in my work.

There are a number of examples of how boundary crossers have assisted the community to initiate, plan and develop projects to meet local health needs while at the same time moulding their plans to meet the requirements of government or other funding bodies. Because of transport issues and the need to provide for its aged population, the Oatlands community needs a dedicated ambulance service with good local knowledge, available 24 hours a day. Tas Ambulance was not in a position to fully fund such a service. The hands-on boundary-crossing behaviour of the local council general manager saw the negotiation of a partnership between the Council and two branches of the state health service (the MMPHC and Tas Ambulance). The partnership combines community resources with state health department funding, in a unique arrangement where volunteer drivers are paid by the council:

> There was a bit of a mismatch where Tas Ambulance has taken on responsibility for the vehicle, all the equipment and the training, we *the council* recruit and pay the drivers...the third party is the MMPHC, who provide the nurses and doctors to sit in it.

In this case, pre-existing relationships established with the same senior health department personnel some years before during the establishment of the MMPHC assisted in negotiating this new partnership.

In Deloraine, the DON worked closely with the community to refine and focus on an achievable project that would link identified community need for aged care respite services and improved local health service delivery, with available Commonwealth and state government funding opportunities:

> There were grand plans, other people had very different ideas and eventually the group developed a bit of an understanding of, well, we can't do brain surgery here, but we can perhaps have a bit more of a primary health care focus, and we can look at potentially expanding our services, and once that was identified as a good thing to do, and I came on board and actually found some funding to build a Centre for Health and Wellbeing...

Evaluation and reflective learning

Boundary crossers can and should play a role in facilitating evaluation and reflective learning regarding community-driven health initiatives. Following the successful establishment of the Centre for Health and Wellbeing in

Deloraine, the steering committee had achieved its original goal and undertook a process of evaluation and reflection in relation to its future direction. The DON facilitated the process by linking the committee to a state health department representative who helped them to identify options and reach a decision regarding ongoing management of the centre and employment of diversional therapists. The DON and several other committee members also attended a workshop on community committee governance processes and structures, which resulted in a change of name to the Centre for Health and Wellbeing committee, and the development of a new mission statement that better reflected their new direction:

We achieved our initial purpose, and then once we had our centre, it became clear that we needed to become a management committee rather than a steering committee...we also needed to revise our mission statement...which is now to create and maintain holistic community-based health services in our area. *(Chair, Centre for Health and Wellbeing committee)*

In Oatlands, the community advisory committee, working with the site manager of the MMPHC, makes a practice of evaluating past actions and initiatives, stating 'we always learn from something that we have done'. It is the plan of the site manager that the committee will become more actively involved in identifying and analysing health needs in the community, developing solutions to meet those needs, and evaluating the impact of those solutions. Through a process of upskilling and capacity-building, and a broader focus on a range of health and wellbeing issues, the committee notes that 'we are tending to look ahead more'.

Implications for external agents

Tapping into boundary crossers' intimate knowledge of the community and its capacity/readiness to engage is a critical first step in the collaborative process. Enquiries through existing local networks help identify boundary crossers. Boundary crossers may not necessarily display specific characteristics or traits that distinguish them from other group members. In UDRH work, boundary crossers have been identified through displays of trust from fellow community members or empowering leadership. Trust is critical for gaining endorsement from the community for any proposed collaboration with the external agent. The boundary crosser can act as an advocate for the relationship. This is an important process as it shifts the overall benefits and risks associated with the collaboration away from the individual boundary crosser onto the broader community.

Through their knowledge of the community and other stakeholder agencies boundary crossers are often aware of other caveats to the engagement process that may need to be addressed. We are aware that a judgement based on a broader perspective may or may not be aligned with community perceptions or needs. There may be a fine line for boundary crossers between helping communities to align their thinking and planning with existing or potential funding opportunities, and between inadvertently stifling community creativity and innovation because of their understanding of external values and priorities and the sorts of projects that are most likely to be externally funded. Similarly, where boundary crossers don't share their knowledge, or don't utilise empowering or enabling leadership practices and processes, they run the risk of creating a dependency culture within the community.

Our experience suggests that more effective boundary crossers, like those discussed in this chapter, are skilled at working with other agencies to better align outcomes to community needs than may have been the case had the boundary crossers not been active. Given the potential influence and impact the boundary crosser may have in the engagement processes it is important that they are not regarded as a short cut in the community consultations process. Whilst boundary crossers have the potential to influence the direction of engagement, many also have to manage conflicting agendas which may limit their capacity to be a positive influence for change. In UDRH's community engagement experience boundary crossers are regarded as part of, rather than separate from, a whole of community engagement approach. This avoids the risk of bias and lessens the risk of a culture of dependency that may arise if knowledge is not shared with the community.

Conclusion

Boundary crossers can have a substantial influence on the effectiveness of partnerships between external agents and rural communities, including by facilitating risk taking and encouraging the moulding of opportunities and effective learning. They have access to knowledge and resources that can influence collaborative processes and the capacity of the community to address health issues. An understanding of the characteristics and modus operandi of boundary crossers provides valuable insights for external agents in designing their approaches to partnerships that build rural community capacity for health, including by drawing on their empowering leadership. The location of the community on the set of indicators of coalition maturity outlined in this chapter should be considered, along with the nature and characteristics of the boundary crossers who are present, to formulate a customised, holistic approach to the partnership process.

This chapter has revealed a gap in understanding of the operation of effective partnerships between rural communities and external agents. The set of indicators developed here requires further testing with other rural communities and in other, non-health contexts. We have suggested several ways in which the potential of boundary crossers could be limited, particularly by not sharing their knowledge or empowering others and inadvertently stifling creativity and innovation. More research is needed to investigate under what circumstances such limiting occurs, and explore what training and support should be provided to maximise the effectiveness of boundary crossers, and who should provide it.

Appendix: Indicators for rural community coalition maturity for partnering with external agents for the purpose of planning and negotiating health and wellbeing services

Indicator	Derived from:
Leadership contribution of community and external agent: reliance on external agents/networks, extent of community initiation of joint projects	Leadership is solely province of external agent at early stages, community is engaged at latest stages (3)
	Health service and community together play an active role in identifying and meeting community needs (4)
	Initiation of projects moves from external (early) to group (mature). Mature groups strong enough to resist external power (5)
Trust and working with the coalition: trust within coalition and partnership, attitudes and sense making of members, professionalism of procedures	Initial stage: build trust and formulate consistent, transparent and workable procedures. Sustaining stage: develop and support close relations and communication between partners (1)
	Effective groups have consensual view of purpose, do strategic planning, and have a cooperative culture built on social relationships (2)

High level of trust amongst partners, health service and community; transparency, accountability and professionalism of processes important (4)

Move from community climate is guarded at denial stage to community supportive at later stages (3)

Early stage: making sense of old realities, mistrust of the new and externally imposed rules and norms. Mature: expect change as the norm, develop and evolve own rules and norms, sharing within group and to and from external actors (5)

External links and networks

Sustaining stage: partners engage effectively with both community and external sponsors (1)

Health service and community utilise extensive external networks (4)

Early stage: few external links; vertical links are one way to and from above. Mature: well-linked to external agencies (5)

Shared vision for community health

Initial stage: Build shared purposes and goals (1)

Ineffective groups concentrate on the operational; effective groups also articulate the underlying vision (2)

Mid stage (preparation): community has modest support for improvement efforts (3)

Health service and community are committed to a vision centred on improving community health (4)

Knowledge, use and valuing of community's resources: by community, health service and external agency

Sustaining stage: recognise partners' contributions and facilitate new and strategic relationships (1)

All available resources must be used effectively (2)

Health service and community value skills of all (4)

Latest stage (professionalisation) sophisticated knowledge of community, high community involvement (3)

Risk taking and moulding opportunities: openness to new ideas, risk taking, willingness to mould opportunities to match vision	Earliest stage (no awareness) 'its just the way things are' (3)
	Health service and community are open to new ideas, willing to take risks and willing to mould opportunities to match vision (4)
	Early: waits for and adopts external solutions. Mature: generates internal solutions; experimentation leads to adaptation and innovation (5)
Evaluation and reflective learning	Sustaining stage: actively reflect upon, review and revise goals, renew commitment (1)
	Effective groups: reflective learning informs planning and action (2)
	Latest stage (professionalisation): extensive evaluation and modification (3)
	Evaluation of partnership (4)
	Mature group: critical reflection leads to new insights (5)

Sources: (1) Billett, Clemans, and Seddon (2005): initial and sustaining stages. (2) Cuthill and Fein (2005). (3) Edwards *et al.* (2000): nine stages from 'no awareness' to 'professionalisation'. (4) Johns, Kilpatrick and Whelan (2006): effective partnerships. (5) Pretty and Ward (2001): early, middle and mature stage groups.

Notes

[1] The concept of boundary crosser was first used by Peirce and Johnson (1997) in relation to community leadership.
[2] Full copies of the two case studies are available from the authors.

References

Billett, S., Clemans, A., and Seddon, T. (2005) *Forming, Developing and Sustaining Social Partnerships*. Adelaide: National Centre for Vocational Education Research.

Buxton, C., Carlone, H. and Carlone, D. (2005) 'Boundary spanners as bridges of student and school discourses in an urban science and mathematics high school', *School Science and Mathematics*, 105(6): 302–12.

Canadian Health Services Research Foundation (2003) *The Theory and Practice of Knowledge Broking in Canada's Health System*. Ottawa, CHSRF (http://www.chsrf.ca/broking/pdf/Theory_and_Practice_e.pdf), accessed 30 May 2006.

Cavaye, J. (1999) *The Role of Government in Community Capacity Building*. Brisbane: Queensland Department of Primary Industries.

Cuthill, M. and Fein, J. (2005) 'Capacity building: facilitating citizen participation in local governance', *Australian Journal of Public Administration*, 64(4): 63–80.

Edwards, R.W., Jumper-Thurman, P., Plested, B.A., Oetting, E.R. and Swanson, L. (2000) 'Community readiness: research to practice', *Journal of Community Psychology*, 28(3): 291–307.

Foster-Fishman, P., Berkowitz, S., Loundsbury, D., Jacobson, S. and Allen, N. (2001) 'Building collaborative capacity in community coalitions: a review and integrative framework', *American Journal of Community Psychology*, 29(2): 241–61.

Johns, S., Kilpatrick, S. and Whelan, J. (2006) 'Our health in our hands: building effective community partnerships for rural health service'. Discussion Paper, University Department of Rural Health, Tasmania.

Kilpatrick, S. and Falk, I. (2003) 'Learning in agriculture: building social capital in island communities', *Local Environment*, 8(5): 499–510.

Kilpatrick, S., Johns, S., Mulford, B., Falk, I. and Prescott, L. (2002) *More Than an Education: Leadership of School–Community Partnerships*. Report on Project UT-31A, Canberra, Rural Industries Research and Development Corporation.

Kilpatrick, S. and Loechel, B. (2004) 'Interactional infrastructure in rural communities: matching training needs and provision', *Rural Society*, 14(1): 4–21.

Lauder, W., Reel, S., Farmer, J. and Griggs, H. (2006) 'Social capital, rural nursing and rural nursing theory', *Nursing Inquiry*, 13(1): 73–9.

Peirce, N. and Johnson, C. (1997) *Boundary Crossers: Community Leadership for a Global Age*. Baltimore, MD: Academy of Leadership Press.

Pretty, J. (1999) 'Can sustainable agriculture feed Africa? New evidence on progress, processes and impacts', *Environment, Development and Sustainability*, 1(3–4): 253–74.

Pretty, J. and Ward, H. (2001) 'Social capital and the environment', *World Development*, 29(2): 209–27.

Sutherland, M., Harris, G., Foulk, D. and Gessner, L. (1998) 'Community partnership development in a rural southern county: a case study in African-American leadership', *American Journal of Health Studies*, 14(2): 57–66.

Taylor, M. (2000) 'Communities in the lead: power, organisational capacity and social capital', *Urban Studies*, 37(5–6): 1019–35.

Williams, P. (2002) 'The competent boundary spanner', *Public Administration*, 80(1): 103–24.

Chapter 15

Co-investigation of social capital

Dave Beck

This chapter reflects on a participative examination of frontline workers' understanding and experience of social capital using popular education techniques. It was carried out by a group of trainee community workers from the Inverclyde Community Apprentice Project, along with an academic from the University of Glasgow and an experienced community learning and development practitioner.

Inverclyde

Inverclyde is an area primarily comprising three small towns on the banks of the River Clyde. Once a major shipbuilding area, Inverclyde has seen an industrial downturn and a declining population, and figures from the Office for National Statistics indicate this trend will continue, with an 18 per cent fall in population between 1996 and 2013. Currently the employment rate in Inverclyde is 64 per cent. This is significantly lower than the average in Scotland of 75 per cent.

The Scottish Executive's response to regenerating areas such as Inverclyde has been the establishment of Social Inclusion Partnerships (SIPs). SIPs are broadly based partnerships, which comprise the local authority and other public agencies such as local enterprise companies and local health boards and the voluntary and private sectors with the aim of redeveloping the most disadvantaged neighbourhoods, so that people living there can take advantage of job opportunities and improve their quality of life.

The Community Apprenticeship Project

As part of the Inverclyde SIP's work to develop community capacity, the Community Apprenticeship Project was established in January 2003 to give local activists and workers access to higher education in the form of the Bachelor of Community Learning and Development, delivered by the University of Glasgow. The rationale for this type of approach has been previously discussed in greater depth (Beck, 2000). The programme gives local activists and workers the opportunity to reflect on the wider context of community regeneration both in terms of broader sweeps of social policy and a range of social theories. It also aims to develop analytical skills with which to understand, challenge and shape the forces which form their lives. As such it fits centrally into the Scottish Executive's policy thrusts of social inclusion, active citizenship and lifelong learning (Scottish Executive, 1999, 2004, 2005). The project's aims are to:

- enhance individual career prospects;
- strengthen the capacity of the local community and voluntary sector to deliver services to disadvantaged individuals and groups across Inverclyde;
- address issues of social and economic cohesion by supporting and encouraging local people to develop the skills required to become effective community practitioners; and
- raise confidence and motivation in communities with the potential to increase the local economic activity.

Its work is specifically targeted at unemployed people in the SIP area who are involved in community work on a voluntary basis, in particular individuals who could be deemed disadvantaged, e.g. lone parents, those affected by disability or others whose circumstances are recognised as a barrier to training and employment.

Social capital

The purpose of this article is not to explore notions of social capital, which is done effectively elsewhere (Field, 2003), but to focus on the research process, and so a brief definition of what social capital is will suffice. The definitions which the research group initially focused on were:

- The skills, resources, networks, opportunities and motivation that a community has which enable it to work together effectively to promote its own wellbeing (Scottish Executive, 2003).

- Whereas physical capital refers to physical objects and human capital refers to the properties of individuals, social capital refers to connections among individuals – social networks and the norms of reciprocity and trustworthiness that arise from them. In that sense social capital is closely related to what some have called 'civic virtue'. The difference is that 'social capital' calls attention to the fact that civic virtue is most powerful when embedded in a strong network of reciprocal social relations. A society of many virtuous but isolated individuals is not necessarily rich in social capital (Putnam, 2001: 19).

- Social capital refers to the institutions, relationships and norms that shape the quality and quantity of a society's social interactions. Social capital is not just the sum of the institutions which underpin a society – it is the glue that holds them together (Narayan, 1997).

- Social capital consists of the stock of active connections among people: the trust, mutual understanding and shared values and behaviours that bind the members of human networks and communities and make cooperative action possible (Cohen and Prusak, 2001: 4).

- Community learning and development is critical to the empowerment of both individuals and communities. For people of all ages it provides opportunities to develop potential, improve the quality of their lives and participate in local and national democratic processes. For communities it contributes to the building of social capital: the skills, resources, networks, opportunities, confidence and motivation which characterise empowered communities (Scottish Executive, 2003).

The other important conceptualising of social capital which was considered by the group was that of Bourdieu. His definition of social capital is 'the sum of resources, actual or virtual, that accrue to an individual or a group by virtue of possessing a durable network of more or less institutionalised relationships of mutual acquaintance and recognition' (Bourdieu and Wacquant, 1992: 119). He focuses on the social capital of the powerful and suggests that this functions to reproduce social inequality. An example he cites is that membership of a private golf club both signals a particular social position and develops a network of contacts which can facilitate business deals, the development of economic capital and therefore power. Bourdieu's idea of social capital links to the Gramscian concept of hegemony (Gramsci, 1971), which suggests that the political and moral leadership of a society is won by a ruling class through state apparatus and by cultural activity within civil society. The cultural forms (or cultural capital) of the ruling class are privileged within that society and transmitted or imposed through education, the Church and the mass media. The cultural forms of the dominated class are seen as inferior and deficient.

The research

The impetus for the work arose from many informal conversations both between the project tutor, the students and the lecturer. From these it was recognised that social capital was a contested and potentially problematic term which was increasingly featuring in the policy of the Scottish Executive and therefore shaping the context and practice of community development workers. This was coupled with a desire to explore research practices which were in accord with the Freirean approaches to education which were of interest to individuals in the group.

Freirean education offers us a framework and methodology to engage more democratically with learners. The approach which Freire (1972) refers to as problem-posing education enables the learners' own experiences and stories to become the focus for reflection and action (praxis). Fundamental to this process is the valuing by the teacher of the knowledge that already exists within the group of learners. This enables a mutual exchange of knowledge and experiences of both the teacher and learner in a co-learning situation since there is a context of mutual respect.

Within this process the educator listens for the issues/topics that reveal strong emotions within the learning group, demonstrated through fear, anger, joy or sorrow. From this information 'generative themes' emerge; these are the issues about which people have a critical curiosity which have the potential to lead to transformative action. The generative theme is re-presented to the group as 'codes' (Freire, 1972); which are concrete representations of the generative theme used to stimulate dialogue. These can take the form of pictures, songs, drama or text. The code does not offer a solution but presents the issue as a problem to be solved by the group, through a process of decodification.

An example of the Freirean decodification process is provided by Hope and

Timmel (1995). First the group are asked to describe the code, and this leads to questions about why the phenomena are happening. Links are then made to real-life situations: Does this happen in your experience, and what problems does this lead to? The group is then asked what the underlying causes of these phenomena are, and finally what action could be taken in light of our new understandings.

The research process described below was informed by this method for gathering and exploring the issue of social capital. The initial phase of informal discussion identified the generative theme of social capital and the events described below explore the decodification process. However; the area of action planning is less well developed. It is hoped to pick this up in further work with the learning group.

Collaborative research

Based on the values of Freirean education discussed above, we designed a research methodology which aimed to treat people as subjects, not objects, and attempted to fully utilise their potential as knowledge makers (Curry and Cunningham, 2000). We attempted to develop knowledge which was a product of the whole group – students, project worker and university worker – collectively examining our experience and understanding of social capital. This draws upon a model of collaborative learning (Bruffee, 1993) in which it is assumed that knowledge is socially, rather than individually, constructed. We worked on the results until a consensus view was reached. Differences of experience and understanding were part of the dialogue and an indispensable element of the learning process.

The fact that the research was initiated by a joint interest of the project and university workers does not invalidate it as an example of a participatory approach, since:

> In practice the participatory research process of intervention is initiated by an external agent, such as a community development agency, an extension service of a university, or a church group. A researcher or a team of researchers working with this intervener enters the community to stimulate the community's interest in participating in the research activity (Park, Brydon-Miller and Jackson, 1993: 9).

Reason and Bradbury's (2001) key features of a participatory research methodology, which they term cooperative inquiry, are outlined below. Their understanding, as ours, is that good research is carried out with, not on, people and that they are able to develop their own understandings through the participative process. Further, they see the need to integrate research and action, picking up on Freire's concern for praxis. Without this integration of thought and action we are left with mindless activism on the one hand or empty theorising on the other (Freire, 1972).

- There is intentional interplay between reflection and making sense on the one hand, and experience and action on the other.
- There is explicit attention, through agreed procedures, to the validity of the inquiry and its findings. The primary procedure is to use inquiry cycles, moving several times between reflection and action.
- There is a radical epistemology for a wide-ranging inquiry method that integrates experiential knowing through meeting and encounter, presentational knowing through the use of aesthetic, expressive forms, propositional knowing through words and concepts, and practical knowing – how in the exercise of diverse skills – intrapsychic, interpersonal, political, transpersonal and so on. These forms of knowing are brought to bear upon each other, through the use of inquiry cycles, to enhance their mutual congruence, both within each inquirer and the inquiry group as a whole.
- There are, as well as validity procedures, a range of special skills suited to such all-purpose experiential inquiry. They include fine-tuned discrimination in perceiving, in acting and in remembering both of these; bracketing off and reframing launching concepts; and emotional competence, including the ability to manage effectively anxiety stirred up by the inquiry process.
- The inquiry method can be both informative about, and transformative of, any aspect of the human condition that is accessible to a transparent body-mind, that is, one that has an open, unbound awareness.
- Primacy is given to transformative inquiries that involve action, where people change their way of being and doing and relating in their world – in the direction of greater flourishing. This is on the grounds that practical knowing-how consummates the other three forms of knowing – propositional, presentational and experiential – on which it is grounded.

- The full range of human capacities and sensibilities is available as an instrument of inquiry (Reason and Bradbury, 2001: 179).

Although in intention this research was to have been a cooperative inquiry, in reality it was nearer to an example of hermeneutical research inasmuch as the data analysis is not a separate process from data gathering (Lawrence, 1997). As a group we discussed our experience and understanding of social capital and then reflected on those experiences and understandings, which in turn developed new knowledge. This is similar to what Gummesson (1991) calls the 'hermeneutic spiral', where each turn of the spiral builds on the understanding at the previous turn. By this process deeper understandings were created within the group and points of action were indicated, but that action was left to the individual to follow up. Had this been formalised in an agreed procedure which incorporated cycles of action and reflection as discussed below, this research would have been more fully within the sphere of co-investigation.

The research process

The group of students were invited to a research day which would explore our understanding of social capital. This was a term that they were familiar with, both in terms of their work experience and from having studied it briefly on the Bachelor of Community Learning and Development course. The day was facilitated by me and the support worker from the Community Apprenticeship Project.

We used a community room in Inverclyde that was well known and accessible to the group, provided refreshments and set the chairs in a circle to establish a relaxed, informal atmosphere. People spoke about who they were and what issues they were working on and why we thought social capital was an important subject to consider. I then talked about the research process, which consisted of a series of focused dialogues and a follow-up evaluation and reflection session. On consideration, there was a missed opportunity to involve the whole group in designing the research methodology, indicating how embedded the socialised role of researcher is.

My co-facilitator introduced a photo language exercise within which the group were invited to choose from a wide range of images, one which had some significance to them. We then shared the image and its significance with other members of the group. This encouraged people to both begin to engage with one another but also to engage intellectually and emotionally with objects.

We introduced codes in the form of statements made by the Scottish Executive and others, as listed above, about the nature and impact of social capital. We then had a series of structured dialogues where we posed the questions: What do you understand? How do you feel about it? How do you experience it both professionally and personally? What do you add to it by what you do, and is there a downside? These cycles of investigation explored the cognitive, affective and experiential understandings of the topic, each cycle deepening the group's understanding. The discussions were recorded on flipcharts in the form of mind maps which enabled us as a group to see and develop emerging themes and recorded the group's consensus view.

After a short break we presented an input on Bourdieu's understanding of social capital and again had a structured dialogue on two linked questions: Does this challenge your understanding? Does this challenge your practice? This enabled the group to reinvestigate their own understanding in the light of a new theoretical framework, allowing them to make connections between local and structural dimensions.

Throughout the research process, we recorded the discussions using mind maps (Buzan, 2003). This pictorial record was used by the group within the dialogues to identify emerging themes and to agree our collective understanding. The content of the maps was written up and circulated among the group for final approval. The results are recorded below.

Results

Understanding

Essentially the group recognised social capital as a bottom-up process, where groups of people act together. If genuine, it should respond to the community's agenda, but there is also a role for the local authority to build community capacity to take an active part in democratic processes. They felt that the greater levels of social capital within communities should result in clearer and more effective challenging of those who had power.

They believed that in order to develop social capital, people had to develop their knowledge. This should not, however be only seen in terms of qualifications, linked to vocational progression, but should also develop a belief that change is possible within the community and beyond.

They recognised that there was a link between social capital and human capital and felt that this could impact on levels of economic capital both at an individual and community level.

Feelings

Dialogue about their feelings in relation to social capital, as implemented through the local authority and other agencies, revealed a much more complex picture. There was a great deal of suspicion that what purported to be community capacity building or social capital development was at best tokenistic and at worst, a continuation of oppressive structures and processes which were being rebranded to appear more palatable. It was similarly felt that the main driving forces were available funding streams and the government policies which were behind them rather than the expressed needs of the community. They were concerned that much of the language used by regeneration practitioners was exclusionary. This, coupled with excessively bureaucratic structures, meant that only the 'same old faces' could participate in local democratic structures – giving the illusion of a locally controlled process but denying access to the majority.

Fuelled by anger at all of the above, there was a desire in the group to reclaim and re-express social capital in a way which could act as a catalyst for transformative social action.

Experience

People within the group recognised that personally, they had significant reserves of social capital in the form of family relationships, their learning colleagues at university, church membership, sports clubs, involvement with other parents through childcare activities and the local pub. These various networks provided a sense of belonging, personal support and the release of pressure, the sharing of skills and a vehicle for working through difficult questions and choices. Conversely they were also a source of questions and conflict. Field (2003) similarly points to a range of conflicts arising from social capital, ranging from subtle pressure not to break ranks to violence.

Professionally, group members were part of formal networks such as the health network and the early-years network. They were also part of informal networks where people with similar professional values would work on issues of common concern. These networks provided a place to share new ideas, share resources and challenge agencies, policies and local practices. These benefits were hindered by a culture of competition created by an over-emphasis on outcomes and chasing new funding. This highlights the contradictory impact of the local authority in both encouraging and inhibiting the development of social capital (Wallis and Dollery, 2002).

What they add to social capital

They felt that their personal experience of working in the same community where they lived was valuable in helping agencies deliver services and engage with the community in appropriate ways. Using a problem-posing methodology (Freire, 1972), they were able to challenge practices which were discriminatory or excluding of local people. They offered a variety of personal supports to local people and other workers ranging from encouragement and enthusiasm to formal mentoring. Organisationally, they helped new groups to form and developed communication systems, processes for sharing resources and piloting new ways of working. Finally, they were involved in a wide range of training and informal skill-sharing activities both on the individual and collective levels.

The downside

The group were clear that social capital is not a cure-all. Groups rich in social capital tended to get the available resources and funding. This had the unintended outcome of further disadvantaging the most excluded members of the community. Also, a strong sense of belonging sometimes leads to increased inter-community tensions; territorialism would be an example of this. In terms of the Scottish Executive's response to social capital development, the group observed that often existing networks were overlooked. This resulted in new structures being imposed on the community which were often detrimental to levels of participation on community activities and informal democratic processes.

Reflections on Bourdieu

The group acknowledged that much of the work around social inclusion and social capital development is based on middle-class values and does not therefore reflect the aspirations of the local community. The changes which are produced are not 'real change'. One group member noted: 'It makes a local and superficial change but does not impact on hierarchical power structures.' This reflects Field's observation that 'High levels of homogenous Social Capital represent a strategy for communal survival without much impact on the wider situation (2003: 80). This lack of real change explained for the group why people are reluctant to get involved and are wrongly branded as being apathetic.

They noted that there is resistance from within the community to people changing and moving on, since that violated some of the cultural norms within the community. This is further evidence of the negative effects of bonding social capital where a group's norms may be limiting in terms of education, employment and other lifestyle choices.

As workers they recognised the danger of being incorporated into the middle-class system which they were critiquing. As they develop new lifestyles, language and values they may lose contact with grass-roots concerns and serve to replicate social inequality. This is indicative of the hegemonic process (Gramsci, 1971) which offers rewards as a way of incorporating and neutralising resistance.

Their response to this was the desire to establish groups which could support people to analyse what was happening in their community and beyond and generate collective social action which would change the power balance within communities. It was observed that many ordinary people had high levels of social capital through friendships, family and workplaces, but that this does not give them access to resources, funding or influence over policy makers. The role of community learning and development could be to provide that critical analysis and the organisational skills to harness those stocks of social capital in order to effect change.

Reflection

Although the group could see that social capital was a potentially useful way of understanding the community and developing their potential for action, there are many deficiencies in the models espoused by both central government and local authorities in Scotland.

The overly optimistic model of social capital which is posited by the Scottish Executive fails to recognise the possibility for conflict which is produced by its development. High levels of bonding social capital can result in oppression of members within those groups. This was exemplified by one group member who had a strong church connection, who felt that her individuality and scope for questioning was restricted by other church members. Tension between highly bonded groups can be seen, for example, in instances of territorialism which is experienced within communities. Finally, groups with lower levels of social capital become even more marginalised, as more developed groups secure greater access to resources and opportunities.

It was appreciated that there is a role for the local authority in developing social capital (Wallis and Dollery, 2002); however, it is one that is fraught with difficulties. Top-down initiatives to develop social capital are seen as tokenistic, counterproductive or as the development of individual skills and knowledge, which is human capital and not social capital at all. Exclusive language and practices further marginalise disempowered groups and create elite volunteers within communities while not changing existing power structures. However, bottom-up approaches which enable communities to think and act collectively can be successful, but current power holders must be willing to give away some power and be prepared to change structures to let the community in.

Perhaps the greatest omission within current models is the lack of critical analysis. Action, not linked to an understanding of structural inequalities, will result in a recycling of poverty, since root issues are neither considered nor tackled. The potential role for community learning and development workers in response to this gap would be in line with Gramsci's idea of the organic intellectual. 'The mode of being of the new intellectual can no longer consist in eloquence...but in active participation in practical life, as constructor, organiser, "permanent persuader" and not just a simple orator' (Gramsci, 1971: 10). It must be appreciated that the potential for role conflict here is very high since this is counter-hegemonic activity; pressure from employers, funders and even colleagues to toe the line will inevitably come. Again, Gramsci's idea of the War of Position is useful here. Workers and community organisations alike build alliances which in turn contribute towards a new hegemony based on different world views and values. Perhaps this is where the notion of social capital is both useful and radical. Developing norms of reciprocity, trust and networks with a view to overturning unjust social conditions is a project worth engaging in. Without this wider aspiration, social capital becomes merely rearranging the seats on the *Titanic* in close, cosy circles.

Evaluation of the research process

In a follow up session, the group reflected on the research process through a series of focused dialogues.

What did you get out of the event?

The group found it to be an enjoyable event where they felt comfortable and able to explore new ideas without feeling that they would be criticised or thought stupid. They felt that they were able to participate in and shape the process, rather than just being passive.

The discussion helped them to realise that they already knew about social capital – it gave words to their experience. It gave them an opportunity to link the theory to their personal and professional practice and to link community development theory to ideas about social capital. Through the process, they felt as if they had developed new understandings as individuals and developed a shared understanding as a group.

What did you learn?

They learned that they had already been operating in ways that developed social capital, but now they had a language to describe it. They also recognised that social capital is something they are involved with and benefited from in both their personal and professional lives. Further, the creation or destruction of social capital is something everyone was involved in.

They have come to understand that if their definition of social capital did not include the idea of change and bridging gaps between the powerful and the powerless, that much of their efforts could result in reinforcing the status quo, even if social capital, by some definitions, has been developed.

If you were exploring the idea of social capital in your community, what would you do differently?

In general, they felt that the principles of the process would be appropriate with community groups. Particularly, they would ensure that people were involved as subjects, not just objects of scrutiny. They would start the process using concrete experiences drawn from people's everyday life to explore the concepts of social capital and then introduce new language and terminology. They felt that an important dimension, from the perspective of community development workers, was that study and research should link to personal change *and* collective action; having understood the world, they would work to change it.

Do you think this is a good way to research a new topic?

Yes. There was time to make people feel safe as relationships were developed. In this context, people were able to explore and investigate new ideas freely. They were also able to help develop one another's understanding through dialogue. However, they felt that this still left scope for differences of view and opinion to be developed and valued.

Is there anything else you would like to tell us?
They felt that this research process would be particularly successful in well-established social groups. They felt that it revitalised the group by giving them fresh energy and vision for the work they were involved in.

Conclusion

Reflecting on the process in light of Reason and Bradbury's (2001) understanding of collaborative research, the short-term nature of the project worked against it fulfilling the potential it had to affect thinking and practice. The exploration did reflect and make sense of the issue in the light of practice, but should have formed part of cycles of action and reflection in order to both develop a robust understanding and to affect practice. This happened to some extent with some members of the group but not the group as a whole.

The process did draw on ways of knowing, drawing on feelings, knowledge, experience and analysis. The process of revisiting the topic of investigation from these different perspectives did develop greater congruence within individual inquirers and the whole group.

It is possible that the most appropriate role for the academy in this type of participative inquiry is to act as a catalyst; bringing practitioners together around common interests and providing the skills and context for in-depth reflection and action planning. The action itself should be taken by the practitioners. However, having started the process we should have gone on to provide further cycles of reflection on that action. This omission was partly due to the fact that this was not the agreement made with the group at the time and partly because time to take a lead in that type of work within the community is not valued by academic institutions. This cycle of action and reflection over a number of years could provide the opportunity for higher education to directly impact on the lives of whole communities, not just individuals. In this case social capital was the topic, but could apply to any and even the most intractable of human problems.

References

Beck, D. (2000) *The Linking of Work and Education to Enable Social Inclusion*. SCUTREA. Paper presented at the 30th Annual SCUTREA Conference, 3–5th of July.

Bourdieu, P. and L. Wacquant (1992) *An Invitation to Reflexive Sociology*. Chicago: University of Chicago Press.

Bruffee, K.A. (1993) *Collaborative Learning, Higher Education, Interdependence and the Authority of Knowledge*. Baltimore, MD: Johns Hopkins University Press.

Buzan, T. (2003) *The Mind Map Book: Radiant Thinking – Major Evolution in Human Thought*. London: BBC Active.

Cohen, D. and Prusak, L. (2001) *In Good Company: How Social Capital Makes Organizations Work*. Boston, MA: Harvard Business School Press.

Curry, R.M., and Cunningham, P. (2000) 'Co-learning in the community', *New Directions for Adult and Continuing Education*, 87: 73–82.

Field, J. (2003) *Social Capital*. London: Routledge.

Freire, P. (1972) *Pedagogy of the Oppressed*. London: Sheed & Ward.

Gramsci, A. (1971) *Selections from the Prison Notebooks*. London: Lawrence & Wishart.

Gummesson, E. (1991) *Qualitative Methods in Management Research*. Newbury Park, CT: Sage.

Hope, A., and Timmel, S. (1995) *Training for Transformation: Handbook for Community Workers*. London: ITDG.

Lawrence, R.L. 'The interconnecting web: adult learning cohorts as sites for collaborative learning, feminist pedagogy and experiential ways of knowing', in *38th Annual Adult Education Research Conference Proceedings, Stillwater, Oklahoma, May 16–18, 1997*, compiled by R.E. Nolan and H. Chelesvig, pp. 179–84. Stillwater: Oklahoma State University, 1997. (ED 409 460) (http://www.edst.educ.ubc.ca/aerc/1997/97lawrence.html).

Park, P., Brydon-Miller, M. and Jackson, T. (eds) (1993) *Voices of Change: Participatory Research in the United States and Canada*. Toronto: Ontario Institute for Studies in Education.

Putnam, R. (2001) *Bowling Alone: The Collapse and Revival of American Community*. New York: Simon & Schuster.

Reason, P. and Bradbury, H. (eds) (2001) *Handbook of Action Research: Participative Inquiry and Practice*. London: Sage.

Scottish Executive (1999) *Social Justice: A Scotland Where Everyone Matters*. Edinburgh (http://www.scotland.gov.uk/library2/doc07/sjmd-00.htm).

Scottish Executive (2003) *Community Learning And Development: The Way Forward*. Edinburgh (http://www.communityplanning.org.uk/documents/ CLDWayForwarddocMay30FINALAPPROVED.pdf).

Scottish Executive (2004) *Working and Learning Together to Build Stronger Communities: Scottish Executive Guidance for Community Learning and Development*, Edinburgh (http://www.scotland.gov.uk/Publications/2004/02/18793/32157).

Scottish Executive (2005) *Lifelong Learning Strategy Update: October 2005*, Edinburgh (http://www.scotland.gov.uk/Publications/2005/11/07161143/ 11439).

Wallis, J. and Dollery, B. (2002) 'Social capital and local government capacity', *Australian Journal of Public Administration*, 61(3): 76–85.

Chapter 16

Sustaining community leadership learning: recent experience in Montana, USA

Larry Swanson

Introduction

The art, science and practice of community economic development (ED) in the USA are changing, as evidenced by recent work and experience in the state of Montana. Past local-area ED efforts have been largely carried out by local agents, hired by local entities or organisations with small boards created for the purpose of pursuing area ED efforts and initiatives, using tools and strategies embedded in national and state ED programmes. There was little community learning or broad-based community leadership learning as precursors to, and continuing components of, local ED efforts and strategies. This chapter is the result of the author's extensive experience with diverse regional civic groups. As Director of the O'Connor Center for the Rocky Mountain West at the University of Montana, the focus on economic and community change has provided insight for the discussion here.

There is growing recognition that advancing a community economically is not a simple matter of increasing jobs or assisting businesses. A community functions within a region which provides a much more complex context. In looking at economic development through such a lens, systemic change must be considered, as Inman and Swanson (2007) noted:

> Regionalism is an integrative approach to policy that follows a geographical focus looking beyond political and jurisdictional boundaries. This allows for the study of social, economic, and environmental issues through the creation and sustaining of

organizations that do not comfortably fit into the established framework of local, state, and federal governments (p. 1).

The 'plate' for ED planning and decision-making, therefore, is much larger than job creation and business assistance. Community economic advancement is much deeper and broader in scope, involving strategies and programmes in infrastructure development, workforce development and education more generally, and attention to all aspects of community decision-making affecting community liveability. Local-area economic advancement is likely to be more successful if local leadership from business, government, education and other functional areas, sometimes partitioned from each other, are linked in a common leadership learning process. But this broad-based local leadership learning can be further strengthened, it is suggested here, by interfacing research and study on how the economy is changing, with information on practical experience from other communities who have already demonstrated success in new and innovative ED programmes and approaches.

This chapter posits that sustained local leadership learning leads to the creation of the types of social capital necessary for conscious, intelligent community advancement. The argument rests on the understanding that social capital at the community level is built upon trust and working relationships among key leaders and strengthened by a well-managed, credible and sustained leadership learning process. This type of leadership learning process is particularly important when it comes to how local communities seek to position themselves for a changing economy. These propositions are easier said than done, but they are being attempted by a private–public partnership entity called *Celebrate Billings*,[1] in the US community of the same name in Montana.

Billings is a moderately sized city of about 100,000 people located in the North American Rocky Mountain West – a mountainous region that has been seeing increased population growth and fairly dramatic economic change and restructuring over the last decade and a half. The region has only a few truly large cities including Denver, Colorado and Salt Lake City, Utah, with much of it sparsely populated, including the state of Montana, where Billings is located. The economy of the American West is modernising, moving away from its 'cowboy' image of the past to one that is more mature, diversified and increasingly urban in character. Traditionally, Montana's economy had been natural resource-industry based and rural in orientation and the state almost prided itself on having no 'real' cities. This contributed to a slow recognition of the importance of small cities like Billings to the region's economic future, even among business leaders and public officials in Billings itself.

The art and craft of economic development programming in this growing and fast-changing region has become one of better positioning small cities like Billings and other communities – their businesses, workers, families, schools and governments – for important aspects of present and anticipated future change. Most forces driving larger patterns of change in the economy and society – technological change, economic restructuring, population ageing trends, monetary policies, global integration, etc. – are supra-community in nature, largely beyond meaningful influence and sometimes comprehension by leaders at the local community level. At the same time, adaptation to change requires well-designed, well-managed and sustained leadership learning. This chapter reports on *Celebrate Billings* as a potential model for other communities seeking to engage key leadership in a process of progressive learning towards community economic advancement.

New imperatives in economic development in the USA

As new patterns and drivers have emerged in the US economy and in the Rocky Mountain West, other forces have been at work leading to new thinking regarding US economic development planning and programming. The growing global interdependence of many long-standing industries, such as manufacturing, energy production, agricultural and food production and other primary materials production, have made many areas heavily dependent upon these industries increasingly vulnerable to faraway influences and international events. This has made many US communities, workers and families feel increasingly economically vulnerable.

At the same time, aspects of government responsibility, including responsibilities for economic development planning and programming, have been steadily devolving, moving from the national and state levels to local levels. As noted in a report by the National Academy of Public Administration (NAPA, 1996):

> The nation's economic development programs will be a critical factor in two of the most significant domestic policy challenges of the coming decades: America's adjustment and response to an increasingly competitive global economy and the recent transformation of social policy from one based on dependency to

one that stresses opportunity and personal responsibility…The primary responsibility for designing and implementing economic development activities must rest with states, regions, and localities. The federal government, by itself, cannot have an enduring impact on economic conditions in the widely different communities and regions throughout the country.

As the federal government has increasingly looked to states to assume areas of responsibility, states have looked to local leaders, particularly large and diverse states containing many different types of sub-regional economies. While it is now well recognised that economic development strategies must be tailored to widely varying local and regional conditions, there is growing anxiety among many local officials regarding their ability to influence the direction of their local economy. The long-standing custom of local leadership in the USA has been to largely defer to national and state programmes and policies when it comes to local economic development programming, tapping into these programmes not only for direction but funding.

There is a growing paradox in economic development. While more and more aspects of the economy are operating at higher and higher levels of national and international integration, responsibilities for economic development planning and programming are being increasingly shifted to local levels of decision making. Development strategies must fit the needs of particular places, but there is often a 'gap' in capacity, knowledge and technical wherewithal at city and county levels – traditional units of local government – to address complex problems and needs tied to an increasingly complex economy. Processes for local leadership learning about the economy necessary to fill this gap have been largely absent or grossly lacking. A report by the Corporation for Enterprise Development (CfED, 1993) notes:

> [T]o build effective plans, communities must understand the economic health of the entire sub-state (or multi-state) economy of which they are a part – and how they fit into that economy… Success will require collaborating with other communities that they may have competed against in the past, because new jobs and economic activity in other areas will strengthen the regional economy and bring benefits to all.

In devising economic development programmes at the national level, policy makers have largely worked on two fronts: one aimed at the problems and needs of cities and metropolitan areas – programming under the guise of urban development and redevelopment – and one aimed at the needs of rural areas, or rural development programming. However, shifting more economic development thinking and doing from national and state levels to sub-state and local levels defies this programmatic differentiation. Sub-state economies have both urban and rural components, and attempting to separate them only serves to limit collaboration and restrict the ability to build local and regional capacity at sub-state levels. As the CfED (1993) report explains:

> [Effective economic development strategies] will not be based on traditional definitions of urban and rural, but on an understanding of the economic and social structure of a particular region, its links to the surrounding economies, and the particular problems and opportunities that these structures and interrelationships present … [Local leaders] must use this understanding to craft policy strategies and programs to build the capacities for taking advantage of new economic opportunities.

Successful collaboration at the regional level also requires 'sustained, broad-based efforts by a spectrum of local leaders and institutions, working in tandem with market forces and producing demonstrable results' (CfED, 1993). Local leaders cannot remake the economy or ignore fundamental trends under way in it. However, well-informed local leadership can take stock of what these trends are and attempt to better position the community – its workforce, schools, governmental bodies, businesses and educational entities – for such changes in the future. Positioning communities for potentially greater prosperity requires a detailed understanding of change.

Building the foundation of economic understanding

It is difficult to interest and engage a broad cross-section of local area leadership in a sustained leadership learning process about the economy. This is essentially why there are so few examples of ongoing, local or community-level leadership learning programmes for purposes of local area economic development. The need is for better and more understandable and engaging economic information among key players in local area development and confidence in facing and addressing the varied challenges.

While there are mountains of data on the economy and on population trends, mountains of data do not easily translate into readily understandable information for a diverse group of local leaders. A database tool referred to as

READ was designed and constructed to address this need. *READ*, which stands for the *Regional Economies Assessment Database*, was developed at the O'Connor Center for the Rocky Mountain West at the University of Montana. It is a computerised database and analysis system designed to facilitate visualisation and comprehension of the economy and economic activity at many different regional scales or levels; including the scale of sub-state, city-centred, multi-county regions.

Features of READ

The primary source of annual and quarterly economic data (detailed employ-ment, labour earnings and personal income data) is the US Department of Commerce, through its Bureau of Economic Analysis (BEA). Most social and demographic data come from the US Census Bureau. National and state labour departments compile monthly and annual data on the labour force and unemployment. Most data are compiled for units of political geography – counties, states and nations. However, most economic activity does not operate within political jurisdictions, and examining change using these units alone hinders careful evaluation of important regional variations in the economy's structure and change.

In *READ* a large array of economic and social data are organised around both political jurisdictions and more carefully defined economic regions and sub-regions. Conditions and trends in the nation as a whole can be compared and contrasted with those for the western USA and important multi-state regions of the West. Conditions and trends for important regions of the West can be compared and contrasted with each other and for many more sub-state regions. Boundaries of meaningfully defined sub-state regions better reflect how the economy is organised and operates at lower, sub-regional and local levels. At these lower levels, economies largely operated around major cities. Recognising this, most sub-state economies generally demarcated in *READ* are referred to as 'multi-county, city-centred, sub-state economic regions.'

The *READ* system is designed to examine how change plays out or exerts itself from one of these regions to the next, carefully accounting for economic differences in the size and nature of different regions and places. Fundamentally, *READ* represents an effort to better understand how the economy actually organises itself in space, region by region. There is no single way to determine the size and reach of an area economy. But, it is clear, regional economies at the sub-state level are largely organised around major population centres and their surrounding, sometimes far-flung, trade and service areas.

There are many different types of regions and regional communities and the classification system devised in *READ* is based upon key differences among them. A 'hierarchy' of regional centres and region types is visualised, reflecting an 'urban–rural' continuum, ranging from regions centred around major metro centres to those centred around progressively smaller centres, proceeding further to regions of sparsely populated, isolated areas that are not closely linked to particular population centres because of their remoteness. This scheme helps in identifying where particular regions and communities 'fit' within the larger economy and helps account for regional variations in different types of economies. This is extremely important in gauging economic development potentials for a particular area or community.

Existing data from a variety of sources are organised for this demarcation of hierarchically ordered regions, telling us much about what we need to know about the economy. Data are never complete and they do not tell us everything we want to know. But, when properly organised and portrayed, they can be an important source of information and understanding upon which to base constructive discussions by local decision-makers. *READ* also assists in devising strategies and initiatives for improving local economies.

READ region 'peer' review

Strategies that can succeed must reflect particular needs and challenges of particular places and the values and goals of the people who live there. In carefully identifying how one economy differs from others and what its unique qualities may be, it is very important to examine local economic data within the framework of an area peer-review process. By carefully identifying and classifying sub-state regional economies by type throughout the western United States, *READ* can be used in identifying regional communities or areas with similar characteristics and attributes. These 'peer regions' can then be used in evaluating how well the economy of one area is doing with regard to the economies of other areas with similar characteristics. These types of comparisons are helpful in identifying area 'strengths' and 'weaknesses', and in gauging how well one area's economy is 'performing'.

Criteria in peer region selection include the population of the region core or centre, the population of the larger region or the centre's surrounding trade area, and area dependencies on certain industries, like agriculture, manufacturing and government. This type of area peer review is important to properly interpret a particular region's situation as well as realistically assessing development potentials. Often area economic conditions, such as unemployment rates and poverty levels, are evaluated against similar measures for the state and nation. However, various indicators of the performance of a 'micro' area economy cannot be objectively judged against non-comparable macro units that encompass many economic regions with vastly differing economic circumstances.

The large array of economic indicators contained in *READ* also can be used in generally constructing a system of regional benchmarks. These are key indicators of economic conditions or trends considered by local leaders as important in gauging how well the community and region is doing economically and developmentally. Measures for these key indicators also can be compared with those for peer regions, thereby allowing the performance of one region's economy to be gauged against other peers. Peer regions which are doing particularly well in certain areas – 'high performers' – can be identified. And, with further focused study of these regions, factors that may be contributing to the success of some regions, both intentionally and unintentionally, can sometimes be identified. This type of analysis is extremely useful when incorporated into a local area leadership learning process. It also helps in making the local leadership learning process engaging.

While local community leaders are being looked to for more and more, they feel capable of actually controlling or influencing less and less, particularly when it comes to the economy. Individual communities are not able to chart their own course irrespective of larger patterns of change as this Corporation for Enterprise Development extract explains.

> [Many] problems that are played out at the local level cannot be controlled at the local level…But there are some real options – as well as some false options – open to our communities…The more realistically we face the options open to us, the more likely our efforts will be more than futile symbolic gestures…It makes sense to consider what our communities now are like, and to relate them to changes going on in the larger society [and economy]. But let us keep in mind that the larger society [economy] is not only out there. It exists in our own community (CfED, 1993).

What local leaders can do within their respective communities is gain a much better understanding of the larger pattern of economic change and how this change is 'playing itself out' within their region and community. Armed with this understanding, they can attempt to identify ways to 'better position' themselves for future change; finding advantages in some aspects of change while attempting to reduce undesirable impacts associated with other aspects of change. They can attempt to make their communities more informed and adaptive and, thereby, potentially more successful and more vital communities.

Montana on the move

New trends in the economy began to redirect the Montana economy in the late 1980s and early 1990s and continue to play out. The state's population grew by less than two per cent during the entire decade of the 1980s, with more people moving from the state than to it. In the 1990s population grew by 13 per cent, spurred by a dramatic turnaround in net migration. Rather than leaving the state destined for places of greater opportunity, more people began to move to Montana, drawn by its beauty and quality of life. An economic expansion began that has continued up to the present day.

In the fall of 2003 the very first forum of what was to be eventually called *Montana on the Move* was convened in Missoula, Montana. The forum was a joint undertaking of the University of Montana's O'Connor Center for the Rocky Mountain West and the mayor's office of the City of Missoula. Several hundred of the community's key leaders were targeted for the forum, which was subsequently held. The first forum was several hours in length, focused upon the sharing of information about changing economic conditions and trends in the region and in Missoula. This information was compiled using *READ*. The information was well received and a second forum was then planned and held to continue the discussion and to move it into areas of potential action. A *Missoula City Club* was formed as a vehicle to continuing the conversation and learning.[2]

Because of the success of the Missoula forum it was decided to expand this initiative to other Montana cities and to do so under the unifying banner of *Montana on the Move (MOM)*.[4] Forums were ultimately held in all seven of Montana's major cities. Each *MOM* forum was planned and conducted by a team of professionals from the University of Montana's O'Connor Center for the Rocky Mountain West and the University of Montana's Public Policy Research Institute.

Working through the mayor's offices of each city, local steering committees were organised in each community to assist in planning the forums. The forums were planned as learning workshops, providing key leadership from each community the opportunity to learn and talk about recent growth trends in their community and in the larger region. Challenges and opportunities associated with this growth and change became the focus of the community leadership learning workshops.

After two years and multiple forums in all of the communities, several common themes emerged from organised conversations among these community leaders. In an economy that seems to be able to go to places of its choosing, attractive cities with attractive surroundings are seeing the biggest changes. Broad cross-sections of key leadership were then asked to conjecture about how to make these changes 'better' and how to best position their community for the type of growth and change that will bring the greatest prosperity. Five common areas of need and opportunity were identified:

1   *Need for quality infrastructure.* Growing cities of quality require quality infrastructure and funding for infrastructure of nearly all types in Montana's cities – streets and other transportation infrastructure, water and sewer, police and fire protection services, educational infrastructure, etc. – lagged behind their growth. Cities built on the cheap with inadequate infrastructure will have underdeveloped economies. Cities that can anticipate growth and that can put into place quality infrastructure as they grow will have greater capacity for sustained growth and prosperity in the future. In Montana, new sources of funding for local infrastructure are badly needed.

2   *Need for quality workforces.* Virtually every facet of the economy where growth is occurring requires quality workers – workers with skills, education and experience, as well as ready access to more training and education as workforce requirements change. A centrepiece of any strategy for area economic improvement is quality workforce development programming and a quality system of education more generally. The design of this programming must be grounded in the communities and regions served and their particular economic needs and opportunities. And this programming must be 'lifelong', addressing the needs of a changing workplace and ageing labour force.

3   *Need for quality growth management.* Becoming 'better' places as they become 'bigger' places requires a shared vision for the

future and careful planning for growth. Nearly all of Montana's cities are facing growth pressures that are straining their capacities to plan and manage this growth effectively and professionally. More attention must be given to the planning needs of Montana's cities by state policy-makers.

4 *Opportunity for proactively pursuing economic advancement.* Past economic development policies and tools at state and federal levels tended to focus on the state's biggest problems with limited success, while largely ignoring some of the greatest opportunities. Given changes in the state's economy wrought by new patterns of growth, state policy-makers need to be much more opportunistic in their orientations to economic development. What is more, because economic growth was mainly coming to cities of quality in the region, the focus of economic development programming needs to be expanded beyond simply business promotion and jobs creation. Successful economic development ultimately hinges upon making Montana's cities and communities more attractive places for people to live and work.

5 *Opportunity for urban–rural partnerships for economic progress.* Past federal programming in economic development had tended to emphasise tools and approaches for 'urban' development and ones for 'rural' development. However, the focus of local development should be on sub-state regions containing both urban and rural components. And as Montana's cities become stronger economically, they will have greater capacity to help in addressing some of the needs and opportunities of their nearby rural neighbours. To do this, these cities and surrounding communities must develop greater trust in working together towards common economic objectives.

Celebrate Billings

Celebrate Billings (CB) is a private–public partnership of key organisations and entities in the city of Billings, Montana, with the express purpose of 'establishing a leadership group that provides our community with one voice, common goals and a platform to successfully pursue regional excellence in the areas of economic development, civic climate, and education'.[5]

There are many existing organisations in Billings that have similar goals to those of *Celebrate Billings* that could and sometimes have led the community forward on different issues. However, most of these are organised for different segments of Billings leadership – such as key leaders in business or education or arts and culture. *Celebrate Billings* is conceived as a leadership development entity that can span and join leadership from across the entire community, including leaders from both the private and public sectors and leaders that are both elected and unelected, formal and informal.

It serves to break down much of the compartmentalisation that has been constructed between key areas of authority and decision making in the Billings community – the type of compartmentalisation that confounds broad-based leadership learning and participation across all of the most important areas of community decision-making.

Adding to the success of *Celebrate Billings* has been its insistence that leadership discussions of key issues be based upon solid and current information about the economy. To enable this, the organisation has relied upon a steady diet of information and analysis from the *READ* system, maintained by the University of Montana's O'Connor Center.

Celebrate Billings was conceived and organised as a private–public partnership of five of the community's most important institutions – the city's two hospitals, St Vincent Healthcare and Billings Clinic, both among the largest employers in the community and region; the city's daily newspaper, the *Billings Gazette*, also the largest and most prestigious newspaper in the State of Montana; the largest institution of higher education in the area, Montana State University – Billings; and the City of Billings itself, through the mayor's office. The Billings-based Foundation for Community Vitality, a private philanthropic organisation working in areas of community development; also later became an important partner in *Celebrate Billings*. And key leaders from other organisations in the community, including those concerned with economic development and education, regularly attend planning meetings of *Celebrate Billings*.

With each new forum and initiative *Celebrate Billings* is steadily trans-forming the community of Billings into a learning community and, in the process, helping to create pathways for better positioning the city and region for future economic prosperity. It is becoming a model for other communities throughout the USA and around the world with the same goals and objectives.

Conclusions

It is becoming increasingly clear to people who have spent a lifetime working in areas of economic and community development that local area economic development is much more than income and job creation. And, even if it were only that, the process of achieving income and job creation is much more than business creation and expansion. Increasingly, the economy – including businesses, jobs and people – is able to locate in places of its choosing. Economic entities are becoming much more footloose and, as they do, the art, science and practice of economic development themselves are changing. A survey of local economic development efforts throughout the USA by the Federal Reserve Bank of Kansas City concluded:

> Increasingly economic development experts are abandoning traditional approaches to economic development that rely on recruiting large enterprises with tax breaks, financial incentives and other inducements. Instead, they are relying on building businesses from the ground up and supporting the growth of existing enterprises…Evidence increasingly suggests that the right approach is usually to focus on developing an attractive and supportive environment that might enable any business, whether small or large, to flourish, and to allow the market to sort out which businesses succeed. Many communities have had success in creating this environment. They have developed and fostered a high-quality workforce through great schools, community colleges, and universities. They have provided lifelong learning opportunities; built and maintained high-quality public infrastructure; created a business climate with reasonable levels of taxation and regulation; and through good government and quality amenities, have created the kinds of communities where highly educated and skilled people want to live and work (Edmiston, 2007, p. 92).

Economic development, or local area economic improvement, increasingly has become a matter of better positioning local communities for current and anticipated change. As Daniel Kemmis, former Director of the O'Connor Center and ardent advocate of bioregionalism states, 'Economic development or local area economic development, increasingly has become a matter of better positioning local communities' (Kemmis, 1990). And doing this successfully requires learning at community and regional levels, particularly among key community leadership. There is no single template for each community to follow in doing this. There is no 'one-size-fits-all' strategy. Economic development is not something finally achieved and then forgotten. It is always a 'work-in-progress', and in order for the work to progress, it must be based upon a sustained and sustaining process of community leadership learning. Many communities aspire to create such a process. Few actually attain it. One that largely has is Billings, Montana, through the hard work and vision of *Celebrate Billings* assisted by the O'Connor Center for the Rocky Mountain West at the University of Montana and the Regional Economies Assessment Database which the centre has developed for local leaders.

Notes

[1] *Celebrate Billings* website (http://www.celebratebillings.com).
[2] *READ* can be accessed through the O'Connor Center for the Rocky Mountain West, University of Montana (http://www.crmw.org).
[3] Information on the Missoula City Club can be found at http://www.cityclubmissoula.org
[4] The results of forums and activities under *Montana on the Move* are summarised at http://www.crmw.org/montanaonthemove
[5] Mission statement on the *Celebrate Billings* website.

References

Corporation for Enterprise Development (CfED) (1993) *Rethinking Rural Development*. Washington, DC: CfED.

Edmiston, K. (2007) 'The role of small and large businesses in economic development', *Economic Review*, 2nd quarter: 73–93.

Inman, P. and Swanson, L. (2007) 'Cities as engines of growth', in M. Osborne, K. Sankey and B. Wilson (eds) *Social Capital, Lifelong Learning and the Management of Place: An International Perspective*. London: Routledge.

Kemmis, D. (1990) *Community and the Politics of Place*. Norman: University of Oklahoma Press.

National Academy of Public Administration (NAPA) (1996) *A Path to Smarter Economic Development: Reassessing the Federal Role*. Prepared for the US Economic Development Administration, Washington, DC, November.

Chapter 17

Who will we become? Power, identities and cultures in the context of notions of social capital and governance

Gwenneth Marshall

Introduction

Evidence of regeneration and regional development programmes – ubiquitous terms in the processes of current development – can be seen in the physical work that is taking place in cities, towns, villages and countryside across the UK. However, the process is neither evenly spread nor uniform in its articulation. Those who inhabit these places may become aware of the process as road closures disrupt their journeys, when a new art gallery or a footbridge over the river appears, when the calendar of local events becomes fuller, when the local farmer changes the way a piece of land is used, or when they become involved through consultation or activity. Educators may find that they have access to specific additional or targeted funding. According to Treasury statistics, the budget of the Department for Communities and Local Government (previously the Office of the Deputy Prime Minister) for 'improving the quality of life by creating inclusive and sustainable communities in all regions' in 2006/7 was £9,570,406,000 (€14,121,685,013.83), with an expected requirement of a supplementary budget of £103,336,000 (€152,444,182.40).

This chapter looks at the identity implications of the processes of regeneration and regional development. It argues that planning processes and rein- vigoration activities, whether they concern the physical environment, cultural activity or the expansion of knowledge bases through learning regions, affect who we are, and who we will become as individuals, groups and com- munities. More specifically, it suggests that those engaged in the processes of development have understandings of who and what the populations, individuals and communities that are being regenerated are, and that this has identity implications because who and what those groups are may change as a result of the decisions that grow out of those understandings. This, it argues, raises questions about governance and inclusivity in development processes and places a responsibility on those involved to understand the potential effects of their actions. In the context of regeneration, the chapter examines development processes through the lens of interactions between power and identity and offers a theoretical perspective on the dynamic interaction between them. Methodological issues which occur in researching the human aspects of regeneration are explored. Articulations of governance are considered in the context of the practice and processes of regeneration and regional development, along with the potential of social capital theory to address human considerations in development agendas, identity formation and development processes. Finally, the chapter considers interventions that could be made in these processes. It offers a theoretical framework as a starting point for the development of systemic and dynamic, but practical strategies, which could be built into, for example, development processes, codes of practice and training.

Regeneration and regional development

Development activity manifests itself at local, regional and national levels. It may be a response to a particular set of local circumstances. The story of Chatham, Kent in the UK can be understood as such. According to the South East England Development Agency's booklet *Chatham Maritime…A Success Story* (2004):

> On 31st March 1984, the Royal Navy left Chatham Dockyard for the last time, leaving in its wake a derelict site, mass unemployment and a bleak future for the people living in the Medway towns. But since then, the 140-hectare site has been transformed into a thriving community where people live, work and enjoy quality leisure time. 400 years of naval history may have ended when the dockyard closed, but the site continues to attract thousands of visitors each year, including many who are now deciding to make Chatham their maritime home.

The regeneration agenda can also be understood in wider terms as a response to late twentieth-century post-industrial decline and, at some levels, to environmental change, which is sited 'in the context of twenty-first century local, national and international efforts and initiatives that seek to absorb, to engineer, and to accommodate global change' (Marshall, 2005, p. 275). Such global change can be understood as taking place in the context of globalised and globalising economies, multinational companies and supranational governance through institutions such as the World Bank and the World Trade Organisation. Green and Voyageur point to an economically based inter-national disciplinary framework that privileges economic concerns over citizens. 'Governments that persist in orienting policy to citizen needs over those of the "economy" or bond rating agencies are likely to be disciplined low credit ratings, devalued currencies and unattractive bond rates, together with a loss of investor confidence, quickly bring these governments to heel' (Green and Voyageur, 1999, p. 148).

It is not a question here of drawing a simple picture in which economic factors are seen as antagonistic to identity. Rather the question needs to be opened up so that the identity issues can be explored. Ellin (1996) gives a comprehensive account of postmodern urbanism that outlines the various modes in which urban design culture and the individual have been understood to interact in the post-industrial world and cites new urban disciplines, including urban sociology and environmental psychology, that focus on 'the relationship between people and their surroundings' (p. 3).

Identity and power

Identity, which can be understood as having relevance to individuals and to groups, is a contested concept that has been the focus of much scholarly debate across disciplines. In part, it is about our own self-perceptions and how others perceive us and define us. It can be argued that who we can be within the frames of social, cultural and physical environments that exist, and that will exist in the future also plays a part in individual and group identities. In this sense, identity can be viewed as fluid, mutable and, in varying degrees, malleable. Such interpretations are supported by a large body of gender literature that links personal identity and subjectivity to external power sources. Some of these sources are cited below; other notable contributors include Friedan (2001), Millett (1977), Greer (1970, 1980), Scott (1988), Faludi (1992) and Spender (1989).

As far back as the eighteenth century, Mary Wollstonecraft was writing of the invasive relationship of external power sources in identity formation, and linking personal identity to broader sources of public power, citing education and social positioning as enfeebling the minds of women. On this basis, she argued against the political systems of the day as well as against Rousseau's approaches to the education of women. Mediations of male identity were similarly identified (Wollstonecraft, 1990). Simone de Beauvoir, in the mid-twentieth century, considered the power issues inherent in dominance as a normative identity framework that underpinned and defined the empowered 'one' and the disempowered 'other'. Personal identity was seen as compromised through internalised status systems that were in turn seen as hegemonically instrumental in maintaining external hierarchical power systems (de Beauvoir, 1972, p. 18). Writing about the power of the state and institutions Foucault, who understood power to be multilayered, decentred, diverse and dynamic, identified historical shifts in how power was exercised, tracing the birth of 'a kind of individualising power' (1980, p. 148; 1982).

More recently Bartky (1988), building on Foucault's work, provides a link between invasive power and the formation of identity and persona: 'Something is "internalised" when it gets incorporated into the structure of the self (p. 77). While much of the literature on identity focuses on how the individual is positioned, suppressed or enabled by external power sources, that is not to say that the individual is entirely powerless. Butler's ideas are interesting because they raise the possibility that power can be reclaimed through the performance of identities and the identity choices that we make (Butler, 1992). Understanding who we are as individuals and groups is a complex undertaking, especially in a world where many of us move around the world or relocate within the country of our birth. Here Brah's (1996) insightful work broadens considerations to include ideas of place and community. Considering the identity aspects of moving across geographical and cultural borders, and of belonging, Brah theorises the concept of 'diaspora space' as 'the intersectionality of diaspora, border and dis/location, a point of confluence of economic, political, cultural and psychic processes' (p. 208) holding that it is 'where multiple subject positions are juxtaposed'.

The ideas outlined above allow for a complex understanding of the identities of individuals and of groups as being, at least in part, the articulation and embodiment of social constructions that change over time and place. Thus it is possible to understand personal and group identities to be the site of power interventions, and power struggles and the slippage between what and who we are, and what and who we believe ourselves or others to be, become significant. Identity is understood as a mutable space in which transformations can take place. In this scenario, the public planning of personal and group futures can be seen as having the potential to change who we are and who we can become.

Conceptualising the relationship between power and identity

As discussed above, identity can be understood as vulnerable to influence and to external power interventions. It can be expected then, that governance, public policy and public activity are likely to have implications for identity. With this in mind, an analytic concept and model based on the understandings of the dynamic interactions of power and identity outlined above may be useful. The concept of the ***power and identity continuum*** and the related model (see Figure 17.1) is offered in response to these needs.

In a theoretical and academic sense, the ***power and identity continuum*** is a response to Foucault's exhortation to consider the 'how' by asking the question 'What happens when individuals exert (as they say) power over others?' (1982, p. 216). The complex relationship between personal and group identities, regulation, governance and the exercise of public power is understood to involve multidimensional, multifarious modes by which identities and group identities are influenced, manipulated, coerced or constructed. Such dynamic interactions cannot be understood in linear terms and are more accurately understood as particular formations of open-ended cycles of empowerment and disempowerment. The ***power and identity continuum*** offers a theoretically informed concept and model that captures the dynamics of the relationship between the two concepts and can help in the detailed analysis of power sources and of interactions between power and identity.

Figure 17.1 shows identity, which is also identified as 'the me or the us' as surrounded by power sources. The left-hand side depicts stronger power sources while the right-hand side depicts weaker power sources (stronger power sources are shown in bold upper case while weaker power sources are represented in bold lower case). While the illustration draws broad distinctions between stronger and weaker power sources, it does not seek to identify who or what those power sources are. This is because the diagram is intended to be generic so that it can be used as a diagnostic tool in diverse sets of circumstances where it may be helpful to identify and insert named power sources. The interaction between power and identity is shown as existing at all points. This interaction is illustrated by lines and by arrows. Where lines

Figure 17.1: *The Power and Identity Continuum* (Marshall, 2005)

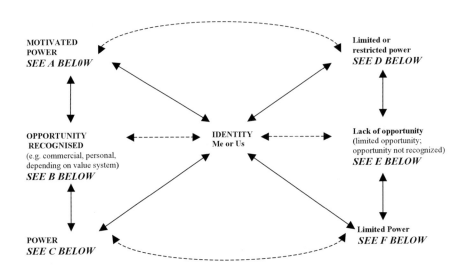

are shown in the form of dashes the interaction is seen as possible but not always present.

The diagrammatic illustration of the ***power and identity continuum*** shown above is designed to help in the process of understanding the power sources that may, either in a motivated fashion or unwittingly, mediate or circumscribe individual and group identities and the identities that are available in the future worlds that are being created. Below is a rudimentary analysis of power and identity in regeneration and regional development using the continuum. The analysis is offered as an example of how the ***power and identity continuum*** could be used and as a starting point for building a more informed picture that may help to create empowerment models for communities and individuals into development frameworks. The analysis is offered in chart form in Table 17.1.

The first three columns show stronger power sources while the last three show weaker power sources. Column A lists those power sources which could be understood as 'motivated' in the sense of having specific agendas. Column B shows power sources that come into play as a result of opportunities in development activities. Column C has been used for other diverse power sources, from the World Bank to conference participants (that is certainly not to say that all conference participants are powerful; rather that some are and that the conference process itself is a source of power). Column D shows

Table 17.1: An analysis of power sources in regeneration and regional development using the *power and identity continuum* (Marshall, 2005) as a diagnostic tool (see Figure 17.1)

A	B	C	D	E	F
Global, international, European, national, regional and local agendas, e.g. ecological, economic, political, professional, artistic, business, professional and personal agendas	Opportunities to further aims/agendas identified and pursued within the regeneration and regional development agenda, e.g. making money/making a living – applies to developers, business investors, regeneration professionals, consultants, other ancillary workers)	The amount of power varies and is not absolute	Each tier can be understood to restrict the tier below, but also as having the potential to restrict the tier above or across, etc.	Individuals and groups who do not have a presence in columns A–D	General population
		World Bank	local governance	Individuals who do not have the time, inclination, patience, resilience, courage or education to become involved in the previous columns A–D	Individuals and groups who fall outside the networks shown in A–D (see also column D)
		WTO	community organisations		
		G8	community activists	Those who do not know about the power networks and funding streams	
		EU	development workers		
		national governance	artists and performative artists		
		DEFRA	members of consultative bodies		
		Arts Council	those who fall within funding criteria		
		regional governance			
		business			
		religious establishment			
		conference participants			

power sources that are limited and limiting. Column E shows sources of power that are limited because of lack of opportunity. Finally, Column F shows limited power sources. The various power sources identified in a particular development process could, as a first step, be listed as they are seen to exist. A second step would involve plotting them on the continuum in Figure 17.1 so that the power and identity dynamics could be understood in a more informed way with a view to creating balance and cycles of empowerment. The continuum opens up identity issues and the opportunity to plot the sources of power in a particular development project.

Researching the people aspects of regeneration and regional development – the issues

The difficulties of developing effective research in the context of rapid change are substantial. Agendas and strategies are often set at national, supranational or even global levels. Adding to the complexities, over the last decade UK policies have increasingly been effected through directives from the Prime Minister and senior ministers and underpinned by directed funding schemes. This style of government, which has been characterised by journalists as 'sofa' government (e.g. Hastings, 2007; Peev, 2007) has made the unpicking of policy-making processes even more problematic. Vaughan counsels against over-specialism which can leave researchers feeling that they 'know more and more about less and less' (Vaughan, 1992, p. 173). She is similarly wary of tying research to organisational forms, academic disciplines, restrictive theoretical frames, or research comfort zones because 'the lack of variation in our choice can inhibit the discovery of theories, models and concepts that are broadly applicable' (p. 174) and suggests that 'the paradox of theory is that at the same time as it tells us where to look, it can keep us from seeing' (p. 195). Saukko sees research methodologies as 'always located, informed by particular social positions and historical moments and their agendas' (Saukko, 2003, p.3). Context is important and may involve 'networks traversed and shaped by flows of transnational media, money, people, things and images' (p. 6). Valid research is multidimensional. She further argues that 'The discourse on "the global" may smack as a bit of an intellectual and popular spring fashion. However, globalisation calls for an analysis of the interaction between the lived, mediated, religious, ethnic, gendered, economic, and political dimensions of the contemporary world' (p. 8).

Researching power and identity in the context of regeneration and regional development: a case study

In a case study designed to investigate the context in which regeneration and regional development were taking place, a total of seven industry-related conferences were observed in the first seven months of the project. In addition, a large body of associated printed and other materials were examined with a view to building up a picture of how the development process is articulated. As part of this phase of the research a detailed case study examination of the context and processes and developments in the rural regeneration agenda was carried out (Marshall, 2005). Two regional network meetings were also observed.

Analysis of the research findings indicated that each conference was underpinned by an economic discourse and that access to funding was seen as key to the process of development in each sector. In the study of rural regeneration, funding was radically reorganised over the course of the research and was, in its revised form, articulated in ways that were likely to enable some identities and to marginalise others. Careful observation and mapping of regeneration, regional development and rural development processes pointed to strategic rather than to democratic forms of governance. Policy was formed and passed through a variety of conferences attended by a large and diverse professional and academic class. Policies and strategies that emerged were articulated through dedicated funding streams and administered through layers of stakeholders. Consent mechanisms included layers of 'consultative' community bodies. Figure 17.2 offers a tracking strategy to show funding and identity influence through the regeneration and regional development process. A significant discourse on consultation practices existed in the conferences, though planning processes typically included consultation at the level of practical implementation rather than at the strategy stage. Some success stories were given in which public consultation was considered to have been effective. The research also revealed two predominant discourses: user engagement strategies involving art, culture and festivals, and the role of social capital.

The discourse on engagement

The first discourse concerns the engagement of people with regenerated environments and puts forward art, festivals and culture as a way of fostering ownership of, and participation in, regenerated environments and as a means of 'breathing life into development and of engaging populations in order that they will take ownership of development and regeneration initiatives' (Matarasso and Landry, 1996). Robert Hughes, the Chief Executive Officer of Kirklees Council, speaking in 1988, said: 'My own blunt evaluation of regeneration programmes that don't have a cultural component is that they won't work' (cited in Evans and Shaw, 2004, p. 2). Evans and Shaw go on to identify gaps in evaluating the wider community effects of schemes involving art and culture (ibid.).

The discourse on social capital

The second discourse considers people from the perspective of social capital. The notion of social capital has emerged as a possible route to extending human considerations in development agendas. Putnam explains that the origins of social capital lie in Hanifan's 1916 writings about the value of strong, supportive community networks. For Putnam, strong networks do not necessarily bring positive results and in some circumstances can be divisive or reinforce inequality (Putnam, 2002). Hall holds that 'social capital turns primarily on the degree to which people associate regularly with one another in settings of relative equality thus building up relations of trust and mutual reciprocity' (Hall, 2002). Writing from a vocational education standpoint, Winch suggests that the term social capital has come to be used in a more individual sense that measures the human social and cultural capital that attaches to individuals. Cultural capital is taken to include cognitive aspects, thus making a link with education and the acquisition of knowledge as social capital (Winch, 2000). Lin explains theories of social capital as trade- and exchange-based approaches to human interaction and to human cultures. Social capital construes social interaction in economic and exchange-value terms and promotes the idea that within neoliberal economies human factors can hold economic and status value for individuals and for groups. These individuals and groups can contribute to dynamic empowerment (Lin, 2001).

Understanding how such discourses may manifest themselves in practical ways involves analysing the details of the development process as it is played out. One city's published strategy declares that it 'engages with and reflects the needs of local communities, develops cohesive communities and leads to sustainable improvements'. This reflects a deficit model of community that is consistent with social capital theories in that it considers what communities need rather than who they are, what they would like to become, and how they would like to get there. The focus on development from such mission statements is likely to be articulated through processes that will bring communities into futures shaped and imagined by others. In this scenario, how people relate to development and regeneration in terms of voice and power is generally considered only tangentially during the end phases of development once strategies have been set, policy frameworks put in place and funding streams determined.

The same city conducted a survey in which people were asked to indicate whether they would like more shopping and leisure facilities. The two questions were collapsed into one and only one tick-box response was invited. This structured choice did not allow a genuinely differentiated choice for instance to curb retail and to increase leisure facilities, or vice versa. Who we are and who we think that we will become are areas for consideration that tend to lie outside democratisation and consultation attempts in current regeneration and development processes and are unrecognised or 'off the radar screens' of many developers and consultants.

Despite its fundamentally economic approach, practitioners and theorists have used social capital as a vehicle for demonstrating the importance of people to successful outcomes in development (Broadbent, 2005; Beck and Martin, 2005). However, the concept of social capital can also be understood as constraining our understandings of populations, cultures and identities by pressing them into a fundamentally economic paradigm that supports and incubates 'enterprise identities' (Marshall, 2005) regardless of the value systems, beliefs, cultures and characteristics of individuals and groups. Thus social capital theories are not the answer to the identity interventions raised in this chapter. New and enabling strategies are needed to assert inclusive democratic processes in regeneration and regional development process and practice. It is therefore important to increase knowledge and understanding in this area. Developing appropriate and effective research and diagnostic tools will help. Some responses to these needs are given in the following section.

Interventions and theory building for researchers and for practitioners

This chapter has argued that power imbalances impact upon identity because they affect strategic decision making, which in current forms of governance plays a part in shaping and enabling some identities and in suppressing, silencing and marginalising others. Successful empowerment and demo-cratisation of process can only be achieved if power imbalances are recognised and addressed at the point of strategic consideration and planning. The *power and identity continuum* (see above) offers a theoretically informed framework for diagnosing power sources and for understanding the potential for unintended and unacknowledged mediations of identity and cultures. The role of perceived and imagined identities envisaged here demands more specific attention and articulation. In order to capture the somewhat convoluted meaning of imagined, understood and perceived identities described, the concept *identity visions* has been introduced. Its significance lies in its potential for rendering the process of identity moderation visible. It refers to the ideas about who communities and individuals are and who they will be in the future and, in doing so, highlights the need for inclusivity. It also carries with it informed understandings that *identity visions* are, in part informed by internal landscapes and history. A related concept – *identity futures* – is also introduced as useful in signalling that the processes of development are likely to have identity consequences in the futures that are being created. This concept is designed to help in identifying exclusionary development processes that could result in deterministic identity formations and cultural outcomes. The processes in question may, as argued above, have embedded within them ideas and perceptions that cluster around or that follow from understandings of existing or future identities and cultures that may permeate decision making and planning. Such identity visions tend to be filtered through value systems that encourage and develop imagined future identities and existing identities and cultures that are deemed desirable. Conversely, other identities may not be included in identity visions, in which case progressive marginalisation, exclusion and suppression may result.

In Figure 17.2, strategy, funding and identity influence are tracked through the regeneration process, demonstrating how perceptions of identity feed into the process at all levels. The chart tracks the dynamic movement of strategy, funding and **identity visions** as found in the research outlined above. The arrows show the directional flows of influence. The top line shows a starting point in which understandings about who individuals and groups are, together with strategy agendas brought into the regeneration process. Strategy agendas may originate in the person at this point but may also originate elsewhere, e.g. professional knowledge; artistic stance; a global, supranational, national body or fund-holder. The holders of these strategy agendas, who have varying amounts of power, also have understandings of past, present and future identity that may be partly or wholly unacknowledged and uninformed. It is these understandings that have been termed **identity visions**. This line represents, for the most part, the many professionals who are engaged in regeneration and regional development. The line of arrows shows the

Identity vision and broader strategy agenda held by each politician, policy maker and regeneration 'doer'
(e.g. developers, festival organisers, educators, artists, creative directors, regeneration consultants, planning department staff)

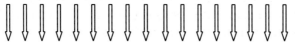

conferences, policy meetings and broader strategy development meetings

Identity visions + regeneration strategies + dedicated funding streams
Based on identity vision inputs and broader strategy agenda, as shown above

Regional development agencies strategy and planning and applications for funding within funding paradigms + consultation obligation

Communities – individuals and groups

Figure 17.2: Tracking strategy, funding and identity visions through the regeneration and regional development process

movement of these identity visions and strategy agendas into the conferences, policy meetings and broader strategy meetings that this group variously and sometimes together attend. The last line shows communities in a 'consultation' dialogue at the regional and local levels. At this point strategic directions are likely to have been set and funding paradigms that had not already been set around strategies that were set outside of the process are likely to been streamed into strategy and into envisioned futures. The diagram shows the potential for identity mediations at each level in the process of planning, envisioning and funding and also shows that the individuals and groups for and to whom development is being 'done' do not have a viable route for inclusion.

Conclusion

Civil activity and governance, at its most altruistic, seeks to improve futures. Even this ideal carries the possibility of suppressing rather than enabling individuals and communities. Spender posited a 'logic of dominance' in which those who order the world tend to be blind to practices that marginalise others (Spender, 1989, p. 88). Others have also pointed to a link between the design and enactment of policy and the internal landscapes of the empowered groups who produce that policy (Millett, 1977; Mohanty, 1988). In contrast, the 1980 catalogue for the Paris Biennale's first architecture exhibition defined urbanity as 'that aspect of a place which illustrates its identity, memory, conflicts and changes, while expressing and nurturing its inhabitants' (Ellin, 1996, p. 38). Interestingly, the utopian ideal that is being held up here is a future that 'expresses' rather than shapes inhabitants. Here Ellin takes planned and built environments as the starting point, but the same principles can be applied to all of the modes of development – art, culture, education, learning regions, community development – that form part of the shaping of our futures, our cultures and ourselves and through which we are attempting to build a sustainable world. With these ideas in mind, all forms of civil activity and governance can be understood as pressing into service histories, knowledge sets, assumptions and experience. However, as demonstrated above, regeneration and regional development is bringing into being new futures which involve not only problem solving but also creative imagination and visions of place and of community. It is these visions that may circumscribe or moderate identity, changing not just how we live, but who we are in the future. It has been argued in this chapter that players in regeneration and regional development, simply by being human, bring with them often unspoken and unacknowledged understandings about who and what populations, individuals and communities are, and that this can mediate the identities of those who will inhabit the regenerated and developed locales that they are bringing into being.

References

Bartky, S.L. (1988) 'Foucault, femininity, and the modernisation of patriarchal power', in I. Diamond and L. Quimby (eds), *Feminism and Foucault: Reflections on Resistance*. Boston, MA: Northeastern University Press.

Beck, D. and Martin, H. (2005) 'Co-investigation of social capital', in *Making Knowledge Work: Building Sustainable Communities through Partnerships in Place Management, Social Capital and Lifelong Learning*, international conference proceedings, University of Stirling.

Brah, A. (1996) *Cartographies of Diaspora: Contesting Identities*. London: Routledge.

Broadbent, C. (2005) 'Like ripples in the pond: building communities of practice for sustainable outcomes', in *Making Knowledge Work: Building Sustainable Communities through Partnerships in Place Management, Social Capital and Lifelong Learning, international conference proceedings*, University of Stirling.

Butler, J. (1992) 'Imitation and gender insubordination', in D. Fuss (ed), *Inside/Out*. New York: Routledge.

Central Government Supply Estimates (2006–7) Spring Supplementary Estimates HC 293 (06/07) 978 010294 4457', HM Treasury, February 2007. London: Stationery Office.

'Chatham Maritime…A Success Story' (2004) 20th Anniversary. Guildford: South East England Development Agency.

de Beauvoir, S. (1972, *1949*) *The Second Sex*. London: Penguin.

Ellin, N. (1996) *Postmodern Urbanism*. Oxford: Blackwell.

Evans, G. and Shaw, P. (2004) *The Contribution of Culture to Regeneration in the UK. A Review of Evidence: A Report to the Department for Culture, Media and Sport*. London Metropolitan University.

Faludi, S. (1992) *Backlash*. London: Chatto & Windus.

Foucault, M., ed. C. Gordon (1980) *Power/Knowledge*. London: Harvester.

Foucault, M. (1982) 'The subject and power'. Published as an afterword to H. Dreyfus and P. Rabinow, *Michel Foucault: Beyond Structuralism and Hermeneutics*. London: Harvester Wheatsheaf.

Friedan, B. (2001, *1959*) *The Feminine Mystique*. New York: Norton.

Green, J. and Voyageur, C. (1999) 'Globalization and development', in M. Porter and E. Judd (eds), *Feminists Doing Development*. London: Zed Books.

Greer, G. (1970) *The Female Eunuch*. London: MacGibbon & Kee.

Greer, G. (1980) *The Whole Woman*. Oxford: Oxford University Press.

Hall, P. (2002) 'The role of government and the distribution of social capital', in R.D. Putnam, *Democracies in Flux: The Evolution of Social Capital in Contemporary Society*. New York: Oxford University Press.

Hastings (2007) (www.official-documents.gov.uk/documents/hc007/hc02/ 0293, accessed 27.6.2007).

Lin, N. (2001) *Social Capital: A Theory of Social Structure and Action*. Cambridge: Cambridge University Press.

Marshall, G. (2005) *A Critical Reflection on the Implications for Identity of Public Funding Streams: Reconstructing the Rural Woman Within Frameworks of Regeneration and Rural Development* in *Making Knowledge Work: Building Sustainable Communities through Partnerships in Place Management, Social Capital and Lifelong Learning*, international conference proceedings, University of Stirling.

Matarasso, F. and Landry, C. (1996) 'Can cities be revitalized without culture?' In F. Matarasso and S. Halls (eds), *The Art of Regeneration: Nottingham March 1996*, conference papers. Stroud: Comedia and Nottingham City Council.

Millett, K. (1977) *Sexual Politics*. London: Women's Press.

Mohanty, C. (1988) 'Under Western eyes: feminist scholarship and colonial discourses', *Feminist Review*, 30: 65–88.

Office of the Deputy Prime Minister (now the Department for Communities and Local Government) (2005) 'Update' (Spring), London.

Peev (www.guardian.co.uk/commentsfreee/story), accessed 1 July 2007.

Putnam, R.D. (2002) *Democracies in Flux: The Evolution of Social Capital in Contemporary Society*. Oxford: Oxford University Press.

Saukko, P. (2003) *Doing Research in Cultural Studies*. London: Sage.

Scott, J.W. (1988) 'Deconstructing equality-versus-difference: or, the uses of poststructuralist theory for feminism', *Feminist Studies*, 14(1): 32–50.

Spender, D. (1989) *Invisible Women*. London: The Women's Press.

Vaughan, D. (1992) 'Theory elaboration: the heuristics of case analysis', in C.C. Ragin and H.S. Becker, *What is a Case? Exploring the Foundations of Social Enquiry*. Cambridge: Cambridge University Press.

Winch, C. (2000) *Education Work and Social Capital: Towards New Conceptions of Vocational Education*. London: Routledge.

Wollstonecraft, M. (1990, *1792*) *A Vindication of the Rights of Women*. Harmondsworth: Penguin.

Part 3

Next Steps

Chapter 18

Converging ideas for building stronger communities

David Adams

This chapter canvasses from the preceding chapters the steady progress of learning that has emerged over the past six years since PASCAL was formed.

PASCAL developed out of the 2001 Learning Cities and Regions Conference in Australia and reflected a broad church of interest in new ideas around place, social capital and learning regions. In particular there was considerable interest in exploring further the relations between these three core ideas. In this book the nature and importance of those original ideas have become clearer, with a number of key themes – four in all – emerging as significant from practice, from policy development work and from research.

The themes are: (1) Integrated place-based strategies to leverage social and economic growth (2) The importance of local knowledge to research, policy and practice (3) Theme 3: Civic engagement and networks as new forms of governance and (4) Research/policy/practice collaboration as the key to coproduction of knowledge. In many ways the successful understanding of these themes and how they play out in settings differentiated by history, culture, issue, resources and capability, can potentially lay down the preconditions for successful learning and community development.

The themes, explored in greater depth below, cover a raft of professions and academic disciplines with no single or clear theoretical home or policy field. The authors move across discourses and methodologies to try and elicit better understandings of the ideas in play and the consequential policy settings that might improve outcomes – for people, for places, for economies and for communities.

The key ideas of lifelong learning, community development and place are themselves all contested. As Hans Schuetze (Chapter 2), for example, notes in relation to lifelong learning, there are at least four distinct normative models (emancipatory, cultural, open society and human capital). There are differing objectives behind each model as well as differing organisational forms associated with planning and delivery. With each model the role of markets, communities and governments varies.

The situation is not dissimilar to that of social capital and place management. Here, we take social capital to mean *the norms and relations between groups which can be used as resources*. For example, within the social capital litera- ture there are ongoing debates about whether governments can or should even be engaged with the idea (Edwards *et al*, 2006). Critics note that the history of government attempts to create social capital have often resulted in its destruction or commodification for political purposes (e.g. Halpern, 2004). For many people social capital is the domain of family and community, not markets or governments.

These points are noted here simply to acknowledge the complexity of the ideas with which this volume is engaged. Indeed, Ingunn Sandaker and Britt Andersen (Chapter 4) nicely capture the theoretical importance of complexity theory as an account of how knowledge and learning are constructed. In order to focus on the intersections between the ideas, many of these contested background issues are muted – not because of their irrelevance – but because we are attempting to explore the ideas through a different lens. It is pleasing to see that there are an increasing number of scholars examining such specific links – for example, between social capital and lifelong learning (Field, 2005) and social capital and the knowledge economy (Westlund, 2006).

Thematic convergence explored

Theme 1: Integrated place-based strategies to leverage social and economic growth
A key trend that emerges from the book's authors is the development of place- based strategies designed to leverage simultaneously social and economic growth. While often associated with regeneration (e.g. John Tibbitt in Chapter 8), they are increasingly being developed as generic learning strategies (Balázs Németh, Chapter 6 and Peter Kearns and Denise Reghenzani, Chapter 7).

As Tibbitt points out, the policy reasoning is shifting. The 'trickle-down' strategies which emerged in the 1980s often failed to materialise or reached the 'wrong' people and places. Such approaches also tended to use blunt instruments such as major projects or job-creation programmes. Tibbitt notes that these are being replaced by more sophisticated strategies which focus on:

- the direct engagement of communities in planning and delivering economic activity;
- a more proactive role for local small to medium enterprises;
- a greater emphasis on place-based rather than functional programmes;
- better alignment of economic activity with labour market skills and training programmes;
- a greater role for tertiary institutions;
- better alignment between industry and labour market trends and skills;
- leveraging the links with social capital formation, e.g. through clusters; and
- emphasising the importance of supportive infrastructure strategies – such as roads, telecommunications and 'creative' facilities.

Such features – which emerge through this volume – reinforce similar findings from earlier research (Duke, Doyle and Wilson 2006; Florida 2007).

Barry McGaw (Chapter 5) provides examples from Australia to demonstrate the benefits of integrating learning strategies into the early stages of planning for new communities. Again, the link between place and learning is at the forefront of this reasoning, as is the importance of understanding how the planning and delivery of infrastructure helps shape the formation of social capital. Internationally, many governments are developing strategies which revisit the importance of place as a key organising principle for the planning and delivery of 'public value' (Victorian Parliament, 2006).

Similarly Anne Badenhorst (Chapter 11) and Carolyn Broadbent (Chapter 12) both argue for the importance of place as not only a site of knowledge production but also as sites for the integration of ideas, resources and co-operative behaviours. In both cases the link between learning and place is made clear.

Theme 2: The importance of local knowledge to research, policy and practice

Many of the chapters (especially 3, 4, 8, 9, 10, 11, 12, 14 and 17) emphasise the importance of local knowledge in learning and community development. Common points the authors make include:

- institutions play an important role in shaping actors and the capacity of communities to reshape those institutions;
- the conditions under which ideas and practices can and do travel across space and time are not self-evident and require specific research and analysis;
- a focus on learning as an inductive and heuristic activity – rather than as a deductive process – is important;
- there is a need to establish and support regional and sub-regional entities to host/promote/advocate change;
- intermediaries (individuals/groups/institutions) have an important role in facilitating (or hindering) learning development and transfer;
- social capital (expressed, e.g. trust relations) is significant as a learning precondition.

Each of these areas warrants further research in its own right, but the more significant insight from the book is the interdependence of these factors. It appears that they are all necessary conditions for the successful emergence and sustainability of lifelong learning and community development. However, the current structure of disciplines in universities, the structure of the professions and the structure of government departments militate against integrative approaches, as does the separation of research from practice and policy.

Government departments, for example, are usually organised around functions such as health, education, justice, agriculture and infrastructure which can hinder place-based orientations by framing the research, policy and practice around functions rather than place-based outcomes. Many of the authors note the significance of regional and other mediating institutions, networks and individuals in trying to develop place-based orientations to research, practice and policy development. A key aspect of this is the role of networks and civic engagement strategies, to which I now turn.

Theme 3: Civic engagement and networks as new forms of governance

Throughout the book, civic engagement and networks are offered as both pre-conditions for the emergence of lifelong learning and community development and for successful policy development. The role of local networks in their own right and in the interface with regional and in some cases global institutions are explored in chapters 3, 6, 7 and 12.

Kilpatrick *et al.* (Chapter 14) not only demonstrate the critical role of local networks in generating ideas and new practices but also the importance of 'boundary crossings' which enable ideas and practices to be transferred spatially for ready adoption and diffusion. Similarly, Strathdee (Chapter 3) identifies the importance of those people who can 'span boundaries' during the innovation process in the New Zealand biotech industry. His chapter is important because it demonstrates the links between networks and economic development – now rightly understood as a form of community development. It provides an example of the intersection of two literatures – network theory from public policy and cluster theory from economics. Both bodies of knowledge give prominence to the role of informal networks in the creation of social capital which can then be used as a resource in building economic capital.

Schuetze (Chapter 2) reminds us that the extent to which lifelong learning strategies will engage with community is dependent on the policy objectives being attributed to lifelong learning. For example, where the objectives relate to narrow constructs of learning for skills development in response to employer demands, there is less likely to be extensive community engagement. The more the objectives relate to 'social justice' objectives, the more likelihood there is of civic engagement becoming a critical component of planning and delivery. Larry Swanson (Chapter 16) also highlights the importance of connecting up decision makers and decision making as critical determinants of the success of lifelong learning strategies. Like other authors, he brings out the importance of the private sector as a key player in the development of lifelong learning strategies.

Most of the authors canvass the important role of social capital in the formation and sustainability of lifelong learning and community development strategies. Some focus specifically on the idea of social capital (Kilpatrick *et al.*) whereas others examine how it can be used as a resource to leverage, e.g. economic advantage (Strathdee). It is interesting to contrast the applied social capital approach of the authors in this volume to the ongoing international debates. Despite the numerous critiques of Putnam – and to a lesser extent those of Coleman and the UN approach championed by Woolcock (Putnam, 2000; Woolcock, 2001). Many of our authors remain cautious about the commodification of social capital and its capacity to be destructive and/or co-opted by specific networks and institutions. These attempts to 'apply' social capital are yielding important insights as to its nature. Five ideas about social capital stand out from this volume:

- The more complex the theorising, the less able the idea is to be researched or applied.
- Social capital seems to be a very local phenomenon in terms of the ability of governments, communities and markets to support its development and apply it to address particular risks and opportunities.
- The link between social capital as an idea and government policy is through networks. Networks are the holders and transmitters of social capital and are more amenable to government intervention that the norms and values that underpin them.
- many of our authors remain cautious about the commodification of social capital and its capacity to be destructive and/or co-opted by specific networks and institutions.
- Social capital and place work well together. Social capital is a community asset and (whilst not all communities are place-based) its formation and growth are facilitated by smart mixing with other assets. McGaw and Kilpatrick *et al*. have all demonstrated the important role of seeing physical infrastructure as a determinant of social capital in the siting, design and collocation of learning facilities.

These ideas are supported by other research (Stilgoe, 2006; Svendsen and Svendsen, 2004; Goldsmith and Eggers, 2004) and in the UK there has been deliberate institutionalisation of the importance of social capital through, for example, the Sustainable Communities Bill (UK Government, 2007).

Theme 4: Research/policy/practice collaboration as the key to co-production of knowledge

In this book we are observing the dissolution of boundaries between research, policy making and practice with a focus on a three-way learning dynamic, and different flows of knowledge can be identified. Rather than the possible directions running in a linear fashion from research to policy to practice, policy determining what research will be carried out or over-zealous reactions to practitioners' experience, they are becoming more dynamic and flowing in all directions. The authors are not only describing partnerships between practitioners, researchers and policy makers as a form of co-production of knowledge but in so doing they are also constructing a much more heuristic approach to policy – one that emerges through practice interfacing with research and which reshapes constantly to adjust to new knowledge and influences. Some of those influences are political; some are driven by policy and research. Dave Beck's (Chapter 15) analysis shows how frontline workers' understandings of social capital are a mixture of practitioner experience, research findings and policy influences – often from formal institutions.

The role of practitioners and researchers in the policy process has been enhanced in recent years as a result of several factors. A push for 'evidence-based' policy emerged in the mid-1990s as part of the renewed emphasis on rationality and managerialism – although of course we should be cautious about just who defines 'evidence' and why the push has led to a re-engagement between policy makers and researchers. This development coincided with the growth of university community engagement strategies (linked to lifelong learning objectives) which created connections both with policy makers and the community. This development is most pronounced in the chapters by Németh (Chapter 6) and Puukka (Chapter 11) which show how the role of the university/community relationship is changing. For many years now university/community engagement strategies have been focused on universities providing intellectual property to stimulate economic growth. This has now shifted in two important ways. First, the concern is now much more with generating overall prosperity and well-being rather than simply economic growth. Secondly, the focus is on the universities as co-producers of place-based knowledge that can give competitive advantage.

During the 1990s, the 'community' orientation re-emerged across many governments internationally and has become embedded with a valuing of local knowledge – the type of knowledge associated with practitioners (Stilgoe, 2006; Parker and Gallagher, 2007). The community orientation continues to grow and is often linked to broader civic renewal objectives – further mandating local-level engagement in policy making and service delivery.

There are some risks here, in particular the possibility that the objectivity and critical role of research could be compromised by proximity to policy makers – where policy makers often have defined agendas on which to deliver. Strathdee and Marshall identify how the dominant discourses of the day shape the way people define issues and frame both understandings and judgments.

As elsewhere in the book, they also illustrate the sometimes tense interactions between community-based networks and more formal institutions in creating and shaping understanding and action.

Conclusion

The four themes elaborated on here are likely to continue as key research areas for PASCAL. The new understandings throughout this book take us a step closer to mapping out and theorising the dynamics driving successful community development and lifelong learning. Within the themes, the intersection between lifelong learning, social capital and place remains the richest area for further research and probably the most important for the emergence of new theory to illuminate policy making. Increasingly, this focus is also emerging in journals (e.g. the *Review of Social Economy*, 2007) where, as in this collection, the linking of scholarly debates with policy debates is informed by practitioner perspectives.

This book provides researchers, policy makers, practitioners and those interested in the relationship between them, first with an insight into how language and perspective vary between them. Secondly, it offers useful references to current policy thinking, practice and research activities across ten countries. Thirdly, the book illustrates the conditions under which successful partnerships between practitioners, policy makers and researchers are likely to emerge and be sustained. It also provides a raft of insights into the conditions under which community development and lifelong learning policies are likely to succeed or fail – including how measures of success and failure can be constructed. Finally, the book illustrates the interdependence of research, policy making and practice. Recognition and utilisation of that interdependence does not guarantee success but it significantly improves the odds.

PASCAL has helped establish that the interdependence exists and that the research/policy/practice interface enables us to better describe the phenomenon we are dealing with.

As practitioners our next step is to build on the findings to date and ensure practice is informed by, and contributes to, further learning. As policy makers our next step is to better understand the causal dynamics that can turn new place, learning and social capital ideas into more effective strategies that promote prosperity and wellbeing. As scholars our next step is to sharpen the theorising and the research, making it more accessible – but still to retain the independence of thought that is the bedrock of the findings and the analysis.

References

Bebbington, A., Guggenheim, S., Olson, E. and Woolcock, M. (2004) 'Exploring social capital debates at the World Bank', *Journal of Development Studies*, 40(5): 33–64.

Duke, C., Doyle, L. and Wilson, B. (2006) *Making Knowledge Work: Sustaining Learning Communities and Regions*. Gosford: Ashford Press.

Edwards, R., Franklin, J. and Holland, J. (eds) (2006) *Assessing Social Capital: Policy and Practice. Cambridge*. Cambridge: Scholars Publishing.

Field, J. (2005) *Social Capital and Lifelong Learning*. Bristol: The Policy Press.

Florida, R. (2007) *The Flight of the Creative Class*. New York: Collins.

Goldsmith, S. and Eggers, W. (2004) *Governing by Network*. Washington, DC: Brookings Institute Press.

Halpern, D. (2004) *Social Capital*. Cambridge: Polity Press.

Parker, S. and Gallagher, N. (2007) *The Collaborative State*. London: DEMOS.

Putnam, R. (2000) *Bowling Alone*. New York: Simon & Schuster.

Review of Social Economy (2007) Special issue on *Social Capital*, 65(1).

Stilgoe, J., Irwin, A. and Jones, K. (2006) *The Received Wisdom. Opening up expert advice*. London: Demos.

Svendsen, L. and Svendsen, G. (2007) *The Creation and Destruction of Social Capital*. Cheltenham: Edward Elgar.

UK Government (2007) *Hl Bill 81; Sustainable Communities Bill*. London.

Victorian Parliament (2006) *Inquiry into Building New Communities – Final Report*. Melbourne: Victorian Government Printer.

Westlund, H. (2006) *Social Capital in the Knowledge Economy*. Heidelberg: Springer.

Index

Index

Index

European Thematic Network of University
    Lifelong Learning (EULLearN) 87
European Union (EU) 9–10, 146–7
    see also individual countries
European Universities Association 83–4, 85, 86
European Year for Lifelong Learning 50, 62
evaluation processes 229–30, 234, 248–50
evidence-based policy/practice 3–4, 5, 293
evolution of systems 58
exogenous development of industry 162
external agent partnerships 220–36

Families Learning Together programmes 190–1
family support 188, 190–1, 195
Federighi, Paolo 11, 133–50
Fein, J. 223, 224
field theory 8, 36, 39–41, 45–6
financing models 29–30
    see also funding/financing
Finland 69–73, 158–60, 164
Florida, R. 35
foreign direct investments 162
formal assessment, Indigenous education 194
formal education 22–3, 27
    see also education
forums 206, 261–4
Foucault, M. 270, 271
Freire, P. 240–1, 242
'front-end' education 22–3, 27
functional approaches 43, 51–2, 201
functional changes, universities 82–7
functional organisation vs. population organisation
    214–15
funding/financing
    identity visions 278–9
    lifelong learning 29–30
    place-based approaches 209
    regeneration programmes 116, 123
    school collaboration 77, 79
    tertiary education 41

GDN *see* Global Development Network
GEAR *see* Glasgow Eastern Area Renewal
gender discourses 269–70
generative themes 240
Germany 71–2, 73
Glasgow Declaration 86
Glasgow Eastern Area Renewal (GEAR) 116, 119
Global Development Network (GDN) 6
Global Learning Villages 104–5
globalisation 2–3, 269, 274
Golden Grove, Adelaide 79
governance 2–3

civic engagement as 291–2
community involvement 207
power/identity/culture 267–86
strategy-led 15
virtual communities 200–2, 204–8
    see also leadership; local government; regional
    government; state involvement
government-dependent private schools 77
    see also private schools
Gramsci, A. 240, 247, 248
Granovetter, M.S. 171
grant-making 207
Green, A. 25–6, 29
Green, J. 269
growth management 262–3
    see also development models
Gummesson, E. 243

Hall, P. 276
health professionals 224
health services 13, 94, 220–36
hegemony concept 240, 247
HEIs *see* higher education institutions
HERA *see* Higher Education Regional Association
hermeneutical research 243
hierarchy of regions 259
higher education 11–12, 92–6
    field theory 40
    financing models 29
    Inverclyde, Scotland 238, 250
    regional development 82–101, 151–66
higher education institutions (HEIs) 154–9, 161–5
    see also universities
Higher Education Regional Association (HERA)
    154
housing programmes 119–20, 122, 126–7
human capital
    advancement 40
    COAG National Reform Agenda 110, 113
    community education 67–81
    definition 239
    lifelong learning model 24–5, 26
Hume Global Learning Village 104–5
Hungary 73, 82–101
hybrids
    local institutions 216
    policy transfer 143

IALS *see* International Adult Literacy Survey
Iceland 72–3
ICT *see* information and communication
    technology
identity 15, 267–86

Index

Index

Index